back today and I'll show you a surfer. Dan Marino? John Elway? Even Joe Montana looks like he just walked off the beach at Malibu. And don't even talk to me about guys like Mark Gastineau and his St. Vitus's dance. A guy like Layne, who once downed so many drinks at half time that I almost passed out when I sacked him and got a whiff of his breath during the third quarter, well, a guy like Layne would take these players today, feed them a bottle of Scotch, and burp them before the two-minute drill.

I swear, all you have to do is look at the guys that get hurt today to realize that all the football world's become a soap opera. I remember one lineman returning three times on one play to jump on my shinbone to make sure he broke it real good. But today a player gets injured and he falls down and he knows he's on camera and damned if he doesn't lay on the ground like he was shot in the head.

So he lays there for fifteen minutes and they have three trainers and the team doctor is usually over him like he's hearing his last confession, and all of a sudden the guy pops up and runs off the field smiling and waving to his mom. Those theatrics kill me. In my day we'd be embarrassed to hell to do something like that.

After that guy jumped all over my broken leg, the trainer taped me up and the coach put me back in two weeks later. I told him I couldn't run, and he said, "That's okay, if they run in your direction just fall down and get in the way."

So anyway, that's what this book is all about. Read it. Enjoy it. Believe it.

FATSO

ARTHUR J. DONOVAN, Jr., and BOB DRURY

Football
When Men
Were Really Men

WILLIAM MORROW AND COMPANY, INC.   NEW YORK

Library of Congress Cataloging-in-Publication Data

Donovan, Arthur J.
  Fatso: how football was when men were really men.
  Includes index.
  1. Donovan, Arthur J. 2. Football players—United States—Biography. 3. National Football League—Biography. 4. National Football League—History.
I. Drury, Bob. II. Title.
GV939.D65A3   1987   796.332′092′4 [B]   87-11313
ISBN 0-688-07340-9

Printed in the United States of America

First Edition

1 2 3 4 5 6 7 8 9 10

BOOK DESIGN BY VICTORIA HARTMAN

This book is dedicated to
my mother, my wife, my teammates,
and especially to Weeb Ewbank,
who made me the player I was.

—ARTHUR J. DONOVAN, JR.

FATSO

1

Still Crazy After All These Years

My name is Arthur James Donovan, Jr., and for twelve seasons I played football in an organization called the National Football League. That organization bears no resemblance to the thing they call the National Football League today. I played with good teams; I played with putrid teams. In fact, I still maintain that the 1958 and 1959 Baltimore Colts were the best clubs to ever take the field, and that includes Vince Lombardi's tremendous Green Bay Packer squads of the late 1960s. And, Christ, you have never seen a football club as pathetic as the 1950 Baltimore Colts or the 1952 Dallas Texans, two squads of which I had the extreme good fortune to be a member.

But my point here is that when I played football, there were wild teams stocked with wild guys playing during wild times. We had fun, not like these guys today with their briefcases and stock portfolios. And even though as a big, fat defensive tackle I made the Pro Bowl half a dozen times and was elected into the Pro Football Hall of Fame in 1968, what I seem to have become most famous for is my memory.

Now I've been asked to put all these experiences down in a book. I might ask, "Why me?" But I suppose someone should get it on the record that the NFL was not always the corporate entity it has evolved into today. No, at one point the National Football League was about as sophisticated as a tong war. And to tell you the truth, I kind of liked it better that way.

First of all, I think the reporters and the announcers writing and talking about the game today try to make it more complicated than it really is. You can't blame them, though. They take their cues from the coaches. Let's face it, these coaches today can blow as much smoke as they want, but football is still a game of blocking and tackling and hitting. Always was; always will be. Maybe the passing game's got a little bit more complicated, but the rest of this space-age terminology to describe every facet on the field is a lot of baloney. You don't have to be a rocket scientist to understand the game.

And another thing, they talk about all this lifting weights and off-season training programs and I have to laugh. The only weight I ever lifted during my career was a beer can, and I have no doubt I could play the game today. That is, if I ever made it through training camp, because I was not a practice player and I couldn't run for love or money. What I'm telling you I couldn't deal with is the Wall Street angle of today's football.

The money side of the game has almost become more important than what goes on between the white lines, and I'm not talking cocaine. And as a result of all this high finance, the signing bonuses and long-term contracts and television deals and deferred payments, today's players are all goddamn businessmen. They certainly don't hang around together in the bars like we did in the old days. With all this money being thrown around, it's no wonder that after practice they all go their separate ways. Whether this is good or bad is for you to decide, after I tell you about the way it used to be.

Now I'm not going to tell you that when I played, from '50 through '61, every team was all one, big happy family, because I'm not going to bullshit you. We had our share of rats on the team. But by and large most of us hung around together, even with the guys on the other team. I love the way they make Jim

McMahon out to be football's Rebel Without a Cause. It's as if they've never heard of a guy who likes beer before. Then again, maybe they haven't.

McMahon is only following in the footsteps of some of the flightiest quarterbacks to ever play the game. Nut jobs like Norm Van Brocklin, Sonny Jurgensen, Otto Graham, Charlie Conerly, Joe Namath, Don Meredith, and Kenny Stabler spring to mind. I'm sure there are more. But there is just one man who rises head and shoulders above the rest when it comes to setting the standard for good times, on and off the field.

That man, of course, was one Robert Layne, a legend in his spare time. Jim McMahon is going to have to burn awfully bright for the next decade before he can even begin to think about picking up the torch Bobby Layne passed down. Bobby died last November at the age of fifty-nine; his liver finally blew out on him. And, true to form, when I called him the morning he died, he was sitting up in his Texas hospital bed reading the racing form and planning a blowout barbecue for his sixtieth birthday party.

Doak Walker used to say that Bobby Layne never lost a game, it was just that sometimes time ran out on him. Bobby began his career with the Chicago Bears but was traded to the old New York Bulldogs after his rookie year in 1948. He once explained that trade by saying George Halas, the Bears' owner, told him, "Bobby, I can't afford to keep three quarterbacks, and I can't make Sid Luckman retire. Sid's Jewish, which means a lot of season tickets. Johnny Lujack's from Notre Dame, which means a lot more season tickets. And you're just a Baptist from Texas. You understand?" Bobby understood.

Bobby went on to win championships for the Detroit Lions before finishing out his career in Pittsburgh, and I remember playing the Steelers once in an exhibition game in the Orange Bowl in Miami. Layne was dropping back to pass when three of us fell on him, really crushed him before he could get the ball off. I looked at him and said, "You all right, Bob?" And he just looked up, smiled, and said, "Yeah, Fatso, I'm all right. But don't do it again because I'm going to meet you afterward. I'm having a big party and you're all invited."

Or take the Colts' first game of the '57 season. We were going against Layne again, only this time he was with the Lions. It was late in the third quarter, and we were putting a helluva lot of pressure on him. He was screaming at his offensive linemen, kicking their shins in the huddle, that kind of thing. And we were all watching him do this from our defensive huddle and busting a gut laughing. He was a wild man over there. Finally Detroit broke their huddle, snapped the ball, and as Bobby dropped back to pass, I hit him a shot, and he went down. I was lying over him and he smelled like an empty wine bottle. I said to him, "Jesus, Bobby, you goddamn reek. You must have downed quite a few last night." He just looked up at me with this silly grin and said, "Fatso, let me let you in on a secret. The way this game's going, I had to down a few at halftime."

But like I say, sophistication was not exactly a hallmark of the early NFL. We were like barnstormers, and we were treated as such. The Colts played the Giants once in an exhibition game in Louisville. It was a brand-new stadium, and the first thing they had in there was the circus. Unfortunately, the Colts and the Giants were the second thing they had in there.

Every time you put your hand down, you stuck it into a pile of elephant shit. But that was okay for us. We were on the defensive line. It was the offensive linemen who were getting the worst of it. Every time the Giant offense set, and their linemen couldn't move, we'd pick up gobs of this shit and throw it in their faces. They were screaming and hollering all day about this indignity, but the officials were at a loss. "Sorry, boys," they'd say. "They can move. They're allowed to move. But after you get into your three-point stance, you guys have to stay still."

Right near the end of the game, an offensive guard for the Giants by the name of Jack Stroud had had enough. He came up to the line of scrimmage, bent down, picked up a fistful of this muck, yelled, "You dirty sonsabitches!" and threw it at us. He got called for a five-yard penalty for being in motion.

It was during that same game that the Giants started a rookie right tackle from Minnesota named Frank Youso, and I had a tough time getting around this big guy. I mean, I didn't know who he was or where he came from. All I knew was that I felt like I was playing opposite a block of granite. I'd walk back to the huddle and say to our defensive end, Gino Marchetti, "Hey, wop, who the hell is this guy who's knocking me on my ass every play?" And Gino would say, "Don't ask me, Fatso, but he's kicking my butt, too."

So this guy Youso went on playing like Superman for the entire game. And the more I thought about it the more I was not relishing facing this guy during the regular season. After the game was over we ran into the Giants outside the stadium as both teams waited for their buses. Johnny Dell Isola, the Giants' line coach, came up to Gino and me while we were waiting and asked us what we thought of his big stud at right tackle. We both deadpanned, "He's lousy, Johnny, get rid of him." And sure enough, the Giants cut the guy the next day. They must have watched films of the game a couple of days later, however, because they brought him back the following week.

Some of my fondest memories are of games we played against the Giants. Toward the end of my career, in 1960, their coach, Allie Sherman, that dirty bastard, he sent a guy into the game to try and break my jaw. Charlie Conerly, their quarterback, had been knocked out of the game, and for some reason Sherman held me responsible. He was yelling at me from the sidelines, and I was yelling right back at him, and toward the end of the game a guard named Mickey Walker was sent in with the express purpose of rearranging my teeth.

Well, on the last play of the game—a Giant punt, as a matter of fact—Walker took a shot at me and he missed, and I started running after him. But he was too fast and I was too tired to try to catch him, so instead I went after Sherman, who was walking off the field. Allie saw me coming and tried to hide behind a bunch of his players, but the Giants knew what was going on and parted for me like the Red Sea. All the Giants began yelling, "I bet you can't catch him!" They were right. But Allie Sherman avoided me for quite a few years after that.

Then one time we were playing the Rams, and Van Brocklin was their quarterback. He was a helluva fellow, a frogman during World War II. He swam around and blew up buildings. You had to be nuts to do that. A lot of people didn't like Van Brocklin. He was pretty arrogant. But he was okay by me. He lived like he wanted and he didn't bullshit anybody, and that's what I respect most in a person.

Anyway, on the line of scrimmage I had this habit of sucking one huge breath into my lungs and waiting for the snap before exhaling and charging the quarterback at the same time. Well, Van Brocklin picked this up, and that sonofabitch used to hurry his huddle and wait at the line of scrimmage until I turned blue before snapping the ball. It was a tough habit to break. But after word got around to the other quarterbacks in the league, it was either break that habit or suffocate to death. I'm still here, ain't I?

Another time, Van Brocklin called an audible at the line, and for about the only time in my career, our coach, Weeb Ewbank, put in this real complicated defense. So Dick Szymanski, the middle linebacker, said to me, "Hey, move over, Fatso, you're in the wrong position." So I moved, but then I figured out that Syzzie was wrong, so I said to him, "Syzzie, you sonofabitch, you're wrong. You move." So he moved and I moved back to where I was originally. Then Syzzie said back, "You fat idiot, no. You're wrong. You move back."

So Van Brocklin was just standing on the other side of the line of scrimmage watching all this, listening to us, and he finally yelled, "Jesus Christ, I can't believe this. Two professional football players and they don't even know where to line up! When you two idiots get straightened out, then I'll start playing again." With that, he called a time-out and walked off the field.

That, however, was about as theatrical as we got on the field. I played and roomed with Don Shula, and whenever I see him I have to ask him about all these showboats playing the game today. Shula was a tough guy when he played for the Colts, and he's refined that image as the coach of the Dolphins. He lets everyone know where he stands, and he's got everyone in Miami kissing his ass and running scared of him, even the newspapermen. But I'll tell you what, Shula doesn't like to see me coming, especially when his players are around, because I've got stories that knock that hard-guy image right on its keester.

We were playing an exhibition game in Milwaukee once, and a bunch of us, naturally, we're drinking in a local bar. Around midnight, most of us left, but Shula stayed there with Carl Taseff, another defensive back. We were back up at the hotel for a little while when suddenly the cops showed up. Uh-oh. One officer walked up to me and said, "We know one of you Colts stole a taxicab. Who was it?" What happened was Shula and Taseff honked the horn of a cab outside the bar, but the driver didn't show up. So Shula put Taseff, who was stewed to the gills, in the back of the cab, put the cabbie's hat on, and drove back to the hotel. And you know, they never would have gotten caught, except Taseff was slow getting out of the cab. He wanted to pay Shula the fare.

Another time, before either of us was married, we went to the Coast, and Shula picked up a good-looking girl on the plane during the flight out. After the game in San Francisco, we had a big party up in the St. Francis Hotel, and Shula brought this girl to the party. Well, he's strutting around the room trying to make a big impression on us with the pretty girl he had picked up. Suddenly I said to him, "Hey, Shoes, look at your young lady now." And when he turned around she was lighting a cigar.

Well, have you ever watched a Miami game on the tube and seen the way Don Shula can get riled up when he thinks the refs have blown a call? That is nothing compared to the way he got this night. She was puffing on the cigar, all right, but the smoke was coming out of his ears. Jesus, he kicked her right in the ass and threw her out of the hotel. I thought he was going to kill her.

Yes, sir, Don Shula was one tough sonofabitch. And he's probably the best coach in the game today. I don't think he has that great a football team in Miami, but he works miracles with the personnel he's got. He truly gets the most out of his players. That's the way he played the game. He was never the biggest or the fastest or the strongest. But he was always the smartest. When Shula was playing it was like having a coach on the field.

It's a damn shame guys like Shula and Vince Lombardi didn't become generals. As Patton and MacArthur said during World War II, "Let's keep going and we'll meet up in Russia." If Shula and Lombardi were generals, we wouldn't be worrying about the Soviet Union today. It would be part of the United States.

You might want to throw Al Davis in with that group, too. In fact, that sonofabitch might be the smartest guy in all of football. I first met Al when he was a coach with an Army football team at Fort Belvoir, Virginia. Weeb would pay him to scout Army personnel for the Colts, and Al used to hang around our training camp all the time. That's how Al Davis got his start in the pro business. He lied on his résumé and said he was an offensive line coach for the Colts. What a con artist that guy is.

But it was obvious from the times Al used to sit around bullshitting with us after practice that the guy had a lot on the ball. I could just never trust him, though. He always looked like a conniver with that duck's-ass haircut and black leather jacket. Listen, Al Davis is a streetwise kid from Brooklyn who says he grew up poor. That's a load of crap. His father was a manufacturer who had more money than anybody in the neighborhood. And I'll bet that when the kids on that block were playing stickball in the street, Al Davis was booking the action on the sidewalk.

I saw Al not too long ago. I was in Pittsburgh doing the color commentary for a Colts game when suddenly here's the man, all dressed in black, stepping out of a limousine longer than the block he grew up on. "Hey Artie, c'mere," he says to me. "I really made it, huh?" I said, "You're goddamn right you did, Al. But you still look like you should be taking the action on some Brooklyn street corner."

Another coach I like is Raymond Berry. I had to root for his Patriots in Super Bowl XX, because Berry's an ex-teammate of mine. Strange guy, that Raymond. He used to wash his own clothes in training camp—socks, jocks, and all. He had some kind of superstition about letting the equipment manager handle any part of his uniform. But man, he was one of the best damn pass receivers to ever play football.

Two years ago, when Berry's Patriots made the Super Bowl, I

was kind of torn, because I like Mike Ditka in Chicago, too. Ditka tells it the way it is. You fool around with Ditka, he's going to rap you right in the mouth. Like when he got rid of Buddy Ryan, his defensive coordinator who took over the head coaching job in Philadelphia. Ditka said, "Good, I'm glad he's gone." He's telling the truth. You can't get in trouble by telling the truth, and the hell with anybody who doesn't like to hear it.

One thing that really bothered me, though, was that Patriot drug scandal after New England lost the Super Bowl. I felt bad for Raymond after that. Evidently, today the drug problem is pretty widespread. But if a guy was putting pot in his pipe right next to me I wouldn't even know what it smells like. In my time, everybody drank beer, everybody was a comedian, and no one took themselves seriously. It seems to me that today these guys have too much idle time and extra cash. Jesus, I'm starting to sound like my old man.

You might remember him—Arthur J. Donovan, Sr., fight referee. They used to call him Joe Louis's personal ref. He was the third man in the ring in more championship fights than any other referee, and when I was growing up he thought I was the biggest sissy in the neighborhood. No matter that I'd tangled in one of the roughest neighborhoods in New York City, fought on Okinawa, played at Notre Dame and Boston College, he was always afraid that I was going to get myself in trouble when I went off to play pro ball. He wasn't far wrong.

Sure, when we played, some of the guys used to take Dexedrine, these little greenies. The trainer would come around and give you a couple right before the game. What the hell, it made you feel younger. But I really think a lot of it was psychological. I remember one time Don Joyce, a defensive end with the Colts, said to me, "Hey, Fatso, c'mere, I got something for ya." And he gave me a capsule before we were playing the Bears in Baltimore.

I swallowed this pill, and I ran out on the goddamn field like I was twelve years old. So I said to Joyce, "You sonofabitch, what did you do to me?" I couldn't sleep for three nights. Every time one of those timed capsules popped in my belly, I ran around like the goddamn Wombat from Mecca. But I can't really compare that to the guys today taking all these drugs. I really feel sad for them. And I can only imagine what my father would say today if I wanted to play pro ball today.

We had another crazy man on our team, a middle linebacker by the name of Bill Pellington. Now, I don't know if Pellington was on drugs or just born with a gland that secreted speed, because this guy was manic. In 1958, a few weeks before we beat the Giants in the championship game since dubbed "The Greatest Game Ever Played," we were beating up on the Packers something terrible in a driving rainstorm in Baltimore. The score was 56–0 late in the game when Green Bay threw in the towel and put in a rookie quarterback named Joe Francis to play out the string.

Joe Francis may not have been the smartest quarterback to ever play the game, but he wasn't stupid. He had been watching us kicking the crap out of the Pack from the sidelines all afternoon. And as luck would have it, as soon as he got into the game, Green Bay started to move the ball. With just a few minutes left they got down to our twenty-yard line, and Pellington screamed at us, "Don't let 'em score! Kill that sonofabitch at quarterback!" So Francis called a time-out, walked over to Bill, and said, "Hey, buddy, take it easy. I don't want to be out here, either."

One night Pellington pulled up to a bar in downtown Baltimore, and since it was a really rainy night he decided to park right in front of the joint. Well, this cop came up to him and said, "You can't park there, it's a no-parking zone." So Bill, being the law-abiding citizen that he is, moved his car down the street and around the corner. When he got back to the place, however, there was another car parked in that spot. The cop had let a girl park there.

"So how come I couldn't park there and she can?" Pellington asked the policeman. And the cop made a near-fatal mistake. He told Pellington, "Never mind, buddy, it's none of your business." Pellington said, "It is so my goddamn business," and with that the cop hit him over the top of the head with his billy club. The club broke. Pellington didn't. He nearly killed the cop. We had to pull him off the guy.

I guess you might say that in my time some guys did take it too far. Once, we were flying home from the West Coast after a win over the Rams in 1959. But first we had to wait four hours for the plane, and of course we all waited in the airport bar. The jet finally arrived, and since our famous coach, Weeb Ewbank, was too cheap to stock our flights with booze, we carried on our own. All of us had beer, except for Big Daddy Lipscomb, who was to wind up dead of an overdose a few years later. Big Daddy liked his VO, and he came strolling down the aisle of our plane with two fifths of whiskey.

We drank all the way back to Baltimore, and by the time we landed, the sun was up and everybody on the plane had a vicious hangover. Everybody piled off the plane in various states of drunken dishevelment except for our tight end, Jim Mutscheller, who halfway down the ramp decided he had to use the head on the jet because he couldn't make it the couple of hundred yards to the airport. The plane was refueling for the trip back to Los Angeles when Mutsch opened the door to the head, and who was sitting on the throne, passed out, but Big Daddy. He had his two fifths of VO, empty, cradled in his arms like babies. They would have flown back West with Big Daddy on that throne if Mutsch could have held his water another five minutes.

One of the best flights we ever had was after a loss in Detroit. Nobody was too happy to begin with, because we should have beaten those guys, and by the time we boarded the flight, half the team had a major-league package on. It didn't take long for the other half to catch up. And up at around twenty-five thousand feet a huge brawl broke out between the offense and the defense. They were gouging and biting and blaming each other for the loss. Well, I was one of the guys trying to break up the fight but having no luck at all. Meanwhile, the plane was pitching back and forth as these behemoths were throwing each other all over the goddamn cabin. Weeb wouldn't get out of his seat because he was afraid somebody was going to throw him out the window.

Finally, the pilot got on the intercom and announced that if we didn't stop, he was going to have to make an emergency landing and we were all going to jail for air piracy or something like that.

That was the only way to stop them. They were crazy animals. And Weeb never said a word throughout the whole trip.

Through my first four years in the league, before Weeb took over the Colts in 1954, I played at six-two, three hundred pounds. I was a light eater. When it got light I started eating. I had a bit part in a movie *Two for the Money* and when the wardrobe people asked me my clothes sizes they told them to check with Omar the Tentmaker. They used to weigh me on a scale downtown at a grain store. But after Weeb came in, I always had a clause in my contract stating I had to play at 270. They weighed me in once a week, and what a show that would be. I'd step on the scale, it would register something like 275. I'd take off my sweat shirt and drop two pounds. My pants would be another pound and a half. And I'd get down to 270 and a half by dropping my underwear. Just when everyone thought I'd be fined for coming in a half pound overweight, I'd pull the *coup de grâce* and take out my false teeth.

Everything went fine until 1959. Toward the end of the season, the Colts were on the West Coast to play San Francisco and Los Angeles. We had to win both games to take the division title. We beat the 49ers and stayed in San Francisco to practice, and that was a big mistake. How can you not gain weight in San Francisco? My tonnage shot to 280.

Weeb was so preoccupied with the Rams game that he didn't have a team weigh-in beforehand. He only weighed a guy named George Preas and myself. Jesus Christ, sometimes I think Weeb would have rather had a good weigh-in than a good game. Anyway, I had a $2,000 bonus clause in my contract. I'd collect if I stayed at 270 all season. Here we were in the last game of the year, and I had blown it. After he weighed me, I went up to Weeb and asked him about a deal. "Suppose I have a good Rams game," I said. His answer: "I'll talk to you about it after the game."

Anyhow, it was about 110 degrees in L.A. by game time. Big Daddy begged out with a bad ankle, although I honestly believe he just didn't feel like playing in that heat, and I had to play the whole game. I was dying. Late in the game, with about three or four minutes left, we were murdering them by about five touchdowns. The Rams finally put in their rookie quarterback, a guy by the name of Frank Ryan, who went on to become a star with the Cleveland Browns and the athletic director at Yale. I said to myself, "Thank God," because I was sure he had been sent in to run the clock.

But no. This guy Ryan got the ball and started running all over the field and throwing bombs. And I was chasing him and screaming at him and calling him all kinds of names. I yelled at him, "I'm gonna kill you when I get you!" But, truth be told, I couldn't have caught him if he was crawling on his hands and knees. So I finally figured the hell with this, and went over to the Rams huddle and said to this guy, "Listen, rook, you goddamn sonofabitch. Give up the ghost. Run out the goddamn clock."

And he just calmly looked up at me and said, "Drop dead, you big, fat SOB." I was shocked. Stunned. I wanted to kill him. Suddenly I realized my teammate Ordell Braase was yelling at me, "Hey, Fatso, you're in the wrong goddamn huddle!" And sure enough, the refs penalized us five yards for being offside. When the game ended I crawled off the field and went looking for Weeb. I wanted to ask him about my money.

"Hey, Weeb," I said after I caught him, "I guess I'm going to get my two thousand dollars back now that we won the game and everything."

"Hell, no, Donovan," he said to me. "You don't get nothing, 'cause you're out of shape."

I asked him what the hell he was talking about. After all, I had played the whole game in stifling heat. And that rat bastard told me that if I was in shape I would have caught Ryan and ended the game that much earlier. I never got the money, either.

But it might have been worth it for that week of food in Frisco. I've never been a gourmet eater. Kosher hot dogs, cheeseburgers, pizza, baloney, and a couple of cases of Schlitz are all I'd need on a desert isle. Once I was in the Knights of Columbus Hall in downtown Baltimore, for some kind of party for the Lions Club of Baltimore, and they had a hot-dog stand set up over in the corner. While everyone else was mingling, I just stood by that stand absentmindedly eating hot dog after hot dog. I got up to about thirty-seven when a buddy of mine came up to me and told me the people in the kitchen were getting pissed off about having to make so many hot dogs. I was so embarrassed I stopped eating, but I could have gone for another dozen. Another time I stopped at one of those hot-dog carts on a corner in New York City and ate the guy dry.

Yet though I may have been the biggest player on the Colts, I was far from the biggest eater. That was a title that belonged to either Gino Marchetti or Don Joyce, and one day we decided to do something about it. We were up in training camp, at Western Maryland College, and after the coaches left, some of the older guys on the team had the cook make up about a hundred pieces of southern fried chicken.

We put up $100 apiece and sat Gino and Joyce down to an eating contest. Who could eat more chicken. The cooks put out a beautiful meal—chicken, mashed potatoes, gravy, and peas. And I had money on Joyce, so I was really ticked off when I saw that Marchetti was just eating the chicken while Joyce was eating the chicken, the mashed potatoes, gravy, vegetables, the works. "Goddamnit, Joyce, don't worry about the trimmings, just the chicken," I told him. So he stopped after two helpings and began concentrating on the bird.

Well, Marchetti ate twenty-six pieces of chicken. And when Joyce hit twenty-five, we said, "Great, two more and we win." But Joyce said, "Hold on, I'm still hungry." He ended up eating thirty-eight pieces of chicken. But the thing is, we hadn't let him drink anything until he beat Gino, on account of we didn't want his stomach to fill up. So when Joyce had his twenty-seventh piece of chicken, he said, "Man, I gotta wash this down." There was a big pitcher of iced tea in front of him, so we said, "Here, have it."

With that, he took four pieces of saccharin out of his pocket and put them in the tea. Then he turned to us and said, "I'm watching my weight."

I never had to watch my weight. I always knew exactly where it was. I knew what I looked like, and I also knew how good a player I was. So I was pretty good-natured about cracks. But every once in a while somebody would really tick me off with some remark about my weight. Gino Marchetti, who played alongside of me for a dozen seasons and was probably the greatest defensive end to ever play the game, still tells a story about me and a running back from the 49ers named J. D. Smith.

The 49ers called the draw play, and I was the only one not faked out when Smith got the ball and came barreling up the middle. I met him at the line of scrimmage and gave him a shot. I thought I might have killed him. I also thought I might have broken my arm, because the damn thing just went numb. Anyway, I got up, kind of grinning down at Smith. And then he jumped up and said, "What do you think you're laughing at, you baggy-pantsed bastard?" Well, I've certainly been called a lot worse during my lifetime, but Gino says I didn't say a word. I just walked over to him and in this hurt tone said, "Gino, can you imagine that guy calling me baggy-pantsed?"

But I was far from the fattest Colt to ever play the game. That title goes to an offensive tackle named Sherman (Big Boy) Plunkett. You may recall old Sherm from his days as a starter with the Jets Super Bowl team. This guy was an ocean liner. We were in training camp once with the Colts when Big Boy was a rookie, and Weeb gave us the night off. So we all went out on the town for a good time, and when we returned, word got around that Weeb was going to have a sneak weigh-in in the morning.

Jesus Christ, we didn't know what to do. So finally we sent somebody into town to buy a case of milk of magnesia. We all started chugging. I know I drank four bottles. I think Plunkett downed about six. I know he couldn't get off the throne all night. He slept there. We had all the lights out in the bathroom because we didn't want Weeb to know anything was up, even though those toilets were flushing all night long.

Sometime in the middle of the night Plunkett was asleep in the stall when our fullback Alan (the Horse) Ameche felt Nature's call and made a beeline for the bathroom. Ameche was the only guy on the team who wore pajamas to bed. He ran in to the bathroom, threw open a stall, dropped his pajama bottoms, and before Plunkett could awaken and let out a scream, the Horse shit all over him. It took about three hours to clean Sherman up.

But I was the one who usually got the jibes about being fat, and for the most part, I didn't mind being the butt of jokes about my weight. Or, for that matter, the butt of any kind of jokes. It was a good thing, because the Colts always gave it to me good.

I was never a fancy Dan as a dresser. When I found clothes that fit me comfortably, I stuck with them. Well, one time I found a sport jacket that fit like a glove, if you can imagine a glove folding over a guy weighing close to three hundred pounds. The jacket began getting frayed around the cuffs and the collar, but I still wore it on every road trip. But when we were out in Long Beach, California, practicing for a Rams game, Marchetti and Dick Szymanski sneaked up behind me in the hotel lobby and ripped the damn thing right off my back. It was funny and everybody laughed and all that, and I took the jacket and threw it in the trash can at the hotel.

A couple of hours later I came back down to the lobby and there it was: The jacket was wrapped around a statue of a nude woman. So I grabbed it again and put it in the trash bin of the lady who cleaned the lobby. We beat the Rams that afternoon and the next day I was getting on the team bus to head for the airport when the bellboy came up to me and said, "COD package for you, Mr. Donovan, and it's got three dollars' postage due." I paid the kid the three bucks, and on the bus to the airport ripped open the box and there's the damn jacket again. I opened the bus window and threw the jacket out. This was in Long Beach, and I figured, "Well, that's the end of that." We arrived in San Francisco and the night before the game another bellboy came up to me in the lobby of the St. Francis Hotel with another package. Postage due, of course. I paid him, opened it up, and there was the goddamn jacket again. This time I threw it down the laundry chute of the hotel.

Two weeks later, at Christmastime, I was back in Baltimore in the country club my wife, Dottie, and I own when I got a special-delivery parcel that I had to pay five dollars for. What the hell if it wasn't that damn jacket again! So far it cost me about $22 to get rid of the damn thing. This time I told my wife to burn it, to throw it right on the Yule log.

About eight months later the Shriners had a gala, and they invited me as a special guest of honor. Sure enough, when I got there they presented me with the jacket. It turned out my teammates were paying people all over the country to fetch this thing after I threw it away. They even got my wife in on it. I thought it was very funny. But I didn't think another practical joke they pulled on me was quite so hilarious.

I hate furry things. And the Colts knew I was a city boy and scared to death of animals. So one time up in training camp in Westminster, Maryland, an offensive lineman named Alex Sandusky went out and shot a groundhog and put the thing in my bed. Art Spinney, another lineman, came up to me that night and told me he had left a six-pack under my covers and not to let Weeb find out. I thought, "Great, I'll have some suds while I watch TV." So that night I went up to my room, pulled back the sheets, and there was this goddamn one-eyed thing staring at me. Sandusky had shot the other half of its head off.

Jesus, I swear to God I nearly died. I screamed, "What is it? What is it?" And Spinney's saying, "Gee, Artie, I don't know." I had to sleep on the floor of another room that night because my bed was a mess with blood all over the sheets and blankets. The next day we were all happy because we were breaking training camp. It was all planned that a few of the guys were going to spike the orange juice with vodka at the last practice. So that afternoon I came whistling into the locker room, opened my locker, and there was that one-eyed sonofabitch hanging there by a string. I ran out of that room so fast I knocked the equipment manager on his ass and nearly got hit by a car. I get the goose bumps just thinking about it.

I guess we were pretty stupid, because we did that kind of stuff all the time. John Mackey, the great tight end, had a thing about bugs, so one time we loaded up the slots where the pads go in his uniform pants with a bunch of locusts that had descended on our training site. He was out on the practice field when suddenly he felt some flapping coming from inside his thigh-pad holes. I've yet to see Mackey run that fast in a game.

They also did something like that to Buddy Young, a halfback who was just like me when it came to animals. They put a live bat in his room one night and unscrewed the light bulb so when he turned on the light nothing happened. He ran right through the window, right through the screen, and he must have gone about a mile before he stopped.

But even if you don't hear those kinds of stories anymore, I do think that the one thing that has probably remained constant throughout the football decades is management's sense of football players as no more than pieces of flesh. I see it today with the way all but the very best are just thrown on to the scrap heap when they're through. And I saw it even worse in my day, when players had no rights whatsoever.

I remember once the Colts drafted a guy named Tom Cosgrove, who was a center from the University of Maryland. He was supposed to be an All-American, but he really wasn't too good. Anyhow, there was a lot of pressure on Weeb to keep this local kid. And Weeb didn't want to. We were playing the Steelers in an exhibition game in Pittsburgh in 1954, and Cosgrove hurt his ankle and told the trainer he couldn't play. No matter, here was Weeb's chance. He put him in the game and, of course, the kid did nothing. A few days later, they watched the game films and that poor bastard Cosgrove was limping up and down the field. Weeb said, "Well, he can never make our team running that slow." And he cut him.

I felt sorry for him because I liked him. He now is a pilot for United Airlines. Everyone on the team used to wear these denim jeans with no underwear on underneath. A bunch of us were at the movies in Westminster one night, waiting in the lobby of the theater to get our seats, and Cosgrove came up behind me and yanked my pants down. My big, fat, white ass was all exposed, and two old ladies standing behind Cosgrove were having apoplexy. Take a look at my mug on the cover of this book and then try to imagine what my ass looks like.

I was so embarrassed, so nervous, that I couldn't pull my pants up. I was yanking and yanking and I finally got the damn things up and I started looking for Cosgrove, on account of I wanted to kill him. But he ran out of the theater and I couldn't catch him, which was lucky for him, because if I had he wouldn't have been around for Weeb to cut after the Steeler game.

Weeb cutting Cosgrove was one thing. He was okay! Not the best. He just had two great centers in front of him: Nutter and Syzzy. But I remember one of my best friends was traded just because of a little accident, if you want to call throwing a pail of water over the coach an accident. I don't know what the big deal is. I've seen the Giants dousing Bill Parcells on the sidelines for two years now, every time they've won a game. But Weeb didn't see it quite that way.

What happened was, we used to throw cold buckets of water on each other, just fooling around and acting like overgrown kids. But one day Weeb sent word out that the next guy he caught throwing water was going to be fined $1,000. In those days, that usually amounted to about one tenth of your salary, a pretty hefty bite. So Marchetti said to Carl Taseff, "Listen, Gaucho, we'll throw one more bucket of water and we'll throw it on the Horse, Alan Ameche. I'll stand here, and when the Horse comes around the corner, I'll nod, and you let him have it."

Anyhow, here came Weeb out of his office, all dressed up to do his television show. He came around the corner and Marchetti nodded and Taseff let the bucket of water go and—oh, my God!—he saw Weeb and he went running after the water trying to get it back in the bucket. Weeb was standing there drenched, yelling at Taseff, "You sonofabitch! You dirty, no-good sonofabitch!" And Taseff was literally cringing, almost crying, "I'm sorry, Coach. I'm sorry, Coach." The rest of us were rolling on the floor. I laughed so hard I cried. But Weeb got his revenge. He got rid of Taseff the following season.

Playing conditions are another thing I hear a lot of guys beefing about today. And as far as artificial turf goes, I think they have a point. That fake grass will unlock your knee for you quicker than any linebacker will. But when I visit a pristine NFL stadium today and think back to the garbage dumps I used to play in, I get nostalgic. Right, the way Rome gets nostalgic for the Visigoths. Aside from the occasional perils of elephant shit, I recall that Municipal Stadium in Cleveland was always a pigsty. And when I played in the Cotton Bowl in Texas, well, if you didn't have the wind at your back, kickoffs would often travel about ten yards. Why do you think the Cowboys have that half roof over their stadium? Texas windstorms, that's why.

But the all-time dumping grounds had to have been San Francisco's Kezar Stadium. First of all, you dressed outside this stadium, in a dressing room so small you had to take turns going in to put your uniform on. Visiting teams always got taped at the hotel, so that was all right. But when you came out of the locker rooms, you had to walk down onto the field through a long tunnel, and they had a lot of gravel and cinders in the goddamn tunnel. Also, it was always so dry you'd become asphyxiated by the dust. But that wasn't even the worst part.

When you went out onto the field at Kezar, you'd walk into a bog that must have played host to a dozen football games a week. Bay Area high schools and colleges both played there, and the field was a disgrace. The middle was so bad that the grounds crew—what there was of it—would throw black cinders on it so it wouldn't completely muck up. Jesus, when you made a tackle your shirt would come up and you'd get all these cinders up under your jersey and they'd go right down your pants and get into your jock and it was horrible. But that still wasn't the worst of it.

Because at about four o'clock, just when you were about getting into the fourth quarter, here'd come the goddamn sea gulls. They'd start shitting on you like they were aiming. And you had to keep your helmet on because this stuff coming down on you would hit you like a bomb. The final indignity was that these sea gulls seemed to be trained only to bombard the visiting team. I found out later that it was because the 49ers always took the sunny side of the field, and the sea gulls felt more comfortable or something shitting in the shade. I'll never forget the look of dread visiting teams wore going in to play San Francisco.

Then there was Stagg Field, where visiting teams practiced when they went to play Chicago. That's where the University of Chicago played their football games, in a big concrete stadium, and a portion of the stands was burned black. We found out one day that scientists from the university worked on the Manhattan

Project, the goddamn atomic bomb, right underneath Stagg Field. The concrete got so hot under a certain section that it turned black. If those people living in that neighborhood had known what was going on under there they would have shit like San Francisco sea gulls. I used to check myself in the hotel room after practice to see if I was glowing in the dark.

Anyway, it wasn't until I began being selected to Pro Bowls that I realized that these sophomoric antics weren't limited to the Baltimore Colts. These days you have maybe one insane team in the league: Davis's Raiders, of course. In those days, one sane team in the league doesn't readily spring to mind. Maybe the Giants, considering they were always so media-conscious. But even those guys went pretty crazy when they got out of the spotlight.

I remember one Pro Bowl party in Los Angeles—the game didn't move to Hawaii until after I retired—where Charlie Conerly and Frank Gifford were sitting at the hotel bar, and Conerly was drunk as a skunk. So Gifford dared Conerly to pour a drink over the head of Lou Creekmur, a gigantic tackle from the Lions. Conerly didn't know what the hell he was doing, so of course he accepted the dare, and he dumped his glass of beer right over Creekmur's head. It was the only time in my life I've seen Creekmur hold back. Lou just kind of picked up Charlie, who couldn't even stand up straight, and told him, "Conerly, you can thank Christ that right now you're drunk. Because I'm going to kill you tomorrow, you sonofabitch."

In fact, that same night we had some trouble with another big tackle, a guy named Bob Toneff, who played for the 49ers. We were at a party where everyone was pretty drunk, and Toneff hoists this girl up onto the bar and starts jitterbugging with her in the most violent fashion. He was throwing her out over the bar and pulling her back in, and all the while I'm scared to death that her neck is going to snap. No matter, Toneff wouldn't let her go.

Finally she managed to squirm away from him, and she ran into a phone booth in the lobby to call the police. Toneff followed her outside and pushed the goddamn phone booth over. So she ran outside to get in her car, and Toneff followed her out to the parking lot and, I swear to Christ, ripped the door right off her Volkswagen. I heard she ended up suing Toneff, and Marchetti was called as a witness because he happened to be walking into the party as Toneff went into his King Kong act.

A few years ago the Colts opened the season against the Raiders, and the NFL threw an alumni party out on the Coast. We all partied hardy for a good five days. And at one point during the festivities, which were really just a bullshit festival for us old-timers swapping stories, I heard the wife of Hugh McElhenny, the great 49er halfback, whisper into his ear, "Hugh, I thought you told me only the 49ers had these kind of crazy times. These guys are funnier than you ever were."

I guess that just about sums it up. I can only speak for what I've seen and heard. And I can only tell you the truth. But what follows is a fond remembrance of the way football used to be played, and the guys who used to play it.

2

"The Greatest Game
Never Played"

In 1958 I was a defensive tackle on the Baltimore Colts, the best goddamn football team to ever play the game. I also earned another distinction that season. I started in what historians have come to call "The Greatest Game Ever Played," Baltimore's 23–17 championship victory over the New York Giants in sudden-death overtime.

Playing in that game was a homecoming for me. I was born and raised forty blocks up the Grand Concourse from Yankee Stadium, where the game was played. I had cousins and aunts and uncles and friends scattered all over the Bronx. I had starred in high-school football in the same borough in which I was about to play for the football championship of the world. And perhaps most important, Yankee Stadium was the site of some of the greatest championship fights my father, Arthur Donovan, Sr., had ever refereed.

A championship season was the culmination of all the frustrating seasons I had spent on the Colts. In five years, we had gone from being the worst team in football to the best. And even though I had been selected for the Pro Bowl the previous five seasons, nothing really washes the taste of consistent losing out of your mouth, and I mean losing by scores larger than the gross national debt of Bolivia, then a world title.

"The Greatest Game Ever Played."

What a load of crap.

When they call that game the greatest game ever played, I have to laugh. As it was, we dug ourselves into a hole in the game and barely got by against a far inferior team. We did the same thing the following season, when we went into halftime of the 1959 championship game trailing those same Giants by a touchdown. But we had learned our lesson. We came out for the second half in '59 and absolutely annihilated the Giants, 31–16. That was more like it. And we weren't even as good in '59 as we were in '58.

Let me tell you something: When we tied it in '58 on Steve Myhra's thirteen-yard field goal with seven seconds left in regulation, and then won it on Alan Ameche's touchdown plunge on the thirteenth play of our overtime drive, we weren't feeling ecstasy. We were feeling relief. We were thirty times better than the Giants and we should have kicked the living shit out of them. We just had too much for them. We knew it. They knew it. Most important, Weeb Ewbank, our coach, knew it. And there would have been hell to pay to Weeb had we lost to that team. We were scared he was going to cut each and every one of us right there if we lost that championship.

There were some pretty fair football names to come out of that game from both sides. People like John Unitas, Frank Gifford, Gino Marchetti, Sam Huff, Raymond Berry, Alex Webster, Lenny Moore, Charlie Conerly, and Big Daddy Lipscomb, to name but a few. But the only reason I can think of for the top billing that game still gets in the annals of football is because it was played in New York, the media capital of the world, and because we played against the Giants, those media darlings.

To this day people come up to me and tell me they watched me play in that game. Hell, in the twenty-nine years since, there must have been a couple hundred thousand who have said that to me. There're probably two million people walking the planet who say they were in Yankee Stadium on December 28, 1958. And that cracks me up, because the game wasn't even a sellout. Only 64,185 showed up, some six thousand shy of a full house.

In fact, nostalgia plays an awfully big part in the myth of that game. I grew up about two miles from Yankee Stadium, on the Grand Concourse in the Bronx, and it seems like whenever I go home, everybody I meet in New York was either there or remembers every minor detail like it was Moses coming off the Mount. But at the time, it didn't even strike people as any kind of momentous occasion. The commissioner of the NFL at the time, Bert Bell, died two years later unaware of the billboard this game had provided for the league.

Yet if you want to call the '58 championship game the most important game ever played in the National Football League, I might tend to agree with you. Because it may have been the best thing that ever happened to the NFL.

You see, football is a television game today, and evidently what made football on television was the '58 championship game. Networks and, more important, advertisers recognized us. The game of pro football went from being a localized sport based on gate receipts and played by oversized coal miners and West Texas psychopaths to a national sport based on television ratings.

When I started in the NFL in 1950, the league ran on Johnson & Johnson tape and beer, and not necessarily in that order. Without either, the league would have folded. By the time I finished, twelve years later, business suits and briefcases were already beginning to abound. And by the time I was elected to the Pro Football Hall of Fame in 1968, every third-string center had a business adviser, a string of accountants, a score of agents, and a valet for his limo. That championship tilt created immediate interest nationally. Total income from the '58 title game, including television and radio revenue, amounted to $698,646. Each player received a $4,700 share, tip money to today's second-string defensive backs. But I don't know much about money and Nielsen points and ratings. High finance to me is enough dough for a hunk of kosher salami, a loaf of Jewish rye, and a case of Schlitz. I'm here to talk about football, and with that in mind I have to go back a little ways to tell you what led up to "The Greatest Game Ever Played."

First of all, in '58 I was the oldest Colt in point of service on the team. I was thirty-three years old. An offensive guard, Art Spinney, had come in with me in 1950, but he missed a couple of seasons when he was drafted into the Army. So going into the '58 season, when we were actually picked to win the Western Conference title, I remembered the dog days when the Colts were the pits of the league and the franchise was folding after every season and you needed calculators to tote up the scores teams were beating us by.

The year before, we had finished 7–5, the first winning season in the history of the franchise. Our offense had finally caught up to what had been, even in the bad seasons, a pretty tough defense. We'd picked Unitas up off the sandlots two years before. And Berry, Moore, and Alan Ameche, the Horse, had turned the team into a veritable scoring machine. We ended up leading the league in total offense and scoring, averaging over forty points a game. But the strength of the team had been and still was the defense, especially the defensive line. It lined up with Marchetti at left end, me at left tackle, Big Daddy at right tackle, and Don Joyce at right end.

And we were mean. Hell, guys like Joyce and middle linebacker Bill Pellington were nuts. They'd rather beat the shit out of the man in front of them than get to the guy with the ball. They were the kind of guys you had to watch in the huddle, because if they didn't think they were hurting the man in front of them enough, if he wasn't bleeding from at least three orifices, then they'd start beating on you.

We had played five games that exhibition season and won only two, both against the Giants. People may recall the big rivalry between the Colts and the Giants, but what they don't remember was that it didn't begin until after the '58 championship game. Before then they were just like any other team to us. In fact, there was more rivalry between the Colts and the Packers, and the Bears, and the 49ers, because those teams were in our conference. The

Giants were in the Eastern Conference and we only played them every so often, whereas we played those other teams twice a year.

So anyway, we beat the Giants twice that exhibition season, 27–21 and 41–21, and we were pretty lucky at that, because Weeb, that rat bastard, didn't want to show anybody any of the offenses or defenses we would use during the regular season. He just wanted to get everybody in shape and that was it.

We won our first six regular-season games, and we started to believe we had a helluva team. I remember being on the plane coming home from Green Bay early in the season, where we had just destroyed the Packers, and Gino Marchetti turned to me and said, "Hey, Fatso, just how goddamn good are we?" I said I didn't know, but the way we beat these guys today, I figured we had to be pretty damn good. I told Gino, "If everybody pulls together, shit, nobody's gonna stop us."

Then in the seventh game of the regular season, we lost to the Giants, 24–21, on a field goal with two and a half minutes left. We were pissed. The week before, while we were crushing the Packers 56–0 in Baltimore, this mean defensive back from the Packers, John Symank, had jumped on Unitas late after John had scrambled fourteen yards. He broke John's ribs. John was lying facedown at the Packer six-yard line and Symank just dropped on his back with both knees. One of John's ribs punctured a lung. Symank coached here after he retired, and I can tell you he was nothing but a dirty bastard.

When John went down, I said to myself, "I'm gonna get this sonofabitch, someday I'm gonna get him." And the following year, we played the Packers up in Milwaukee's County Stadium, and he did the same thing to Raymond Berry, our All-Pro offensive end, right in front of our bench. We all jumped up and I figured this was my chance, I knew I was going to get the guy sooner or later. He was in the middle of a bunch of Colts who were all pushing him around on our sideline.

But I figured if I hit him I was going to get caught. So I kicked him as hard as I could, twice, right in the shins. He was screaming and hollering and he turned around and saw Carl Taseff, one of our defensive backs who was standing right alongside me. Symank punched Taseff in the mouth, and Taseff threw a punch back at him and got thrown out of the game. Whoo, baby, I laughed my ass off.

In any case, John missed two games with the punctured lung, including our next game, in New York. The Giants were coming off a big 21–17 upset of the Browns the week before, but we were still the better team. George Shaw started at quarterback, and he had a helluva day. In fact, the statistics in that game were enormously in our favor. Shaw outpassed Charlie Conerly, that tough thirty-seven-year-old coot from Mississippi, 238 yards to 188 yards. But we just screwed it up by fumbling the ball all over the field. Joyce and Giants' offensive tackle Rosie Brown resumed a war they had begun in the summer during an exhibition game. Rosie was a quiet guy, but during the exhibition season Joyce began banging him upside the helmet like there was no tomorrow. I thought Joyce was going to kill him. Finally Rosie just had enough of that crazy bastard, and the two of them began swinging and rolling around in the dirt, gouging, biting, the whole bit. I'm telling you, Joyce went nuts. During the regular-season game he hit Rosie a shot and Brown was taken out of the game and to St. Elizabeth's Hospital with a fractured cheekbone.

And I remember after Pat Summerall kicked a twenty-eight-yarder with 2:40 remaining, we couldn't move the ball, and the Giants got the ball back. And at the end of the game as they were letting the clock run out, the Giants were standing there laughing at us. Laughing right in our faces. That was a mistake.

When the gun went off I stood up and I said, "You dirty bunch of bastards, we'll stick it up your asses before it's all over." And then I started scooping up anything I could find, rocks, dirt, turf, and throwing it at them. And they just walked off the field laughing.

Afterward, Conerly wrote a story in one of the New York newspapers, I don't remember which one, saying that the Giants had "outgutted us." I don't know why Charlie would say something like that. He wasn't a braggart type of guy, at least I didn't think he was. I know Unitas would never say something like that. In fact, none of the older guys on our team would say anything like that. We kept our mouths shut, or, I should say, Weeb made us keep our mouths shut.

He used to say, "If the reporters want to find out anything, tell them to come and see me." It's not like that bullshit today, when they get each player for twenty minutes on the tube after the game. We had to keep our mouths shut, period. If a guy asked us how we felt, we'd say, "Terrific." That's it.

So as if we needed it, Conerly's story really ticked us off more. Weeb had the story hanging from every available wall space in the locker room. Weeb was big on that insult stuff. I suppose most coaches are. Before every game Weeb had articles hanging all over the locker room. Christ, sometimes it looked like a pressroom when you walked in there. I think that's a load of crap most of the time. We were all professionals and we all did our jobs no matter what someone wrote about us. But I believe that in this instance, after the laughing bullshit and the newspaper arrogance, all of us started secretly rooting for the Giants to win the Eastern Conference. We wanted to meet them again.

Anyway, Shaw started against the Bears the next week and we shut them out. And Unitas returned the following week and we murdered the Rams, 34–7. The Giant loss seemed long ago and far away. We were 8–1 when San Francisco came into Baltimore for a game that could clinch the conference for us. The 49ers were a helluva good football team that year, but I want to tell you something: If there is a game in the history of the NFL that deserves to be called "The Greatest Game Ever Played," it was the Colt-49er game of November 30, 1958.

I believe that's the greatest game a football team ever played, and I know it was the greatest game the Colts ever played. I mean, I've seen Colt teams come back from deficits, both while I was playing and during those great years they had in the 1970s when Bert Jones was quarterbacking. But for sheer annihilation, I mean absolutely clobbering a team in the second half of a game, there was no better comeback. We left the 49ers positively shell-shocked.

We were down 27–7 at the half, and naturally, San Francisco

figured it was all over. Their quarterback, Y. A. Tittle, who had spent a year with me on one of the worst football teams of all time, ran in for a score about five minutes into the game. And Unitas, who was wearing some sort of aluminum breastplate to protect his ribs, had one of the worst halves of his career. At halftime, what with that metal corset, he looked like a medieval knight who had just lost to a dragon.

But on the first play of the second half, Lenny Moore broke loose for a sideline-to-sideline seventy-five-yard touchdown run, a real thing of beauty. He must have really run about 150 yards, considering all the cutbacks he made. And suddenly it was 27–14 and the wind was picking up a little bit on our sidelines from the air blowing out of the Niners' sails.

Aside from defense, I played on the Colts' Big Ass teams, and they were just what they sound like. The guys with the biggest bulk were thrown out there to form a human wall of beef to block for field goals and extra points. In the second half of the San Francisco game we didn't kick any field goals, but we scored four touchdowns, and four times I trudged out to block for the extra points. I was the right guard on the Big Ass team, and Leo Nomellini was the San Francisco left defensive tackle who played across from me.

He would line up, and I'd look at him and say, "Hey, Leo, ya big bastard, ya gonna come?" And the first couple of extra points he did come, trying to block them. He'd say, "Get ready, Fatso, I'm comin'," and he'd really give me a shot. But by about our third touchdown of the second half, they knew it was all over. Unitas was just eating them up all over the field. They were going nowhere on offense, and on the extra point I looked up at Leo and he had this look on his face that said, "What the hell happened to us?"

Their whole team was in disarray. So I said to Leo," You still comin'?" And he said, "Hell, no, Fatso, it's all over now." And that was it. We won, 35–27, and clinched the Western Conference title. The last two games of the season were anticlimactic. We traveled to the West Coast for two games and lost to the Rams, 30–28, and 21–12 to the Niners, who gained back some measure of re-

spect. Weeb was always a big bullshitter, and he went around telling all the newspaper guys how overconfidence led to those
defeats. He was wrong, of course. That may have had a little to do
with the losses, but the main reason was that after we clinched,
Weeb was giving everybody on the team a chance to play.

Shaw quarterbacked both games to give Unitas a rest, and we
were up on the Rams, 28–14, when they scored a touchdown to
close to within seven. I remember Weeb on the sidelines had been
a little distracted up until then. But when they scored all of a sudden he awoke and said, "Aw, what the hell, let's win it." And we
could have if we had wanted to, but Weeb wanted to give everybody a chance to play. So he kept the second team in there and
they beat us.

But I want to get something straight right now. We were never
overconfident. None of us had ever been on a championship team,
and there were still quite a few fires stoking from that Giant loss
back in November. The Giants and the Browns tied for first place
in the Eastern Conference with 9–3 records, and New York took
the title with 10–0 victory in the playoff game. The stage was set
for revenge.

The championship game of 1958 was billed as a clash of
cultures: blue-collar Baltimore vs glamorous Gotham. The billers
weren't far wrong. Something like three special trainloads of Colt
fans had rolled up for the game, twelve thousand people in all. I
understand they partied hard in New York. That's understand-
able. This was the first championship game Baltimore fans had to
cheer about since Wee Willie Keeler paced the old Baltimore Ori-
oles to a pennant in 1896.

The fans were all staying downtown in the Manhattan hotels.
Weeb wanted to keep the team away from everybody, so he put us
up on 161st Street in the Bronx, in the Concourse Plaza Hotel, a
joint I used to steal beer from at American Legion dances when I
was a teenager. The fans wanted to go out on the town, and the
Bronx, even then, was no place to go out on the town.

During the season when we played the Giants, Weeb had let us
bring our wives up to New York, and we had stayed down at the
Manhattan Hotel. I swear to God, Weeb to this day believes the

reason we lost that game was on account of our wives being with us. Naturally, no wives were allowed to stay with us prior to the championship game.

I was at home in the Bronx. I'd been born and raised forty blocks north of Yankee Stadium, in an apartment at 3034 Grand Concourse. And I'd gone to high school at Mount St. Michael's, up at the top of the borough. Saturday, the day before we played, we checked into the hotel, and as we were walking down to Yankee Stadium from the Concourse Plaza, all these Jewish guys I knew were out on the street sunning their kids in the baby carriages. One of them yelled to me, "Donovan, you guys are gonna get killed!" And I yelled back, "Yeah, we're gonna shove that title right up your ass." In fact, on the morning of the game, we were getting off the team bus at the stadium when a voice rising out of a group of cops standing near the players' entrance boomed out at me, "Hey, Donovan, I hope you're better than you were when you played at Mount St. Michael's." I couldn't answer that one. I was laughing too hard.

Going into the game, I really believe the Giants thought they were better than we were. How they could think that, I don't know, but I believe they did. Of course, they were only kidding themselves. Man for man, there was no contest. Frank Gifford was a good football player, but I thought Kyle Rote may have been better. Conerly was a tough sonofabitch, but no match for Unitas. Even with Andy Robustelli and Sam Huff on defense, they definitely weren't as good as our team. Playing in New York may have gotten them all that publicity, but don't ever put Huff in the same class as our middle linebacker, Bill Pellington. And there was no match in the league for Gino Marchetti.

We knew we were good, but Weeb wasn't taking any chances. In the locker room before the game, he started in with the big pep talk.

What a big delivery! He should have won an Oscar. He went down the roster one by one, telling every guy on the team how he had been rejected. We were a string of castoffs and rejects, he said. "Pittsburgh didn't want you, but we picked you up off the sandlots," he told Unitas. "Detroit didn't want you, but I'm glad I got you," he told Milt Davis, one of our starting cornerbacks. To Spinney and Alex Sandusky, our starting offensive guards, he said, "You couldn't play offensive end, and you were too small for defensive end, but we made offensive guards out of you."

It was a real three-hankie affair. He even dragged himself into it, saying how he had been the second choice, after the Browns' Blanton Collier, to coach the Colts five years previously. He may have said something about me, he must have said something about me, but I wouldn't know. I was in the men's room throwing up. I'd been doing that before every game since I was playing at Boston College.

There was one guy in the head with me, a defensive back named Bert Rechichar, a good old boy from Tennessee. Bert was also our substitute kicker and our third end, behind Berry and Jim Mutscheller. For some reason, I can't even remember why, Weeb was mad at Bert and vowed not to let him play. So Bert saw me puking in the bathroom and sidled up to me and said, "I'll show that little weasel bastard. I'm gonna get in this goddamn game."

Later, during the game, Mutscheller made a great catch but was knocked unconscious. And Bert went in for him and Weeb didn't even recognize it for three or four plays. Finally Weeb saw him and started hopping up and down on the sidelines, yelling, "Get him outta there! Get that guy outta there!" I'll never forget the look on Weeb's face. He looked like he was having a heart attack.

And for a while, I thought Yankee Stadium was going to see thirty-three Colts have heart attacks right on the field. Throughout the game, the Giants ran away from my side. Somebody wrote that in films of the '58 championship game Art Donovan looked like a big marshmallow covered by a number 70 jersey trailing after every play with his sweat socks drooping low. And that's about right. Vince Lombardi, the Giants' offensive coordinator, put in a pretty goddamn good offensive strategy for the game.

Jim Lee Howell, the Giant coach, had two men on his staff who were destined for coaching greatness in Lombardi and Tom Landry, their defensive coordinator. I remembered Landry from the early fifties, when he was a defensive back, and even when he was playing he was always like another coach on the field. And of course we had heard about Lombardi, but we didn't realize that the guy would turn out to be perhaps the greatest football coach who ever lived. I mean, how are you supposed to know that stuff? I played with Don Shula. I lived with Don Shula. And when I think back to when we were single guys playing and living together, who the hell would ever believe that Shula would be the great coach he is today? A coach, sure. But as good as he is?

Anyway, Lombardi knew our defensive line was going to put a landslide rush on Conerly. And he knew that rush was going to come primarily from me and Marchetti on the left side. So what they did was have the quarterback roll to his left on almost every play, away from me and Marchetti and toward Joyce and Lipscomb over on the right. They made it look like there was going to be a pitchout to our right, we'd gear up for that, and suddenly Conerly was peeling back to our left with the ball, giving him time to look for the pass. And whoops, we'd have to change direction and chase that sly bastard over to the other side. And that was a helluva strategy, because they did manage to neutralize our rush to an extent.

On one of these runs to their left, when they didn't fake it and just ran right at our right outside linebacker, Don Shinnick, Gifford broke loose for thirty-eight yards, a helluva run. That was really the only good run I can remember Gifford ever having against us in all the years we played against him. We really had his number, and Jesus Christ, we couldn't believe it. There was about eight of us an inch from bringing him down, and if someone had just gotten in his way for a split second, he would have been buried. But the defensive flow just couldn't catch him. That set up Pat Summerall's field goal, and the Giants took the lead, 3–0.

A few series later, the Giants had the ball on their own twenty-yard line when Gifford fumbled and Big Daddy smothered the ball. I remember picking Gifford up when he tried to come through the hole, and I didn't even know he had lost the ball. Unitas alternated hand-offs between Moore, Mr. Outside, and Ameche, Mr. Inside, and when the Horse took it in from the two a few plays later, we led, 7–3.

After another Gifford fumble deep in our territory—Don Joyce recovered it this time—Johnny U. just picked them apart, leading us on an eighty-six-yard scoring drive. He finally found Berry for a fifteen-yard touchdown toss and we were up, 14–3, with two minutes left in the half. Let me tell you, in the halftime locker room we figured we were on our way.

Right before the half one of the funniest incidents I can remember during my playing days occurred. Sam Huff had this reputation as a real mean player, but in fact he was as dirty as the day was long. After Raymond Berry caught a pass right near our sidelines and was already down on the ground, Huff came up to him and buried an elbow in his face. Our assistant trainer, a guy named Spassoff, was standing right there, and he started to give Huff some lip. Huff, naturally enough, went after him. So here came Weeb, raising his dukes as if he was planning on throwing a haymaker at Huff. The papers the next day said he did hit him, but let me tell you, Weeb never got near the man.

Weeb clenched his fist as if he was going to punch him, so Huff jumped up and squared off. Weeb thought we were all right there behind him. But while he was staring down Huff, the whole team had backed away. Suddenly Weeb turned around and noticed that we had all cleared out. Well, you never saw a man hemming and hawing and stammering like Weeb in that instant. It was hilarious. "Uh, well, uh, hey, Sam, you know . . ." What a riot. Weeb turned beet red and, vroom, made a beeline behind a group of us as Huff walked back onto the field.

In the third quarter we should have gone up 21–3, but we screwed up royally and gave them a chance to get back in the game.

We had the ball first-and-goal from the Giants' three midway through the third, but four cracks at the goal line produced nothing. The turf was frozen down at that end of the field. Twice Unitas handed off to the Horse, and twice Ameche slipped on the ice. On third-and-goal, John tried to quarterback-sneak it in, but they stacked him up at the one. Finally, on fourth down, Weeb decided to go for the touchdown instead of the field goal, to really put the game out of reach. Unitas pitched the ball out to Ameche, who looked for a moment like he had an avenue into the end zone. But one of their linebackers, a guy named Cliff Livingston, sliced in and knocked the Horse off his feet at the five, a four-yard loss. To this day I'm convinced—though none involved will ever admit it—that Ameche ran the wrong play, that he was supposed to go up the middle, where there was a hole the size of the Holland Tunnel.

It didn't take long for Ameche's loss and our failure to score to come back to haunt us, because suddenly we were fighting for our goddamn lives. The Giants narrowed the gap to 14–10 on a touchdown that was set up by one of the wildest plays in football history. After the Giants took possession, Conerly hit Rote with a bullet of a pass, and Rote carried it all the way to our twenty-five-yard line, where he fumbled the ball—right into the arms of Giant fullback Alex Webster. Webster carried the fumble to our one, and a play later Mel Triplett banged in for the score.

We took the kickoff with about four minutes left in the third quarter, and our situation went from bad to worse. John's pass protection broke down, he was dumped on his ass a couple of times, and we were forced to punt. Conerly hit Bob Schnelker with a couple of long passes, and Charlie eventually found Gifford for the touchdown that put them ahead, 17–14. On the sidelines, we were devastated. As the fourth quarter wound down with neither offense moving the ball, we began to look at each other like we were at a funeral. In essence, we were: our own. I remember turning to Gino and saying, "Jesus Christ, what a shame to lose this goddamn game when we know we're so much better than these guys."

Finally, with time running out and the Giants holding the ball, the game came down to one crucial defensive play. On third down and four from their own thirty-nine, Conerly sent Gifford around Marchetti's end. Gino lunged and grabbed Gifford's ankles and I came in and got ahold of his shoulders and we dragged him down well short of the first down. To this day Giant fans swear the officials spotted the ball wrong, but don't let them kid you. We nailed him well behind the line.

Gino also broke his ankle on that play when Big Daddy, who was trailing the play, piled on. That sonofabitch was always piling on, and I swear I lost more teammates from Big Daddy coming in late than I did from the other team. One year he put about four of our guys in the hospital. In this case, as we were holding Gifford down, I spotted Lipscomb out of the corner of my eye, charging in, and ducked just in time. He missed my head and snapped Gino's leg.

The Giants' Don Chandler punted, a move Howell took some heat for, and with two minutes to go, Unitas took over on our own fourteen-yard line. I don't know if the Giants underestimated John or if they just thought their defense was good enough to hold us. Either way, they should have realized that their defense hadn't really been doing anything all day. John had all the time in the world to throw, except during that one third-quarter possession when he'd been knocked on his keester.

Unitas was just a calm, cool, calculating quarterback, maybe the best who ever played. He knew he had time to throw the ball, because despite an occasional lapse, our pass protection was fantastic. He'd stand back there and pump his arm three or four times before he'd let it fly. In fact, in practice, the defensive coaches were always on our ass about rushing the passer. If the quarterback could pump his arm more than one time, the defensive line wasn't doing a good job getting to the guy. And against the Giants that day, Unitas looked like a traffic cop waving and waving behind our offensive wall.

On that final drive, John methodically picked them apart, completing seven in a row, the last three to Berry. Berry's last catch was to the Giant fifteen-yard line. There were seven seconds left in regulation time when the Big Ass team was sent in to block for the tying field goal. As I was running onto the field for the kick I noticed Gino stop the stretcher-bearers who were carrying him to the locker room. He lay there by the tunnel leading to the locker room waiting to see if the kick was good.

As I said, on the Big Ass team I was the right guard, just to the right of the center. Jim Parker was the right tackle, just to the right of me. Big Sherman Plunkett, a moose of a man, was to Parker's right. As we lined up for the kick, I saw that the Giants were trying to block it. I also saw that they were going to put a game on, and that they were going to come right over me. They had done it earlier on an extra point: Two defensive linemen gang-blocked me and laid me low while another ran over my face trying to block the kick. It had almost worked then. I was scared shitless that it was going to work now.

So right there on the line I screamed to Parker at the top of my lungs, "Parker, you gotta block in! You gotta give me a hand!" And he yells, "No, no, Fatso, they're coming over me!" I yelled back, "You sonofabitch, you—" But just then the ball was snapped. Well, if you ever see the game films of that kick, you can see me flat on my ass, laying right where the Giants knocked me. Two of them hit me and one of them ran right through the hole. They didn't block Myrah's kick, but it was goddamn close.

After we tied the game I started screaming at Parker as we were coming off the field. And he was screaming back, "Hey, don't bother me, don't bother me! I'm nervous!" Listen, we were all nervous. I wanted to strangle the guy.

There was a five-minute break before the first overtime game in the league's history. Then the ref flipped a coin and the Giants won the toss. They chose to receive. After the kickoff, we stuffed them on four plays. It was time for Unitas to put this one away. He moved the club downfield, mixing the running and passing like a maestro until finally he hit Berry at the Giants' nine-yard line.

On first-and-goal from the nine, Ameche carried for two. And then John crossed everyone up by hitting Mutscheller with a little flare pass out in the flat. Weeb had told him to play it safe and not to throw any passes down there, but John knew what he was doing. Mutch would have scored had he not slid on the ice and slipped out of bounds at the one. But while the defense and scrubs were all cheering on the sidelines, Weeb was going bullshit.

I thought it was a hell of a good call, and don't let that weasel bastard Weeb kid you. He was just as choked up from pressure as any player was out on the field. I think John was just showing that he was always his own man on the field.

On the next play, the Horse took it in through a hole up the middle I could have run through, and all hell broke loose. Bal-

timore fans came pouring out onto the field and ripped the goalposts down. They hoisted the Horse up on their shoulders, and
Buzz Nutter, our center, had to chase across the field a guy who
had swiped the ball. Down in Baltimore, one guy who was listening while he was driving ran his car into a telephone pole. And
another guy who was watching on television jumped so high as
Ameche crossed the goal line that he had to be taken to the hospital for stitches in his hand where he had smashed the light bulb in
his ceiling.

Ed Sullivan invited Unitas and the Horse on his show, but only
Ameche could make it. Unitas flew back to Baltimore with the rest
of the team. We voted Marchetti the game ball, and they had to lift
him onto the plane with a mobile freight hoist. The Colts were met
at the old Friendship International Airport by thirty thousand de-
lirious fans. They climbed on top of the bus carrying the players,
and the police picked up fourteen of these fans on a deserted dirt
road about a mile from the airport. A police cruiser was crushed
when fans jumped on top of it to catch a glimpse of the conquering
heroes, and traffic was so bad that the state police asked radio
stations to broadcast a plea for people to stay away from the airport.

Colt fans were crazy for us. They proved that earlier in the season when fifty-six thousand of them all stayed to the final gun of
our 56–0 shellacking of Green Bay in a driving rainstorm. But now
the city was really turned on its ear. The *Baltimore News-American*
sold eighteen thousand extra copies, their largest extra run since
V-J Day. And the mayor of Baltimore declared Thursday, December 18, as "Colt Day."

A fan poll to pick the most valuable player of the Colts was
declared a thirty-six-way tie for first because the *Baltimore News-
American* received so many votes for the team as a whole that they
just decided to award each Colt a plaque. As I said, we all made
$4,700 for the game, and we received nearly another $5,000 apiece
from anonymous donors. We all figured quite a few of those anonymous donors had taken the Colts and the points.

More to the point, there are a lot of people who feel that Weeb
went for the sudden-death touchdown, instead of playing it safe

with a field goal, because the Colts' owner, Carroll Rosenbloom, had a big bet on the game. The scenario makes sense. The Colts were laying anywhere from three and a half to five points that day, and old Rosey definitely struck me as the kind of man who didn't mind playing it fast and loose. I remember when he drowned off the coast of Florida in 1980, I called Ordell Braase, an old teammate, and said, "Well, the Sicilian frogmen finally got to Rosey."

I've often heard and read that the reason we went for the touchdown was because Rosenbloom was such a dear heart to his players in setting them up in business and dishing out private loans. Bullshit. Let me just say that the farthest thing from my mind when I was on that goddamn field was to "win one for Rosey." Some of the other players may have thought that way, although they never mentioned it to me, but I was out there busting my hump for one person and one person only: Arthur J. Donovan, Jr.

Our locker-room celebration after the game was also in stark contrast to what goes on after games today. The win was something nobody on the team had really ever experienced. And there wasn't a lot of screaming and hollering and shouting. Everybody just felt good that everybody had contributed to the win, and there was none of this pouring of champagne all over each other. I really detest that when I see that on television. I think it makes these guys look like big, overgrown babies. In fact, we didn't even have beer. Weeb wouldn't allow it in the locker room. I celebrated with a bottle of soda, got dressed, and went up to my mother's house for a party.

So I won't give you the wrong impression, don't for a minute think that there wasn't a veritable flood of suds at the house at 3034 Grand Concourse. While the rest of the team went back to Baltimore, I stayed in New York to celebrate my newfound notoriety. All my uncles and cousins were at the party, and they had been Giant season ticket holders for years and years. In fact, the only Colt fans present at the affair were my wife, my mother, and my father. But I didn't really give anybody the big razz. And actually, the family was happy that we won, happy for me.

So the next day, I was standing in front of Mr. Goldberg's candy store, a place where I always hung out when I was a kid, and I was feeling my oats. All my friends were coming up to me and saying what a great game I played and what a great football player I turned out to be, when I spotted a man named Mr. Sherman coming down the street. Now, Mr. Sherman was a longtime neighbor of our family. I was born in an apartment next to Mr. Sherman's house. As he got near me I thought he was coming to shake my hand, so I put out my hand. He just looked at me and said, "Why, you big bum, you. Are you out of work again?"

Old Mr. Sherman never even knew I played football. I guess everything is relative. Of course, that was something I should have already realized from growing up in the Bronx.

3

Da Boy from Da Bronx

I was born on June 5, 1924, on the same bed on which my mother was born. In those days you didn't go to a hospital for a little thing like a baby coming into the world, although in my case I understand it wasn't such a little thing. Our family physician, Dr. Thomas Shaughnessy, said that when I came out I weighed close to seventeen pounds. My poor mother, Mary, couldn't walk for three weeks.

Eleven of my first cousins were born in that bed, in my grandmother's house at 252 East 202nd Street, the Bronx, New York City. I was surrounded by aunts and uncles and cousins up in the Bronx. They were mostly from my mother's side. But a couple of my father's brothers lived up there, too. My father's family was generally more spread out. They had moved to such exotic locales as New Jersey, Long Island, and Westchester County. They could have been on the moon for all I knew.

Both sides of my family had come from Ireland in the nineteenth century for the same reason: There was nothing to eat over there. They had this thing going called the potato famine, and since the potato is the only vegetable that has passed these lips in the past fifty years, usually in the form of that wonderful recipe supplied by the French, I kind of understand how they felt. One look at me, however, usually lets people in on the secret that I've never really known true hunger.

My mother's parents, Margaret O'Keefe and James Wall, met in New Jersey and, after they were married, settled in the Bedford Park section of the Bronx. My grandmother, Margaret Wall, was an Irish washerwoman and she also took in boarders. She had eight children—six daughters and two boys—and most of the boarders she took in were Italian immigrants brought over to work on the Third Avenue el, the elevated subway train. None of these guys could speak English when they came over, and as they slowly learned the language, they all picked up a thick Irish brogue. You haven't heard anything until you've heard a Sicilian with an accent like he just got off the boat from Mayo.

My grandparents lived in a big old house, and my mother's father was always complaining that there were too many doors in the house for all his daughters and all these Italian guys running around. James Wall was a gardener, and he was Irish to the core. It was as if he refused to believe he had ever left the old country. He used to have these Irish dances at the house, go the whole nine yards. Every Mick from the Bronx would show at my grandfather's jigs.

My grandmother was completely different. She was really Americanized. She used to say that she would have starved in Ireland, so when she came to a country that would feed her, the least she could do was adopt its customs. She was shrewd, too. One of her favorite sayings was, "There's money in dirt," and to prove it, she would buy a house, fix it up, sell it for a profit, and buy a bigger house. She did this regularly until she wound up with what for those days was a mansion, on 202nd Street. When I was a kid one of my older cousins told me that if the Depression hadn't come along, she would have made a million dollars. At any rate, she didn't, but she was never poor. In fact, I'd have to admit that growing up, we were one of the richest families in the area.

The parents of my other grandfather, Mike Donovan, came to the United States around the same time as the Walls and the O'Keefes. The Donovans settled in Chicago, and when Mike was seven, his mother died and his father skipped town. Word was he took a riverboat down the Mississippi to try out the gaming tables and whorehouses of New Orleans. At any rate, Mike never saw his father again.

Mike was raised by an aunt, and at fourteen he ran away and enlisted in the Union's Irish Brigade in the Civil War. He was an infantryman. I never knew him—he died in 1918—but my father used to tell me stories about what an amazingly tough guy he was. He was with the army that reinforced Grant at Chattanooga. He marched to the sea with Sherman. And he fought at Antietam, stopping Lee's advance in what they call the bloodiest day of the Civil War.

It's funny—a few years ago I drove through the Antietam battlefield, right out in western Maryland. I was on my way to a speaking engagement at the Horticultural Society of West Virginia. And damned if I didn't get goose pimples all over my body when I drove past that battlefield, just thinking about old Mike Donovan. Then I had to laugh to myself. I doubt if my grandfather even knew what a horticultural society was. I sure as hell didn't. Thought they were goddamn florists. Turned out to be apple growers.

After the Civil War my grandfather was discharged in St. Louis and fought his way to New York as a bareknuckle prize fighter. He eventually fought his way to the middleweight championship of the world. He was a special favorite of Wyatt Earp and Doc Holliday when he was fighting out West. And he fought heavyweights like Jack Dempsey, the Nonpareil, and John L. Sullivan, who knocked him out of the ring in four rounds in Boston. Sullivan admired the little guy's moxie, though, and they went touring together, putting on exhibitions all over the country. That's when he met up with Earp, Holliday, and the Wild West boys. Finally he broke with Sullivan and trained Gentleman Jim Corbett, who took Sullivan's title in a bloody brawl.

After seventy bareknuckle fights my grandfather retired to become the boxing instructor at the New York Athletic Club, a job he held for thirty-eight years. He became Teddy Roosevelt's personal boxing tutor while Teddy was New York's police commissioner. And after Roosevelt became vice president and, later, president, Mike used to take a weekly train to Washington to spar with him. My father told me Mike told him old Teddy had a pretty good right cross. Mike even published a book, *The Roosevelt That I Know*, in 1909. In fact, when Roosevelt was elected to a full term as president in 1904 and heard that Mike Donovan was going to lead the New York veterans' contingent in the inauguration parade, Teddy called him and made three requests. Well, I guess you might call them orders.

He told Mike to wear his Grand Old Army of the Republic uniform. He told him to make sure he was riding a white horse. And he wanted the band to be playing "Garry Owen," the old Irish marching tune that had been adopted by the Irish Brigade (and, later, by George Armstrong Custer, who had his fife and drum corps break into this rouser as he marched into the valley of the Little Big Horn). Well, Mike filled all these bills, and as the New York veterans marched past the reviewing stand, Roosevelt jumped up and yelled, "Bully! Bully boys!" much to the wonderment of the politicos sitting around him.

Mike Donovan died at the age of seventy-one, on March 24, 1918. He caught pneumonia recruiting soldiers for World War I up at the old New York Armory—but not before marrying Cecilia Butler of Pennsylvania and fathering fourteen children, including my father, Arthur Donovan, Sr., who took over his boxing instructor's job at the New York Athletic Club and held it for fifty years to the minute.

My father's whole life was teaching boxing and refereeing. It was my mother who really raised my sister Joan and me. My father couldn't care less if the sun came up, as long as the New York Athletic Club was still standing when he got down there to work. After he became the most famous referee in the world—I guess about the time I was ten years old—we saw him even less. He would work from three in the afternoon until nine at night, and afterward he would go out with all the millionaires who loved to hear his fight stories.

He'd been a pretty fair fighter himself, but little things like wars kept interrupting his career. He fought with General John O'Ryun and Black Jack Pershing on the Mexican border. When my grand-father died they gave my father leave from his Army camp in Spar-tanburg, South Carolina, to come to the funeral. And three months later he was over in France, dodging bullets in the trenches of France with the 27th New York Infantry Regiment. I even ran into that tough old sonofabitch during World War II in Guam, when I was with a machine-gun outfit in the Marines.

But like I said, we didn't see much of him at home. I remember my mother sending me out to the candy store every night to buy the evening *Journal-American* for him to read when he got home. She'd also slip me a couple of pennies for candy, and I had a good scam going there. But when I'd try to wait up to see my father come home and read the paper, I could never quite make it. We saw him on weekends—Sundays, really—and sometimes he would take me down to the club to box with the rich kids, or we'd go sailing out on some millionaire's yacht. For the most part, how-ever, he spent his time down in Manhattan slugging sparring part-ners and slugging back drinks.

For the first seven years of my life, I lived in a small apartment at 3001 Briggs Avenue, with my parents and my sister Joan, who was two years younger than me. It was about a block and a half from my Grandmother Margaret's house. Then, when I was seven, my father started making good money refereeing fights, and we got high class and moved two blocks up the street, to a six-room apartment at 3034 Grand Concourse, apartment 1B, on the east wing of the ground floor of a United Nations building, if you know what I mean—Irish, Jews, Italians, Germans. I grew up in a poly-glot environment.

But the hub of the neighborhood was always my grandmother's house. We had what seemed like a million cousins hanging around that place. I had twelve first cousins alone who lived within a two-block radius of my grandmother's house, and a bunch more who were right up the road in Yonkers. Whether you were Italian, Jew-ish, Irish, German, family, or nonfamily, everybody in that neigh-borhood passed through my grandmother's home. Sometimes it seemed like everybody in the Bronx passed through. She orga-nized Easter egg hunts, and fifty guests for Thanksgiving and

Christmas was a small affair. Everybody used to come by and say hello. I can even remember the bootlegger, Mr. Politucci, coming down with his patent-leather bag bringing her the whiskey for her party.

Everybody was invited—it was more or less an open house—and when we'd all sit down to dinner, here it came: the leg of lamb. Holy Christ, I must have been ten years old before I realized you weren't required by law to have leg of lamb on Sunday. The only difference was whether you had it with baked potatoes or boiled potatoes or potatoes roasted right around the lamb.

On weekdays, my mother would feed us the usual Bronx Irish fare: Chef Boyardee spaghetti or pork chops or hamburger meat. But you might say my culinary tastes strayed from the norm when I was somewhere around ten or twelve. For the past forty-five years I haven't eaten anything but kosher salami, kosher baloney, corned beef, cheeseburgers, pizza, and, like I said, French fries, my concession to the vegetable family. Never steak—I don't like anything you have to chew on. And never, never, any other vegetables. I'll worry about scurvy when I get it. When I was a kid, my mother and aunts used to try to make me eat my vegetables, and what I would do is eat my baked potato and stuff all the vegetables inside the potato skin so they wouldn't know I didn't eat them. But give me some kosher cold cuts and I'm in heaven. Since I was six years old they've called me the Baloney King.

About the first thing I can remember was being about six years old and going to classes at St. Philip Neri parochial grammar school. That was right up the Grand Concourse, at the end of 202nd Street. My sister and I both went there, and most of the nuns who taught at the school were girls who had grown up in the neighborhood. Almost all of them knew my mother, and she used to sort of sandbag them a little bit to take care of me, because I wasn't the greatest scholar in the world. To be blunt, she'd either have about six of them over to dinner or she'd take them for rides in her car just so I would pass a course. She'd go over to the convent and pick them up and motor them out to Long Island, or up to Rye Beach, anything to get them out of the city and me out of second grade.

To tell you the truth, the nuns all liked me. I was sort of their fair-haired boy. But it really got to the point where I wasn't doing my homework or anything else except hanging out with the gang from the neighborhood. We always hung out either in front of Mr. Goldberg's candy store or at the playground of Public School 8, which was right across the street from our Briggs Avenue apartment. Sometimes, when we were feeling really adventurous, we'd head down to the vacant lots by Mosholu Parkway. I did what every other kid growing up in the Bronx did in those days: went to church, played sports, and hung around the candy store refining my bullshit technique.

When I got old enough to play football, the older guys in my neighborhood all took a shine to me. I guess they figured that maybe I was going to be a pretty good football player one of these days—I was born big and I stayed that way—and they'd let me play with them. I was still in grammar school, and these guys were in high school. But I was big enough so that when I played with them they treated me just like everybody else.

They'd get mad at me and they'd chase me and they'd whip the hell out of me. But I guess I was always sort of the older neighborhood guys' pride and joy. A couple of years ago I went to the funeral of one of my best friends up in the Bronx. His name was Al Arater, and when I walked out of the church I saw all the old gang. They had all moved up to Westchester County or Connecticut, and when they saw me they all said, "Well, Artie, you sure had a great career." I felt very proud when they said that to me that day.

I spent a good number of my formative years going to baseball games at Yankee Stadium. The kids from the neighborhood would go with the Police Athletic League, or with the Catholic Youth Organization. And believe it or not, I always liked baseball better than I liked football, even when I got to high school. Joe DiMaggio was my man, and I had pictures of all the Yanks hanging in my bedroom, surrounded by pictures of Notre Dame football players and, of course, the Fordham Ram football team. Joe D was a close second in idolhood next to the football stars from Fordham.

Unfortunately, I was born way ahead of my time. I would have made a tremendous designated hitter. About the only way I could get on base was by hitting it over the fence. I wasn't what you'd call extremely fast. And I had an iron glove when it came to fielding. But I could slam the hell out of that baseball. I knocked a couple out of Macombs Dam Park, right next to Yankee Stadium, that my coach said were the longest balls he'd ever seen hit. And though I wasn't fast, Christ, I was quick.

I mean, everybody in the neighborhood played stickball, or strikes and balls against a wall, or handball, or three-on-three basketball over at P.S. 8, and that's where I developed my quickness, especially from handball and basketball. Years later, when Weeb Ewbank took over the Colts, he used to race all the rookies against me for fifty yards, and anybody who couldn't beat me would be cut. "Lose to the fat man Donovan," he'd say, "and you don't deserve to play professional football." But Lord, nobody could beat me over those first three, four, or five yards, as a lot of overconfident offensive linemen were to find out when they saw the fat man with the droopy socks line up against them.

Despite the family heritage, I never took to boxing. First of all, my father wouldn't let me. And second of all, I didn't like it. I just never seemed to enjoy getting rapped in the mouth. Not that I didn't have my share of fights. You couldn't live in the Bronx and not raise your dukes at some point. I was born and raised with Steve Belloise, who grew up two blocks from me and fought Sugar Ray Robinson for the middleweight title. Steve's older brother, Mike, won the featherweight championship of the world in 1936. We all hung together. My mother used to call me a house devil and a street angel, and I suppose what she didn't know didn't hurt her. I especially remember all the Italian kids at St. Philip Neri getting on my case when my father would ref a fight and the Italian guy lost.

None of the fights we used to have up in the Bronx were racial, but each nationality tended to hang out in its own packs. Every time my father would referee a fight between an Italian and an American (even though the Italian was really an American, too; in those days boxers changed names and nationalities like we change our underwear), if he gave the decision to the American, the Italian kids at school would beat the shit out of me. They'd rip off my clothes and chase me home, and the weird thing was that my mother knew all of their mothers. Not that that stopped them.

I go home to the neighborhood now, and all those guys who used to beat me up are still around there. My old neighborhood's the cleanest in the Bronx because all those Italian kids are now inspectors in the sanitation department. They all walk around like Italian generals, with the green uniform with the epaulets on their shoulders and the scrambled eggs on the front of their caps. When they see me they yell, "Hey, Artie, remember when we used to kick the hell out of you? We were crazy!" And I yell back. "Come on, try it now!" That's when they tell me that now we're friends. Those sonsabitches.

We had some crazy people living in the neighborhood. There was this kid named Eddie McCarthy—he lived on 202nd Street, in a tremendous home two houses from the Grand Concourse. His mother had died, he lived with his father, and I swear to God Eddie McCarthy was crazy. He formed this army—we called it Eddie McCarthy's Army—and he signed up all the kids in the neighborhood. There were younger kids like me, but there were some older fellows, too, guys who were in the Naval Reserve and whatnot. Most of our fathers had fought in World War I, war was once again in the air, and more than a few kids from the neighborhood expected to be fighting in World War II.

So anyway, Eddie would pass out these .30-caliber rifles he had—I don't know where he got them from, probably from his old man—and we'd go down to DeWitt Clinton Park for maneuvers, things like close-order drill. The primary thing you'd have to remember about Eddie McCarthy's Army was that Eddie McCarthy was the boss. And if you did something wrong, like step out of line during close-order drill, he'd take you down to the basement of his house and tie your hands to the pipes hanging from the ceiling, and the crazy sonofabitch would shoot BB's at you, like you were being executed by firing squad.

You know the way those potato chips come in those long cans today? Well, that's the way cookies used to be sold. And Eddie McCarthy made a machine gun, or a cannon-type thing, out of this cookie can, and he'd line us up and tie us up and take off our shirts and he'd shoot the goddamn cannon at us.

I'd go home at night and my mother would say, "What happened to you?" I'd say, "Nothing." And she'd say, "Don't tell me nothing, you're bleeding. You were at Eddie McCarthy's house again, weren't you?" What a beauty this guy was.

Nonetheless, everybody kind of liked Eddie, even the nuns at St. Philip Neri. But everybody was also a little afraid of the nut job. The back of his house abutted ours after we moved up to the Grand Concourse, and one day my mother gave him a dollar to string a clothes line from our bathroom over to a small telephone pole that was in his backyard. He climbed up that pole and yelled, "Hey, Mrs. Donovan, look at this!" And he was swinging around the goddamn pole like Tarzan. Of course, the pole broke, and he nearly killed himself.

But Eddie McCarthy's best adventure always had to do with war or weapons or something like that. Like I said, his father was wealthy, I think he was an insurance executive, and he owned this big back lot, it must have been an acre, right behind his house. They built garages on the lot, which Eddie's father rented out. And next to the garages Eddie had his own little hut. He was always mixing gunpowder and stuff in there, and one time he blew the roof right off the fucking thing and burned every hair off his head. Another time, over in the playground of P.S. 8, he was experimenting with a new type of bomb. He had laid a flat rock out on the ground, poured a pile of gunpowder on it, and then climbed up on to the roof of one of the school buildings, toting another big rock. He dropped the rock on the gunpowder, there was a giant explosion, and the rock that he had dropped broke and sent stones flying in all directions. One of the stones nailed Eddie right in the forehead, and he fell off the roof and broke his arm. Like I said, Eddie McCarthy was crazy.

There were two other kids who were crazy little bastards from the neighborhood. One was named Charley Moran. He was a cripple who needed crutches to get around. The other was Jimmy O'Toole, Charley's best friend. I used to serve Mass with these two, because we were all big Fordham football fans. In those days, the Fordham Rams were the end-all and be-all as far as football was concerned in the Bronx. That was the era of Fordham's Seven Blocks of Granite, and if we got up to serve six-o'clock Mass, the priest, Father Mulcahy, would take us over to Fordham football practice in the afternoon. There were also fringe benefits to being an altar boy. I began my altar boy career as a benchwarmer, fifteen or sixteen of us sitting on a pew over to the side during high Mass. But soon I became a favorite of the sexton, and when you were called out of school to serve a ten-o'clock funeral Mass, the priest would have to leave right after the Mass to get to the burial. So after he left, we were always in the back taking off our cassocks and chugging down that wine. I also used to be called to serve six-o'clock Mass for the Ursuline nuns in the St. Philip Neri convent. That was a great deal. After Mass, they'd always sit you down to a big breakfast, and it was great chow. Any chow was great chow.

The pastor of St. Philip Neri parish was named Father Shalara, the only Italian priest in the parish. He used to come into school and drag the Italian kids out of class and beat the crap out of them after they did something wrong, hit their mother or something like that. Well, Father Shalara eventually threw Charley Moran and Jimmy O'Toole off the altar boy squad for good.

They were always pulling pranks on the priests. And one day a priest named Father Muldoon was in his rectory when he heard a big crash in the church. So he put on his cassock and ran downstairs, and there was little Jimmy O'Toole all upset. Jimmy was shouting, "Father, Father, something terrible has happened! Charley blessed himself with the holy water in the back of the Church and he threw away his crutches!" Well, Father Muldoon got all excited and went down on his knees then and there and started genuflecting. He was blessing himself and shouting, "Oh, faith and begorra, a miracle has happened in my parish!"

So then Father Muldoon stood up and grabbed Jimmy O'Toole and asked him where Charley was. Jimmy looked up at him and said, "Hey, Father, where in the world do you think he is? He's flat on his ass by the holy water fount." Needless to say, I didn't attend any more Fordham football practices or chug any more wine with Jimmy O'Toole and Charley Moran.

Like I said, I guess you could say the Donovans were one of the richest families in the neighborhood, between my grandmother and my father, who not only had a steady job but who also was beginning to referee the big fights more often. I remember there were times when he'd referee three a week during the mid-1930s. But even my mother's drives to the beach were starting to wear pretty thin with the nuns at St. Philip Neri. I was being tutored three nights a week by Dr. Shaughnessy's wife in spelling and arithmetic and English, but it didn't save me from being left back in the seventh grade. I was lazy. I could have gotten good marks if I had wanted to, but I was too interested in horsing around the neighborhood. I swear, those nuns did everything they could to try to get me by.

If I had finished St. Philip Neri, I'm sure I would have gone to Fordham Prep High School. But I didn't finish. The nuns called my mother and, ah, suggested that she get me to a Catholic brothers' school for some discipline. And the only two Catholic brothers' schools in the Bronx that had grammar schools were All Hallows, about two blocks from Yankee Stadium, and Mount St. Michael's, which was all the way up at the top end of the borough.

So my mother pulled me from St. Philip Neri, and it was just my good luck that my father had a good friend whose son went to the Mount. I was aching for All Hallows. I remember the Monday morning my mother took me up there to register, she told the Marist brother in charge, "I don't care what you have to do to him, but teach him some discipline and make him study." That was 1937, and Jesus Christ, were those brothers tough after my having my way with the nuns. It was like going from a feather bed to a chain gang.

I was a big kid at the Mount, although, unlike grammar school, some kids there were just as huge, and tougher, too. Something happened there to me early that I'll never forget, and I really believe it's affected the way I've gone through life.

While I was in the grammar school at the Mount my football idol was the captain of the 1938 high-school football team, Bud Kohlman. He was my hero. When I became a freshman at the high school, my mother gave me money to buy a new pair of football cleats to try out for the team.

When my hero Bud Kohlman, the captain of the team, saw me walking out of the gym with my new shoes hanging over my shoulder he said, "Where do you think you are going with those shoes?" When I told him I was going to try out for the team, he laughed at me. I remember as if it was yesterday. I was never so embarrassed in all my life. I was really heartbroken. Here was my knight in shining armor laughing right in my face. I know what he does now—he works for New York Telephone Company, that's how much this thing stuck with me. I said to myself, "Why would a guy ever do that?" And Bud Kohlman taught me a lesson. From that day on I vowed I would never make fun of anybody who was trying out for anything—sports, a job, whatever. And I haven't.

But even though I was going to school somewhere up near the North Pole, I still managed to get around the neighborhood a fair amount of time. By now I was in my teens, and church was fading to a distant third behind sports and bullshitting in a Bronx boy's priorities in life. I remember we had a softball league around our block. It was called the Ray Loftus League, after the man from our neighborhood who put all the athletic programs together at St. Philip Neri. And my Uncle Bert Broome, the husband of one of my mother's sisters, was the head umpire. He was an old World War I veteran. He really never umpired in this league, he was just in charge of all the guys who did. But one day he was behind the plate calling balls and strikes and he called a strike on me.

So I hollered at him, "Uncle Bert!" And for the rest of the season, every time I stood up at the plate, I'd hear a singsong chorus from the stands and the opposing team, "Uncle Bert! Uncle Bert!" Now, that was cause to go behind the iron gate. The iron gate was a door in the P.S. 8 schoolyard that separated center field of the baseball diamond from the school playground. When Eddie McCarthy invented his bomb, he fell off a building right onto the iron gate. Anyway, when kids were going to have a fight, they'd say, "Okay, meet you behind the iron gate." They finally tore it down—not because of fights, but because they tore down most of P.S. 8. But I still shiver when I think of the iron gate.

Although I was growing at a sizable rate—I was six-one and 220 pounds by the time I was a junior at the Mount—I certainly wasn't a regular behind the iron gate. I never enjoyed that kind of stuff, and when I saw some of my best friends from the neighborhood go at it back there over something as silly as a ball game, I actually became embarrassed. Fistfights, however, were a way of life in the Bronx. If you didn't duke it out, you were a sissy.

Soon enough, however, I was developing a passion for something better than fighting, a love that has stayed with me to this day. And that passion is beer. I was six years old when I had my first sip, in a speakeasy, and I loved it. When I was little, all the uncles would have to baby-sit when my mother and her sisters went out shopping, and they used to take me over to Mr. Tooley's, an old Irishman's speakeasy on Jerome Avenue and Bedford Park Boulevard at 200th Street.

I found out soon enough that there was a price to pay for everything, though. One of my uncles would take me over to Mr. Tooley's. His name was Pierce Wall, and they used to call him Bully Wall because he always loved to fight. Trouble was, when he was taking care of me, this sonofabitch would make me fight, too. If some strange kid came came into the neighborhood, Uncle Pierce would say to me, "Go out and fight that kid." I'd say, "But I don't want to fight that kid. I don't want to fight nobody." And he'd say, "Come on, boy, don't you want to grow up and be like your Uncle Bully?"

Frankly, that was the last thing I wanted to do. But if I voiced that opinion I was likely to get a smack in the snoot. And given the choice of fighting either a kid at least near my size or taking on old Uncle Bully, I usually ended up rolling around in the dirt with some stranger I had nothing against. Pierce Wall was mad as a hatter. We'd be driving in his car and someone would holler something, and for no reason at all this bastard would stop the car and tell me, "You go out there and fight him." I was seven years old, for Christ's sake. But with old Bully, you were never too young to start learning to take your lumps. But the one good thing about it, win, lose, or draw, was that Pierce would end up at Tooley's springing for beer.

It seemed like Tooley's joint was always crowded on a Saturday afternoon, men at one end of the bar watching all the kids at the other end of the bar while all the wives and mothers were out. I guess Tooley's was where a lot of our gang got their taste for the hops.

As I mentioned earlier, when we got old enough we used to head down to the Concourse Plaza, the hotel where I stayed with the Colts for the '58 championship game. It was opposite the Bronx County Courthouse, which has long since been razed, and they'd always post when they were having the American Legion dances. The Concourse Plaza was always one of the finest hotels in the Bronx, and their dances were real shindigs with only top-shelf orchestras. So on a Saturday night, we'd sneak in and hide behind a curtain, and when the swells all got up to dance, we'd air-raid their tables and swipe bottles of beer. We'd go out into the corridor and drink them and wait for the band to strike up another tune everybody just had to dance to.

And when I think back to some of the kids I used to run with, it's a wonder I've survived this long. One of them was Lefty Weisberg, who was one of my best friends and one of the only Jewish guys I ever knew who could go beer-for-beer with me. Lefty was a rear gunner in a bomber during the war, and he was shot down over Germany. He spent a year and a half in a prisoner-of-war camp, and while he was a prisoner, his family got a telegram from the War Department saying he was missing in action and presumed dead.

When he was liberated, he never bothered to call his family to tell them he was alive and well. They brought him back to the States, he disembarked in New York, and while he was walking up the street one way with his duffel bag slung over his shoulder, his mother was coming down the street from the other direction, going shopping. So here came this goofy bastard, he ran right into his mother, and she fainted dead away on the street. I'm surprised he didn't give her a heart attack.

Lefty got out of the service and enrolled in art school. I used to take the train down to Fifty-seventh Street in Manhattan to meet him at the Art League. He fell in love with an Italian girl from the neighborhood after the war, and the two of them got married. That just wasn't done in the late 1940s, and both of their families kicked them out of the house and disowned them. Lefty was a great Giant fan, a real nut about it. One time we played the Giants in an exhibition game in New York in 1961, and Lefty was there, and he claimed that I hit somebody illegally. I got a letter from him a week later, and it said, 'You used to be my best friend, but I'll never talk to you again. You're a dirty football player.'' And I haven't seen him since.

Another of my closest friends was a guy named John Brady. He was five or six years older than me, but he was one of the guys that really took a shine to me and I looked up to him like a big brother. He took me under his wing when I was about seven and got me into football games with the older fellows in the neighborhood. He became a cop in New York and rose to the rank of inspector. During the '58 championship game he got drunk on the Colt bench— he and my father were sharing a bottle to keep warm. And he was yelling at me, telling me what to do, and I was yelling back, "Brady, will you just keep quiet!" Finally Weeb went up to one of the policemen ringing the field and told him to throw that guy out. The cop just looked at him and shrugged his shoulders. "Can't do that, Coach Ewbank," he said. "The man you want me to heave is Jesus Christ around here." So Weeb just steamed and that was that.

When I was a junior at the Mount I got a letter from Fordham University asking if I would like to try out for a football scholarship, and it was Brady who went down there with me.

I told you, I was a Fordham nut, and all of a sudden here comes this postcard with a scholarship offer on it and I was likely to die. Aside from serving six-o'clock Mass so I could watch them practice, my mother used to give me $5 every year—and that was a lot of money for those days—so I could go down to the RKO Fordham and attend their football rallies after the bowl games. I'd go and stand outside the Lido restaurant, where Kingsbridge Road and Fordham Road meet. And the team would go in there and have dinner and I'd wait for them to come out. Then I'd follow them up to the RKO Fordham for their pep rally. Then I'd walk home by myself, my feet never touching the ground.

Anyway, I don't know why they invited me to a tryout, they obviously didn't know I was only a junior, but they sent this postcard to me at Mount St. Michael's and not to my house. I used to ride to Fordham from the Mount every night with my high-school coach, Howie Smith—it was only a twenty-minute ride—and Howie used to pick up a friend at football practice and the two of them would take night classes. Howie Smith must have told his buddy on the team that I was a fairly good football player, and somehow that translated into the postcard.

So the next Saturday morning Brady and I walked over to Fordham's practice field for my tryout. My own father didn't even go with me. When we got there I turned to Brady and said, "Jesus, these guys are big." And he said to me, "What the hell are you talking about? You're tougher than anyone else on that field." So I went down to the locker room with all the other tryouts, and all the others kids down there were Polish kids and Italian kids. I was the only Irish kid in the joint. Fordham's equipment manager, John Cannell, was an old Irish guy, and he gave me the best equipment, which didn't exactly get me off on the right foot with my peers.

While I was dressing, I looked around at these guys telling each other how good they all were and I thought, "What the Christ am I getting into here? These guys are going to embarrass the shit out of me." We went out to the field to do calisthenics and warm up, and finally to line up to take shots at the offensive line coach, Ed Franco, who was one of the Seven Blocks of Granite as well as one of my all-time heroes. As I watched the guys hitting Franco, my confidence was slowly creeping back. I figured I could hit harder than they could. And when it was my turn, I really hit him hard.

He said, "Okay, kid, hit me again." And I was feeling my oats now. I hit him again and he knocked me flat on my ass. He hit me a shot—I still see stars when I think of it. I got through the rest of the day, and after practice the head coach, Jim Crowley, came around and asked me if I would like to come to Fordham. I said, "I sure would love to, sir. The only thing is, I'm only a junior."

And he just nodded. I planned on seeing him next year. I never did.

As for Brady, we kept in touch literally until the day he died. It happened sometime in the early 1960s. I received a letter saying if I wanted to see him alive, I better do it quick, because he was dying of leukemia. I drove up to New York and met up with Al Arater and his brother-in-law, Vinny Maggio, a pilot who had been blown out of his cockpit during the war. We all drove down to Mount Sinai Hospital in Manhattan to see John. I knocked on his door, and Brady said, "Who's there?" I said, "It's me, John, Artie." And he said, "Artie who?" I said, "Artie Donovan, for Christ's sake," and he said, "Did I call for you?"

I told him I just came to see him, and he said, "Unless I call for you I don't want to see you." He was embarrassed that I would see him lying in bed like that, because he knew he was the big brother I never had. And I never did see him before he died.

I have a picture down in my den. It's a picture of me at about ten years old and another kid about my age. I'm wearing a jacket and knickers and the other kid is wearing a three-piece suit with long pants. On the back of it there's an inscription: "From this picture the mighty Donovan grew." The guy who wrote that, the other guy in the picture, is named Abe Goldberg. And he and his twin brother, Duvvie, were two of the craziest Jews I ever knew.

We called them Abie and Duvvie Goldberg, and their father owned the Grandview Hand Laundry, the neighborhood dry cleaners. Duvvie joined the Navy and stayed in the Navy, despite the fact that he once drove his motorcycle off the flight deck of an aircraft carrier. But then again, that was par for the course for Duvvie. Right after the war—he was one of the last to get back— we were all hanging around Mr. Goldberg's candy store and Duvvie wanted to show off his new motorcycle to us. Well, he came roaring down the street, and I guess he was just learning how to ride it, because he couldn't find the brake and drove right through the plate glass window.

Of course, both Goldberg boys were very familiar with that candy store window, because when we were kids I was swinging Abe around by his heels one day and suddenly lost control of him.

He flew right through the glass. The Goldberg brothers were also a couple of Jewish kids who didn't mind a potable solution or three, and after repeal I used to hang at the bars with them and a kid named Vinny Angrisanni, who was the quarterback on the Mount St. Michael's football team.

Every Saturday night we'd have a big night, and we'd go to the Cranford Bar on the corner of 241st Street and White Plains Road for sixteen-ounce bottles of Schaefer. They cost a dime at the time, which left us more than enough money for the pizzeria across the street. Three pies, with everything on it and get my friends whatever they want. Well, maybe I'm exaggerating. But just a little.

I mean, a growing boy needs his strength, and I certainly needed mine. For it was about then that I began to realize that I was better than just about everybody else my age in sports.

At the Mount, I could hit the hell out of a baseball, and I was a catcher in the field. Can't you just picture me squatting down there behind the plate with all that catcher's equipment on? I looked like a human backstop, and that's just about all my high-school baseball coach, the same Howie Smith, thought I was good for. Howie would only let me play, other than to pinch-hit, when this guy Lefty Hanrahan was pitching. Lefty could throw blue darts, but he was wild as hell. He threw every other pitch over the backstop. So Howie would just put me in there to stop Lefty's aspirin tablets from becoming wild pitches. I tell you, it was tough to get a passed ball by me. Anyway, I always thought I was better than the first-string catcher, and one day I went marching up to Howie with an ultimatum.

"Hey, Howie," I said, "if I'm not good enough to play baseball for ya, then I'm not gonna play football for ya next fall." Howie just turned to me, nonchalant as you please, and said, "That's okay with me." Whoa, that pulled me up real short. I went up to him a few minutes later and said, "Wait a minute, here, Howie, let me rethink my whole premise." Because the last thing I could do was not play football. I loved the goddamn game.

I remember my uncles taking me to the Giant football games at the old Polo Grounds. We used to lean over the railings near the locker rooms just to see what those dirty, old, beaten-up locker rooms looked like. Another one of my boyhood idols, right up there with Joe D, was Alex Wojciechowicz, the All-American center from Fordham who was playing in the NFL. In fact, my first two years were his last two years in the league, and both of us were inducted into the Pro Football Hall of Fame at the same ceremony in 1968. If you don't think that was a thrill; I would have needed a calculator to count the goose pimples.

Anyway, I'd be leaning over that railing at the Polo Grounds and I'd say to myself, "Boy, would I love to be in there someday." It was every kid's dream, or it used to be, anyway. I would stand in front of a full-length mirror at home in the apartment and practice stances, pretending that maybe someday I'd be a pro football player.

The Mount had an excellent football program, both grammar school and high school, and I took to it right away. Aside from being the varsity football and baseball coach, Howie Smith was also the varsity basketball coach and taught phys ed to all grades. So I got to know him well while I was in the seventh grade. Somewhere along the line, somebody must have seen something in me, something that told them I was going to be a pretty good football player. Because even as I was playing on the Mount's grammar-school team, I had the feeling I was being groomed.

By my freshman year in high school, in 1939, I was scrimmaging against the varsity. No freshman had ever played varsity football at Mount St. Michael's. Well, there was one, a guy named Red Rosengrave, whom they brought in on a scholarship my freshman year. But he was the only one. And I knew I was doing well in these scrimmages. I went both ways, played on both sides of the line, and I remember brothers coming up to me after practice or between classes and saying things like, "Well, Donovan, I hear you're going to be a pretty fair country football player." I was never one to blow my own horn. I'd just answer them with a "Well, I hope so." But I knew I was holding my own.

My only drawback, as always, was speed. I was quick, but over the long haul they timed me in the sprints with an hourglass.

In my sophomore year, we started fall practice during summer vacation, and I showed up there with shorts, a T-shirt, and sneakers. Howie asked me where my cleats and sweat pants were, and I told him I was only going to be there for a day. I told him my family was taking us on a vacation for a week to Long Beach, Long Island. That didn't sit too well with him, but what was he going to do? He rustled up some equipment and put me at first-string defensive tackle for the day, and when practice was through I figured, "Well, that's over with, it's going to be hard to get back on the first string after missing a week of practice." You have to understand the mentality of football coaches here. They're like generals in a war: stubborn and loyal. If a kid practices for a week with the first team, he doesn't just get knocked aside when somebody better comes waltzing in and decides he wants to play. The same reasoning applies to injuries. If a first-stringer hurts himself, the job should still be his when he's well enough to play again.

So the family went to Long Beach, and after I returned I figured I'd have to play my way up the depth chart. But lo and behold, Howie put me back at starting tackle, and though I felt bad about the guys who had been practicing in the spot for the week I was gone, I didn't feel that bad. I started at tackle from then on and never lost the job. I came very close, though.

After my junior season, I discovered I had osteomyelitis, some kind of bone marrow disease. I've hidden it from every coach and team doctor I've played for since. And, truth be told, it really hasn't bothered me all that much. But that junior year in high school, man, I hurt so bad I just wanted to die.

It was Eastertime of 1941 when I first noticed something was wrong. We had a two-week vacation, and my left shin began itching me something fierce, really bothering me. I remembered a guy had kicked me in football practice sometime before—kicked me twice, as a matter of fact. But after the initial pain I hadn't thought anything was seriously wrong. Now, I didn't know what the hell it was, but it was hurting. One day we were out playing baseball, and it just blew up on me. Hurt like hell. I remember showing my leg to this kid we called Babe because he knew every baseball stat in the world, and he nearly fainted when he took a look at it.

When I got home, I told my mother. And of course she put iodine on it. In those days, you had a broken arm, your mother would put iodine on it. But the iodine didn't help. The leg kept getting worse. It really began swelling up. So my mother took me over to Dr. Shaughnessy's house, at 201st Street and the Grand Concourse (it's a funeral home now, by the way, the same one I laid my father out in), and he looked at it and I'll never forget the look on his face as he studied it. Christ, what a black look. I was sure then and there they were going to have to amputate, and I was already trying to figure train schedules to Cucamonga.

Finally, Dr. Shaughnessy decided he was going to have to do something about this. He didn't know if it was just a really deep boil that had become infected or something right on my shinbone. He gave me some salve to rub into my leg, and I went home and to bed. The next morning, there was a knot on my shin as big as a lemon. So it was back to Dr. Shaughnessy's office for the Torquemada routine.

He got out a peg and a hammer, put me on the sofa in his living room, and started banging a big hole in my shin. Jesus Christ, I nearly died on the spot. Nothing came out but blood, what looked like about all I owned. He sent me home again with another salve, some kind of drawing agent, and he had my mother cover the leg with a bread poultice that night when I went to sleep. I woke up the next morning and the bed was full of blood and pus and, ugh, it was disgusting.

So here we go again. It's back over to Dr. Shaughnessy's, and he begins kneading my calf and suddenly this humongous chunk of pus pops out the front of my shin. And right in the middle of it was this piece of bone I had chipped. He squeezed it out. It was unbelievable. It was diagnosed later as osteomyelitis, and though it hasn't bothered me seriously since, it always kind of aches. And to this day, I know it's there, because every time I touch my shinbone I feel these ridges, like a serrated knife.

I went back and played senior year with no problem. Little did I think I would eventually become during my high-school years the best defensive lineman to come out of New York City. And if I do say so myself, I think I became the second-best football player to ever come out of the Bronx. The best was a guy I played against named Jim White, an end, a tackle, a fullback, an all-everything for All Hallows High School. He went to Notre Dame. Then he played for the Giants. And if he never quite lived up to expectations in the pros, I'd still have to say he was the best goddamn high-school athlete I've ever seen, a tough, dirty sonofabitch. But good.

As for me, well, the Mount didn't have such a splendid record during my years there. At best, we hovered around mediocrity. I didn't even make any All-Star teams. Okay, I did make All-City, but that wasn't what I wanted. One of the saddest weeks of my life was sitting in my bedroom after my senior season waiting for the telegram to be delivered informing me I'd made the *New York World-Telegram*'s All-Metropolitan team and to come down to the newspaper office to have my picture taken. I stayed home every night waiting, and I'm still waiting for that one. I can't even take solace from the fact that I've outlived the goddamn newspaper.

Even though I'd been invited out to Notre Dame on a football scholarship (so you expected maybe nuclear physics?), I hurt that week. And I felt sorry for the offensive lineman, whoever he may be, who lined up against me when I reached the land of the Fighting Irish. I guess I shouldn't have felt too sorry for him. Because it was a fistfight on the practice field with that guy that helped get me thrown out of the school.

4

The Third Man

My father, Arthur J. Donovan, Sr., was the most famous fight referee of all time. He worked in New York when New York was the boxing mecca of the universe, and he reffed championship fights, including nineteen of Joe Louis's title bouts. In all divisions he reffed more than 150 championship fights. It became so monotonous to see Arthur J. Donovan as the third man in the ring during a Louis fight that the sportswriters began calling him Arthur (What, Again?) Donovan in their columns.

I guess he started reffing the really big fights around 1932, when he was forty-two and I was seven or eight. The first big one I remember seeing my father work was over in Long Island City, in Queens, when Primo Carnera took the heavyweight title by knocking out Jack Sharkey twenty-four days after my ninth birthday, in 1933. It was after he began making good enough money working the big fights that we were able to move out of the Briggs Avenue apartment and on up to the six-room digs on the Grand Concourse. But things never came easy for him, I can tell you that.

Mike Donovan taught my father to fight when he was five years old. And after he graduated from the Merchant Marine Academy in 1909 he decided professional boxing was the path he was going to pursue. My dad fought as a middleweight for five months under the name Art Davis until my grandfather found out about this. Then my grandfather said, "If you're going to fight, do it right." And he began instructing him on the finer points of the pugilistic arts.

My dad went into the Merchant Marine weighing 117 pounds, but climbing that rigging built him up into a solid 157. Once, he made a summer cruise to England on a gunboat, a barkentine, square-rigged forward, and fore-and-aft-rigged on the main and mizzen. He was in Plymouth Harbor when some English cadets came aboard. The English skipper asked the American skipper if the Yanks had any boxers aboard, and my dad's skipper said he guessed he could oblige, and they set up a tournament right there.

My dad was boxing this English fellow and threw a jab that the Limey ducked right smartly. My dad fiddled around a little and threw another jab. And as the Limey started to duck, my dad fired an uppercut that knocked the guy clean overboard. He used to say that harbor was full of Limey cadets pulling their chums out of the water.

Another time, in Havana Harbor, a big English mate slapped my dad during an argument. Well, the guy was about 250 pounds, but my dad couldn't take that shit, especially from an Englishman. So he hit him a hook and flattened him. And that's kind of when he decided that he might make it as a professional fighter.

So when he got out, after his fling as Art Davis, he boxed for five years as a middleweight on and off, promoted by two brothers out of the Olympic Athletic Club on Twenty-first Street down in Manhattan. But the Mexican border skirmishes with Black Jack Pershing and fighting in World War I in France with the 27th Infantry Regiment of New York really robbed him of the prime of his career. And when he realized he was never going to be good enough to win the title, he retired to become an assistant to my grandfather at the New York Athletic Club. When Mike Donovan retired from his boxing instructor's position at the NYAC after thirty-eight years in 1914, my dad took over. He was hired on

September 1, 1915, at 3:00 P.M. He retired fifty years later, to the minute, on September 1, 1965.

My father always said he never had any intention of becoming a referee until once in the early 1920s, when he was accosted by Big Jim Farley, the chairman of the New York Athletic Commission, one night while he was coming out of the fights at the Garden. "How could a man named Donovan leave boxing flat? Get back in the game, son," said Farley, and my dad said he was so ashamed that the next day he went down to Farley's office and applied for a referee's license.

He debuted as a ref in a place called Dexter Park, a typically small boxing club with a top seat of $2 for a busload of bruisers. The remotest seat in these joints was well within bottle range of the center of the ring, and my father's dexterity in ducking guided missiles was called to the fore perhaps more than he had planned on. In fact, he was once knocked flat by a flying shank of pastrami. He used to describe those small boxing halls to me as a place "where customers buy blood and bruises, and always insist on the gentlemen in the ring disassembling each other at the earliest possible moment."

He also did some wrestling refereeing. But then, as now, if boxing is the sweet science, wrestling is the sour livelihood of lunatics. He realized one night that officiating a wrestling card held no charms when he was paid $50 for semaphoring six wrestling bouts and ended up with a $20 pair of pants shredded at the knees with blood showing. From then on it was boxing or nothing for Arthur Donovan, Sr. Needless to say, there was an awful lot of boxing and very little nothing.

Dad was still working as a boxing instructor at the New York Athletic Club while he reffed, and he was never so presumptuous as to assume he would be called to ref a fight on the day of the battle. So when he went to work at the club on the morning of a big fight, he would never bring his refereeing togs with him. That chore would be left to me. Dad would get a call from the New York Athletic Club sometime around 3:00 P.M., letting him know he'd been chosen to be the third man in. And he, in turn, would call home and say to my mother, "Mary, I'm working. Bring the bag."

The bag contained his gray flannel pants, his gray flannel shirt, his high-top black leather shoes, and his black bow tie. Before I was old enough to bring him his equipment by myself, my mother would pack my sister and myself up and he'd meet us either at the entrance to Yankee Stadium, or at the Polo Grounds, or at the subway stop at Eighth Avenue and Fiftieth Street, outside the entrance to the old Madison Square Garden. We'd take the subway downtown—the D line ran right under our apartment—and walk up the stairs and wait for him. And after we'd deliver his bag, my mother would take my sister and me over to the Taft Hotel for something to eat at the fountain, usually a baloney sandwich for me. Then we'd go next door to the Roxie and see a movie. Then we'd go home. My mother never went to the fights.

And the next morning I'd awake to find my father sitting in the kitchen with my mother, reading the newspaper and talking all about the big fight the night before. Christ, it seemed like every time there was a championship fight, he reffed it. I remember one year he refereed three in one week. The money was never extraordinary, maybe $100 for a good night's work. But that was nothing to sneeze at during the Depression. And my father got more than his share of fights to work.

When I was old enough, I began running my father's bag to him whenever he got the call. I remember once when I was about thirteen, Joe Louis was fighting somebody in the Polo Grounds, my mother was away, and I had the bag packed and was waiting by the phone for the call. It came and I was off, all excited because I thought Dad was going to take me into the fight with him. But somehow our communications got mixed up, and I waited where I thought I was supposed to meet him for an hour and a half before I saw my father coming toward me. It was barely moments before fight time, and steam was escaping from his ears.

He asked me where the hell I had been, and before I could explain anything, he grabbed the bag and took off, leaving me just standing there in upper Manhattan. Now, the Polo Grounds was across the Harlem River from the Bronx, and I didn't have any money to take the subway back home. So I went up to a policeman and said, "Excuse me, sir, but my name is Arthur Donovan, Jr., and I just dropped my father's refereeing gear off to him for the fight. I wouldn't be bothering you now, except that my dad was so mad at me for being late that he didn't leave me any money, and now I've no way to get home." Sure enough, the cop gave me a nickel to get through the turnstile, and I'd be lying if I said that I never tried pulling that scam again.

Between working during the day and refereeing and squiring the millionaires from the NYAC around town at night, my father really lived his own life. My mother, Mary, really raised my sister and me. My father's life was another world. He drank with all the club members, especially the high-rolling sports families of New York who were always dying to hear him talk about the fight game. He was on intimate terms with the Stonehams, who owned the baseball Giants, and with the O'Malleys, who later owned the Dodgers. And he was a regular at places like Toots Shor's and Mickey Walker's and Jack Dempsey's. That was his life, going out with these very wealthy men. And it never really bothered Joan or me that much, because we understood that was his life.

I suppose today you could use that kind of childhood as a defense in a court of law after you've committed a mass murder. The old deprived-childhood routine. But I don't think my father loved us any less because he spent so little time with us. In fact, I really grew up a spoiled kid. And we certainly didn't love him any less because of it. He did, after all, bring home the bacon. Or, in my case, the baloney.

And whenever he got a day off, which was usually on a Sunday, he'd take me places I never could have dreamed existed. We'd go out for a day on some millionaire's boat in Long Island Sound, and Jesus Christ, I couldn't believe people could own ships so big. I thought I was on an ocean liner. These millionaires would always play up to me because I was Arthur Donovan's son. And though I never knew where the hell we were sailing, I cared even less.

I recall a man named Whitneybelle, a member of the New York AC who owned a mansion up in New Rochelle, New York. This Whitneybelle had a gym on the top floor of his home, and my father would go up there quite often to give the man private lessons. Rather than take payment, Whitneybelle would give my father a new car every three years.

When I was about ten my father began bringing me up to Whitneybelle's house while he gave the man boxing lessons, and it was *Babes in Toyland* revisited. Whitneybelle had a kid about my age, and this kid had every toy ever conceived. The only problem was, this kid was a real bastard. We'd take the bus from Fordham Road to New Rochelle, and all I could think about on the ride up was getting on this kid's new bike, or playing with his train set, or swimming in his pool.

But every time this miserable little sonofabitch would catch me playing with his stuff he'd go screaming to his father, and it embarrassed my father no end. He knew the kid was a prick. But the kid's father was picking up the tab, so what could he do? Soon enough, I stopped traveling to Mr. Whitneybelle's mansion with my dad. But my father also used to take me down to the NYAC to box with the members' kids every Saturday. And since I was bigger than most boys my age, his only words of advice were, "Let the rich kids win, Arthur. Don't hurt any of them." And I always did let them win, although I could have knocked any one of them on their bony little asses if I had really wanted to. But what the hell did I care? I was having too much fun.

Actually, I don't want to be too harsh on those kids, because so many of them were nice enough despite the fact they had bucks up the kazoo. I've met a lot of them along the line in my life; they always come up to me and say, "You may not remember me, but my name's so-and-so, and you let me knock you on your keester when we were little kids at the NYAC." I guess they got a kick out of boxing with me. I also guess they eventually learned what the score was.

But just because my father worked like a monk didn't mean we never saw him. On any given summer Sunday my father would pack up the family and we'd drive out to the beach on City Island in the Bronx. On special summer Sundays we'd head all the way out to Long Island. Or as often as not, my mother would gather Joan and me and tell my father she was taking us on a vacation for a week, and he'd get up to see us when he could. My mother always had her mother and sisters around, so she'd think nothing of taking off for a couple of days. And if we didn't head to the beach, we'd escape the summer heat in the mountains, where Dr. Shaughnessy had a cabin in the Adirondacks he'd let our family use.

I remember the big thing for the family was New Year's Eve, when my mother and father would take Joan and me down into Times Square to witness the mayhem firsthand. Those were the days, of course, when a family could spend New Year's Eve in Times Square without worrying about getting out alive. Then there was the night before Thanksgiving. That was my parents' wedding anniversary, and the four of us would always go out to dinner with my grandmother.

I knew from the beginning that my dad had a different kind of job from the other fathers in the neighborhood, who were always around to help their kids with their homework, or play catch in the street, or even just shoot the shit. On the one hand, my father was the toast of the town. No millionaires went out of their way to shake hands with Al Arater's old man or Duvvie Goldberg's dad. And I was proud that my father was a great referee and that the neighbors all held him in high regard. Yet on the other hand, I missed my dad growing up, and I always wonder what it would have been like to have had normal parents. You know, two of them.

But what the hell, it never really bothered me that much. And I had a great family life. Like I said, my grandmother's house was the hub of the neighborhood, and there was always a cousin or an uncle or an aunt to get into trouble with. My grandmother had what seemed like a constant card party going on in her parlor. And all of her sons-in-law were always playing. For the most part they were a bunch of bullshitters. A few of my uncles were inspectors in the New York Police Department. And one was an electrician. Another sold insurance down on Wall Street. And another was a purchasing agent for the city. At these card parties they'd talk a blue streak trying to outimpress each other about their fame and fortune.

But my father was a shy man. He never really had much to say whenever he had time to show up in my grandmother's parlor.

And as much as they asked, he never really liked to talk about the fight game with the family. He never brought any of his boxing cronies up to the apartment. And because of that reserve in him, I think my grandmother liked him best.

My mother's side of the family was all very religious. All the aunts would go across the street to St. Philip Neri Church every Sunday together, and they'd be dragging all their husbands along with them. My father always went, of course, but I don't think his heart was ever in it. The only thing his heart was ever really in was the fight game. Surprisingly, being a famous referee's son didn't automatically mean I saw a lot of professional fights. In fact, I probably attended fewer fights than the average Irish kid growing up in the Bronx.

I saw Louis maul Johnny Paychek when I was fifteen. Louis hit him so hard in the first round the kid's mouthpiece flew out into the crowd. Paychek came out for the second round, and, boom, Louis hit him once and he crumpled to the canvas. When I was seventeen I saw my father ref the fight the night Willy Pep took Chalkie Wright's featherweight title. And when I was sixteen I watched my father ref as Fritzie Zivic, perhaps the dirtiest fighter who ever lived, knocked out Al (Bummy) Davis in ten.

My father was highly respected for the way he controlled a fight. When he instructed fighters to break clean, they followed his instructions. And he also kept tough fights going. If there was an illegal punch thrown, he gave the fighter who took it extra time to recover.

The two most famous fights my dad was ever involved in were the Louis-Schmeling bouts. In their first meeting, on June 19, 1936, Max Schmeling, hero of the Third Reich, knocked out the unbeaten Louis in the twelfth round. My father always said Louis took a bad break from a late punch in that one. "The bell rang ending the sixth round and I was moving toward them to break them when the German hit him a terrific punch," he told me once. "It was after the bell, but you can't withhold a punch once it goes. And the way I saw it, Louis never recovered from the shot."

But my father always said the German had trouble with his movement and couldn't retreat. My dad thought Schmeling had fallen arches. He also figured the German carried his right hand too low, and he was surprised Louis's camp didn't have their man adjust to his odd stance. It was that odd stance, he figured, that caused Louis so much consternation, because the big kid from Detroit couldn't get his jab inside Schmeling's right. Once, when I was with my father at a boxing testimonial, I asked Max Baer, another tough old heavyweight, just exactly what Louis's jab felt like.

"What did it feel like?" replied Baer. "It felt like a bomb bursting in your face."

Two years later, almost to the day, Louis and Schmeling met again for the rematch in Yankee Stadium, this time for the title. I've never seen my father as nervous before a fight as he was before that one. After it was over, after Louis destroyed the German in one round, my father sat down and wrote his reflections of the whole scene in a diary. I still look through it every now and then. It reads:

June 22nd was one of those days when the weather was like a woman in a millinery shop. It couldn't make up its mind. At noon, after a wondering night, I dressed in teaching togs at the N.Y.A.C. Two o'clock came with word that Louis and Schmeling were weighing in. The wind had shifted, which meant that the rain had missed us and the big, outdoor fight was on.

After refereeing a still-life preliminary to the second Louis-Schmeling go, I hopped from the ring, wondering what was next. Yankee Stadium was a horseshoe jammed to the inch with roaring thousands. Schmeling climbed to the canvas amid a tremendous ovation. Louis, in purple trunks with red-hemmed silk, came next, to milder roars punctuated by ecstatic screams from Negro throats.

I was one of three refs standing at ringside waiting for the big tap on the shoulder, and as I paced the canvas lip the nerves in my spine tingled like electric shocks. The fighters warmed up in their respective corners while Dempsey and Tunney, Braddock and Baer bowed and grinned in a ring clotted with handlers and trainers and seconds and police. Where was the tap on the shoulder? Notables and notorieties smoked and laughed and talked foolishly all around me.

Came a tap on my right shoulder.

"Go in there, Donovan," ordered Chairman Phelan of the New York State Athletic Commission.

Strange how the nerves vanish when the action is on.

I talked to the two fighters just as to a pupil in the boxing gym, except I added something—not meant for the fighters— something I'd never have to tell a pupil.

"If anybody from either side so much as puts his head—I almost said 'puss,' but checked myself just in time—into this ring, there will be drastic consequences."

Newsmen glanced up puzzled. What's the idea? They were soon to find out.

Louis came out, making a winding motion with his right forearm—the very same gesture with which he had come to the ring center for his first battle with the German.

"Hasn't he learned anything from that one?" I asked myself.

In twelve seconds Louis answered with a jolt to Schmeling's jaw that staggered the German. Then another, and another, and another. There was no dropped guard after the hitting.

"He's learned all he needed to know," I said to myself.

Schmeling tried to counter the fusillade of ripping rights and lefts. Louis jerked back. Schmeling touched a light one. Louis ignored it. Louis smashed home a right that would have dented concrete, wheeling Schmeling face-front to the ropes. But as bad as the German was hurt, he still managed to throw a right that was lucky for Louis that it landed high on his cheek, or it would have knocked him out right there. After that miss, Schmeling had no chance.

A vicious right to the kidneys and Schmeling screamed in pain—the most terrifying sound I ever heard in a ring. Max struggled to lift his right arm to grab the spot. The man was paralyzed. I stepped between them just as Louis poised another bomb.

"Get away, Joe," I said.

He blinked and backed away, cold eyes boring in on the German.

I shouted for a count. But no count began. Max refused to go down. He was utterly helpless, and would have flopped but for the ropes. His head rolled like rubber as Louis advanced to end the carnage. Joe laced him with a swishing hook, with rifle twist on it. It made my hairs on the back of my neck stand on end. It also made the German drop, but the amazing kraut staggered up on knocking knees.

"You're done, Maxie," I thought, "when you've forgotten how to grab at a count when one's offered."

Again Max went to the floor, and as the knock-down hammer banged, something white came floating into the ring and nearly hit me in the face. I thought it was a piece of paper, but it turned out to be an illegal towel. I threw it from the ring and glared at Schmeling's corner. That is exactly what I had warned those bums against.

I knew I couldn't be wrong stopping the fight. The German corner was admitting defeat when they threw in the towel. But they weren't going to take the play away from me by saying they stopped it. It was my responsibility and I was the one who stopped the fight.

Schmeling crumpled for keeps, and I breast-stroked with both arms to keep Louis away. That was the end of the massacre. Max went to a hospital with polysyllabic fractures. I don't like to speculate where he'd have gone had Louis struck another lightning bolt to his kidneys.

Not bad, huh? And you probably thought I was the only Donovan with literary sensibilities! As a postscript, thirty-five years later they reunited Louis, Schmeling and my old man in the ring at a special ceremony in Long Island's Nassau Veterans Memorial Coliseum. We all went up to New York for the occasion and had a helluva good time in the bars afterward.

I found out that night that for all the stories written about my father being Joe Louis's personal referee, the two never even spoke in public until 1963, long after Louis had retired. My father was crossing Fifty-ninth Street heading to Central Park, and he was reading the paper and not looking at traffic when a car roared past him and nearly knocked him over. The car came to a stop and a man got out and said, "Close call." It was Joe Louis. He and my father finally had a conversation.

But I know my dad always loved the man in the manner that athletes love each other. My father and I watched Joe Louis fight Rocky Marciano from our apartment in the Bronx on October 26, 1951. Louis was just a former shell of himself. He was in the ring strictly for the money. And when Marciano knocked Joe out in the eighth round, my father had a tear in his eye seeing this great fighter going down the tubes. My father rarely if ever showed any emotion. I don't even think he cried when my mother died. But when Louis lost that night, it shook him.

My father never kept pictures of himself or newspaper articles about him and the fighters he chummed with. Around our apartment there were a few photos of old Mike Donovan in fighting poses, but none of his son Arthur. Mrs. Shaughnessy, our family doctor's wife and my special academic tutor, did start a scrapbook, however, and now pictures of my dad decorate the country club Dottie and I operate outside Baltimore.

When people remember my father as a famous referee, the thing they tend to forget is that the guy could really fight, because for fifty years all he did was teach people how to box. Once, in the late 1960s, a few years after I retired, I was sitting in one of the liquor stores I owned when I got a call from my sister in New York.

"You've got to come home right away," she said.

"What the hell for?" I asked.

"Because they're going to lock Pa up."

Holy Christ, what did he do this time? I mean, the man was about seventy-seven years old. What kind of trouble can a seventy-seven-year-old man get into? So I stopped home for a change of clothes and drove straight to New York, and I remember it took me three hours exactly to get from the country club to the Bronx.

I got to the house, and there he was sitting, all sullen and offended. He just jerked his thumb over his shoulder toward the living room. And when I walked in, my sister, who had left work, was sitting on the sofa between two policemen. The cops were guys from the neighborhood, they knew the whole family as they were growing up, and one of them just shook his head and said to me, "Little Arthur, you've got to stop your father from hitting people around here." Hitting people? They explained what happened.

My father was crossing Fordham Road when a guy came up to him and tried to bum a cigarette off of him. When my father told him he didn't have a cigarette, the guy said, "Well, then give me a dime so I can buy one." My father said, "I don't have a dime, either." And the guy replied, "You're a fucking liar."

Boom! My father decked him. The man was seventy-seven! Then some other guy joined the fracas and jumped on my father's back. In the meantime, all these retired cops and firemen who hung out in the park on Fordham Road saw what was happening, and they in turn jumped on the second guy and pulled him off my father. The first guy was still out cold on the sidewalk.

So the cops came along and put my father in the police cruiser and drove him the mile up to our house, where he called my sister. So I said to my father, "Dad, you can't keep doing this kind of stuff." And he said, "If a guy calls me that name again, I'll flatten him again." The cops finally said, "Oh, the hell with this." And no charges were pressed. I think they secretly got a kick out of the whole scene, anyway.

Let me tell you, that man was a tough old bird until the day he died. Another time I was down in Baltimore when I got a phone call from one of my uncles. It seems my father was crossing the Grand Concourse to get a paper one night and a car hit him and broke his leg. Some greenhorn from Ireland who didn't even have a driver's license just plowed right into him. It was right around the same time as the fight with the bum, he was in his late seventies at the time, so I was pretty worried.

I drove up to New York the next morning, and my sister and I went to visit him in Fordham Hospital. Here was a man who had been in three wars, and I felt he deserved to be in a veterans' hospital, so I got an ambulance to transfer him to the VA hospital on Kingsbridge Road in the Bronx. That tough old guy spent a year to the day in that hospital and walked out without a limp. He was just tenacious as hell. And oh, man, was he ever a dude. He was the kind of guy who put a shirt and tie on to take out the garbage. And by the way, that's the only chore he ever did around the house—take the garbage out. After my mother died in 1959, my sister would have to take an hour subway trip up from her job on Wall Street just to cook dinner for the old man.

But like I said, he was a fighter. A few years after he broke his leg, when he was eighty, Dottie and I had him down here for Easter dinner when he began complaining of stomach pains. A few days later, back up in New York, my sister got him to a hospital, and after an examination, the doctor told us he was suffering from some kind of bowel cancer. The doctor was a sharp guy and he wanted to operate. But I said to him, "Bullshit, you're not going to operate on him. Jesus, let the man die in dignity. He's eighty years old."

But the doctor said, "I'm telling you right now, your father has the body of a sixty-five-year-old man. He's in great shape. So let us fix him up."

My sister and I discussed it and finally gave the medicos the go-ahead. He came through the operation all right, but he refused to believe that he wasn't just fine when the doctors told him not to get out of bed. At any rate, he made such a pain in the ass out of himself trying to walk around, breaking stitches and whatnot, that they finally had to tie him to his bed. I knew right away that was a mistake. It was like flashing a red flag in front of a bull. But they kept him in there a month hog-tied like that.

Finally, my wife and I came to see him and he begged us to untie him. He was yanking on the ropes and he said to Dottie, "If you untie my arms I'll go to Baltimore with you." This was quite a statement from a man who thought anything outside a twenty-mile radius of New York was camping out in the boondocks. So my wife untied him and goddamn if he didn't pull that colostomy right out of his side. They had to go back in and reroute the whole thing again. But the old rooster lived eight more years.

Eventually my father lost his fear of traveling out of New York. And after a while, from 1954 to 1962, he used to come down to the Colts' training camp and spend two weeks with us out at Western Maryland College, in Westminster. This was two weeks of his

NYAC month's vacation, and the Colts really became his whole life in a sense. He lived up in training camp in one of the dorm rooms, just like the players. And he got a real kick out of it. The players loved to listen to his great fight stories. And every out-of-town newsman who swung through camp intending to do some kind of preseason profile on the Colts invariably walked away with a notebook full of old fight stories from the fat defensive tackle's old man. Every August 10 the team would throw a birthday bash for him. And suddenly he began to realize that Baltimore wasn't such a bad town after all.

He'd come down to all our home games before my mother died, and she used to love coming down here, too. In New York, she was just another woman from the Bronx. But down in Baltimore, she was Arthur Donovan's mother.

Every two weeks she'd get on the train and I'd pick her up at the station and bring her out to our house. And I used to remind her of the times when I was single and I'd come home and take her to her card parties where she'd always be saying to me, "Oh, Arthur, look at all these people, what wonderful children they all have. Mrs. O'Leary's son's an architect and Mrs. O'Boyle's son's a lawyer." That kind of crap. My mother just couldn't believe that I could be a success just playing football until I started getting her down here and they started treating her like the Queen Mother. She changed her tune about football right quick.

During the training camp summer of 1959, the year after we took the first championship game from the Giants, my father and I were down here when he got a call from my sister saying my mom was sick.

It was a Saturday night after an exhibition game, so my father and I were in Baltimore rather than Westminster. And for the life of us neither of us could figure what was wrong. My mom was sixty-nine, but she had just had a checkup and everything had come up roses. Now my sister was telling me that my mother needed an emergency operation the following day. Just like that. I couldn't believe it. As we were packing up my father's clothes to get him on a train back North, Joan called again: "The doctors have found some kind of tumor."

My father went home, but I had to go back to training camp. But I just couldn't stand the waiting and not knowing. I was running to church every chance I got. Finally I went to Weeb Ewbank, our coach, and told him I had to leave. "There's nothing you can do about it up there," he said. "I don't care," I said, "I'm going home."

It was the weekend before we were going to meet the college All-Stars in an exhibition. Two friends from Baltimore picked me up in Westminster, drove me to the train station, and I guess I rolled in about ten o'clock at night. The whole family was at the house, and I could tell right away my father really needed me there. He had always been this stoic old Irishman, he wasn't used to venting his feelings, and I could tell he had so much churning inside him and no one to let it out to. We stayed up all night talking, and the next day the three of us went to the hospital.

We sat by her bedside—she was unconscious. We went back to the neighborhood, walked around the block thirty or forty million times, then went back to the hospital again. Finally the doctor came down and said the tumor was so big he couldn't take it out. I'll never forget that moment: We were waiting in the hallway to get the results, and as soon as I saw the look on the doctor's face walking down that hall, I knew it was bad news. And another thing I'll never forget, and this seems incongruous in the context of what was happening, but there was some kid in the hallway waiting to be admitted into the hospital and the kid was making so much noise I thought my father was going to kill him. Strange, the things you remember at times like that.

My mom was in Yonkers General, and they operated on her again that day and she pulled through that one. There was relief in the family despite the fact we all knew things weren't going well. My aunts had my mom transferred to Miseracordia Hospital in the Bronx, and she hung on for another eight weeks.

I went back down to start the season. After every game I'd rush up to New York to spend the night with my sister and father and all day Monday with my mother. I was working full time selling liquor for Schenley Distributors then, and I'd tell both the Colts and my bosses at Schenley not to try to get in touch with me for anything on Mondays, because I had important things to do. Everyone understood.

Finally, on a Sunday in late October I reached the Bronx and my sister just shook her head as I walked through the front door. Mom was on her way out. I went to see her that Monday, and this goofy old lady told me that as a dying wish she wanted a lobster dinner before she walked through the Pearly Gates. I'm beside myself with grief, and at the same time I'm wondering just where in the hell I'm going to get a goddamn lobster on a Monday afternoon in October in the Bronx.

So I walked out of the hospital and up the hill to White Plains Road and spotted a fish market. I walked in and said, "Mister, I don't know whether you can help me out or not, but I have a strange request. See, my mom's dying in the hospital down the street. I don't think she's going to last more than a few days. She's dying and she wants a lobster."

There was an Italian guy behind the counter, and he said to me, "Son, not only am I gonna get you a lobster, but I'm gonna cook it for you. Because you played football with my son in high school and my son always told me that you treated him well even though you were the star of the team." I nearly fell over.

So I got the lobster dinner and took it back down to her. Of course, she never even ate it; she never even touched it, she was too weak. I returned to Baltimore that Tuesday morning and the next day got a call from one of my aunts. "That's it," she said. "She's gone." She died on October 29, 1959. I went back up for the funeral. They buried her on the last Saturday in October. The hardest thing I ever had to do in my life was bury my mother. It was the worst thing that ever happened to me. It was like my whole world collapsed around me.

I came back down to Baltimore that night and suited up against the Browns the next afternoon. I don't know how well I played; I was in a daze for some time. It was the worst time I ever had to go through in my life.

My father lived another twenty years. We spent as much time with him as we could when we could get him down to Baltimore. But he never really lost his New Yorkerness.

He once told me that he harbored a private dream of roaming through Ireland and finding some big, redheaded faction fighter, "preferably as freckled as a pomegranate." He wanted this fictional kid to weigh about two hundred pounds and meet the tests of toughness and tractability, fighting spirit and endurance. He wanted this kid to have the "it" of the ring—a flair and a fast, devastating left. Then he'd say he'd take that broth of a boy and nurse him along like an orchid orchard or a Derby winner. And if he turned out to be only a good second-rater, that would be fair enough. But if he made it to the top, my father said, the kid would be a gold mine in gloves, a gate-smashing Kid Galahad.

"But Arthur," he'd tell me after reciting his dream, "the curious thing about this dream of mine is that somebody is always discovering somebody else who finds it comes true. It would be nice if it happened to me. But a man can only expect so much good fortune in one lifetime. I believe I've had more than my share."

Arthur J. Donovan, Sr., died on September 1, 1980, at the age of ninety. He was the toughest man I ever knew. I still miss him.

5

A Few Good Men

I went out to South Bend for my first semester at Notre Dame in December 1942. I received a scholarship offer from the Irish during my senior season at the Mount, and I had enough credits to graduate early. I didn't really want to go, but my mother made me. Now, it might strike you as astounding that an Irish kid from the Bronx would be disappointed about a scholarship to Notre Dame, but as I've said, my first and only football love was the Fordham Rams. When Howie Smith received the scholarship offer, I pleaded with him not to tell my parents about it. I wanted to wait to hear from Fordham. But Howie said he couldn't do that in good conscience, and when my mother found out, there was no arguing. I was going to Notre Dame.

I knew I'd be out there for only a few months. I had already received my "Greetings" letter from Uncle Sam, and I knew it was only a matter of time until my opponents were going to transform from Purdue and Michigan State into Japs and Nazis. The armed services beckoned, and, truth be told, they didn't really like me at Notre Dame, anyhow. I don't think they liked any New Yorkers. Right away, if you were from New York, you were a wise guy.

Whether you were or not, that's how they pegged you. I arrived there and suddenly I was a zoot-suiter, a drugstore cowboy, a guy from a strange land who didn't even speak American.

I remember in speech class once, the professor got me up in front of the class to read this fancy goddamn poem, I think it was William Blake, and I couldn't even pronounce the words much less read the thing in the King's English. Everybody in the class was laughing at me as I'm struggling through this thing, but that really didn't bother me. I felt I looked rather silly myself, this big knucklehead standing up there spouting poetry in an indecipherable Bronx accent.

But suddenly I looked over and noticed that the professor was laughing at me, too. Now, that burned me. I was giving the poem my best shot, and I didn't need that sonofabitch standing over in the corner giggling. I said to him, "Hey, Professor, I don't mind these guys laughing at me, but you don't have to make fun of me, too. So what if I'm a New Yorker and I don't speak right. I'm still up here trying." I've been down here in Baltimore for thirty-five years, and I still talk like a New Yorker. Anybody who changes the way they talk is a phony, I think. So what's the big deal about a Bronx accent? The speech professor just laughed harder.

I had a physics teacher out at South Bend by the name of Professor Plunkett, and three of us were sitting in the back of the classroom one day, minding our own business, when this Professor Plunkett decides to make a big deal about the way I speak. He called me up to the front of the room and began giving me the business. You know: "Where are you from, kid, that you talk so funny?" Stuff like that. He went on like that for the rest of the year, another zinger every day. I just didn't understand it. He thought I was a wise guy simply because I came from New York.

He couldn't have been more off base. I've never been a wise guy in my life. In fact, I recently got a Christmas card from a kid I haven't seen since high school. He wrote, "I was very proud of you when you were elected into the Professional Football Hall of Fame. I often wondered how such a nice, easygoing, gentle fellow could be a professional football player." I suppose he won't be wondering after he reads this book, but I swear to God, I was only tough when I had to play. That's what these professors like Plunkett just didn't understand. During the last week of the semester I went up to him and said, "Professor Plunkett, my old football coach asked me to say hello to you. I believe he was your roommate when the two of you attended Notre Dame." He asked me who I was talking about, and when I told him Howie Smith, well, lo and behold, I suddenly became Professor Plunkett's pet. He asked me why I hadn't told him about this earlier. I was just a dopey kid. I didn't want to polish the apple. He was, of course, a day late and a dollar short with his Mr. Nice Guy routine. By then, I had come to the full realization that Notre Dame was just not my type of school.

For example, I lived on the third floor of a freshman hall, Breen Phillips Hall. And there was an older guy who lived up there with us named Joe Signaigo. Signaigo was on the varsity, and he actually played in the NFL for two or three years before becoming a Miller Beer distributor in Memphis. I still run into him every once in a while. At any rate, someone threw a carton of sour milk at our door, and of course it splattered and stunk up the whole third floor. Our proctor, the priest who was the boss of the hall, was named Father Holdredth. Father Holdredth—or "Black George," as we called him—was also the golf coach. After the milk incident, Black George summoned everyone from the third floor downstairs to get to the bottom of this heinous crime.

When he asked who threw the milk, my roommates and I tried to explain to him that we certainly wouldn't be throwing sour milk on our own door. Nonetheless, he said, "There's only one boy in this room who I know would not pull a stunt like this, and that's Joe Signaigo. I know, I met his family. He's too fine a young man." Of course, Signaigo was the guy who threw the goddamn milk, but Black George just let Joe and his roommates go. Then he took the rest of us, about thirty kids, down onto the campus, and in the middle of a raging snowstorm he made us march for ten hours between Breen Phillips Hall and the administration building to the circle in front of the school and back to Breen Phillips Hall all night long. I nearly caught pneumonia, while all the while that sonofabitch Signaigo was nice and toasty up in bed. To this day I think priests are all half nuts.

To be honest, Notre Dame may have come to the same realization I did regarding my presence there. The football coach, Frank Leahy, and I got off to a bad start almost immediately. During spring practice I thought I did fairly well. In fact, the guy who was going to be the captain the following year, Pat Filley, told me one day that I was one of the only recruits kicking ass during scrimmages with the varsity. But I got into a fight with an offensive tackle during one of the first days of spring practice, and it turned out that the guy was one of Leahy's protégés. He was a big old tub of lard from New Orleans named Tiny Thorpe.

The guy had been holding me all practice. And I had warned him, "I don't like you as it is. Keep holding me and we're going to get into a fight." He did. And we did. Those things happen on the football field, and the incident itself didn't bother Leahy as much as the fact that I wouldn't shake hands with Tiny after they separated us. The guy was a jerk, and shaking hands with him wasn't going to make him any less of a jerk. But Leahy told me right in front of the whole team that he didn't like or need my type around there.

I still don't understand what Leahy's type was. He was a strange man. I got the measles when I was out there, and they put me in the infirmary. Leahy came and dragged me out of the infirmary and made me go to practice. So then I got the double measles, or at least that's what they called it at the time. I was sick as a dog, locked up in that infirmary for a week and a half. I thought I was going to die. I didn't know what the hell was wrong with me. Leahy came again and took me to practice. Finally the school doctor forbade him to take me out of there again.

But like I said, it really didn't matter. Most of my buddies from the old neighborhood were already in one branch of the service or another, and staying that semester at Notre Dame was like doing time. There was a war on, and I knew once the semester was over, it was *sayonara* South Bend.

Colleges ran war-shortened semesters then, and I returned to New York in early April. Before I had even left for South Bend a half dozen of the guys from the neighborhood had gone down to Grand Central Annex, right above Grand Central Station in midtown Manhattan, which was where they had all the recruiting booths set up. We walked in and there they were: Army, Navy, Marines, Coast Guard. Some sergeant from the Army called us over and said, "If you guys join up right now we'll give you all good jobs." "Doing what?" we asked, and he told us they'd make us all cooks and bakers. A couple of the guys went for it, but I was thinking, "To hell with you. I ain't gonna be no cook in the goddamn Army for the rest of the war." So I went over and joined the Marines. I told them I was going to Notre Dame in January and they said they'd be calling me up after the semester was over.

I went home that night, and my father said, "So Arthur, you're going into the Army, huh?" And when I told him no, I had joined the Marines, Jesus Christ, he began hollering at my mother, "Kiss him goodbye, Mary, he's going to get killed! He's going to get that fat ass shot right out from under him!" I tried to explain to him that I had to join something and that the Marines seemed to promise the most action. But he wouldn't hear any of it. Through all his years in the service, the Marines were always the ones my father had seen die first. Needless to say, he wasn't real happy with my choice.

So about a month after returning from Notre Dame, I was on a train headed for boot camp in Parris Island, South Carolina. They put us on a barge to cross the Hudson into Jersey and from there on the B&O railroad down to Washington. We followed the coastline down through Yemassee and Port Royal, South Carolina, and finally reached that mosquito-infested swamp where the Marines train a few good men.

I was six-two, 240 pounds, just back from Notre Dame, and probably in the best shape of my life. I sailed through boot camp. It was a hell of an experience. They worked my ass off, but it was great training. And I loved it. It may sound conflicting with a world war raging, but I felt like I didn't have a care in the world. Some guys didn't quite feel the same way about boot camp. I recall waking up in the morning and seeing empty bunks where the night before a trainee had been sleeping. But nobody ever said the

Marines are everybody's cup of tea. My drill instructor was a guy named Hal Feinstein, and he was one of the finest men I've ever met. He was a graduate of Lehigh, but he had turned down an officer's commission when he signed up. He wanted to do it the hard way. Next time I saw him I was on Okinawa. I don't know what ever happened to him.

In boot camp they taught me how to shoot guns. Big guns. I fired 40-millimeter and 20-millimeter babies off the gun sponson of an aircraft carrier. Those sonsabitches put some kind of fire out. More important, the Marines taught me how to eat like a king, all the baloney I wanted. Man, that Marine chow was great. Of course, I never had any bad chow in my life. From boot camp I went to sea school, because I was assigned to the Sea Corps of the Marines.

I was transferred to the *San Jacinto*, an aircraft carrier in Norfolk, Virginia, and from there we steamed through the Panama Canal. The first action I saw was in the Mariana Trench, just southwest of Guam. I was the second loader on a 40-millimeter twin mount, and those goddamn Jap dive bombers and torpedo bombers kicked the living shit out of our Navy in '44. I remember one night at dusk, these Japanese planes got between two of our ships and while we were shooting at the planes we were actually hitting each other. We almost destroyed one of our own ships; it was really terrible.

But all in all, it was an okay assignment. The Navy guys loved us. After all, we were stopping those goddamn dive bombers from blowing them out of the water. There were a lot more Navy gunners on the *San Jacinto* than Marine gunners. The only reason there is a sea school of the Marines, as a matter of fact, is because of the Marine anthem. You know, ". . . on the land and on the sea . . ." The Marines had to keep a contingent at sea for tradition's sake. But we only manned about eight guns compared to the Navy's hundred or so on the *San Jacinto*. There was a good, friendly competition between gunnery crews, and despite being outnumbered by the swabbies, we more than held our own.

We invaded the Mariana Islands on June 7, 1944, the day after we invaded Normandy Beach on the other side of the world, and the tide of the war began to turn. I was still assigned to the *San Jacinto*, but when the Marines put out word that they were looking for volunteers for the FMF—the Fleet Marine Force—I raised my fat paw real quick. The Marines were taking 10 percent of their seaborne complement and bringing them on land, and I was kind of looking forward to getting the hell off that ship. Because by then the sky was becoming blacker and blacker as it filled with more and more kamikaze planes.

Those goddamn Japs, they were coming down and blowing up our ships left and right. We nearly lost the Navy to those wild bastards. And I figured it was only a matter of time and percentages before the *San Jacinto* took a hit and went down. So I volunteered for the FMF, and a couple of days later I was straddling a rope between the *San Jacinto* and a Navy tanker waiting to take about fifty of us to Okinawa. When we got there, I was assigned to a machine-gun squad, heavy weapons. There were eight guys in the squad, we fired a .50-caliber machine gun, and I was an ammunition handler. I never fired the gun. My job was to make sure the guys who did were never empty.

I spent two months in Okinawa, and though the island was allegedly secured, there were Japs all over the place. You'd never really see them, you'd just hear their bullets whistling past your ear when you'd get into a fire fight. But it still beat hell out of facing the goddamn kamikazes. After Okinawa, I was reassigned to the 3rd Marine Division. Guam was just like Okinawa; it was supposed to be secured, but there were Japs all over the place. Probably still some of them hiding out in that jungle today. You could hide on Guam for years, for Christ's sake. One night they came down out of the hills and stole the tent over our commode, and we had to go out looking for them. At night. We couldn't find them, and I think everyone was kind of happy. Nobody wanted to get killed over a tent from the goddamn latrine. They stole the tent. What the hell did we care? Let them steal the tent. Those guys never gave up. They always went down fighting. And Guam was a big island.

Pretty soon, however, it seemed to get smaller and smaller. First I ran into Al Arater, my old buddy from the Bronx. His submarine had been sunk and half the guys hadn't made it out. He was one of the lucky ones. My name had made the church bulletin back home, and Al's mother had sent him the bulletin. When he got near the island, he swung a three-day pass and the two of us went on quite a bender, using some of the local hooch as the stimulant.

Then a few weeks later who do I run into but my old man. He had been a commander in the Merchant Marine, overseeing trainees out in Sheepshead Bay, in Brooklyn. But he was transferred to an overseas USO tour to referee fights. So one day he just showed up on Guam, and boom, I got the best seats in the house for the exhibition fights he was reffing. But my most memorable experience in the South Pacific wasn't for fighting. It was for stealing. Or, I should say, getting caught stealing.

One night we were working all night on the docks near Agana, Guam's capital, emptying cargo ships and getting all this stuff ready for the invasion of Japan. We were sure it was going to be ordered any minute. At about four in the morning, I and a couple of other guys found a case of Spam down in the hold of a troop transport. So I grabbed it, loaded it onto our truck, and finally stashed it under our tent.

Well, the next day there was a typhoon, a real gulley-washer, and wouldn't you know it but that's the day this young lieutenant just in from the States, a real greenhorn, picked to pull tent inspection. Jesus Christ, can you imagine tent inspection in a war zone? Anyway, he looked under the floor of our tent, and the rain had washed away the dirt we had dumped on the case of Spam. He said to us, "What's that?" Nobody said nothing, so he ordered us to pull it out. Finally he asked, "This is government property. Where did you guys steal it from?" Still nobody said nothing. He asked again, "Who does it belong to?" After a long pause, I told him it was mine. He asked me where I got it, and I lied to him. I told him I found it on the side of the road.

The greenhorn left, and the next thing I knew a runner came up and told me to get dressed in khakis and go see the regimental adjutant. The adjutant's name was Joe McFadden, and he was from New Jersey. He was also the former quarterback of

Georgetown's football team. I stood there shuffling my feet and finally Major McFadden asked, "Donovan, where'd you steal the Spam?" I told him I found it laying by the side of the road and he said, "Goddamnit, Donovan, don't lie to me." So I admitted that I took it from the hold of a troop ship we were cleaning out. And he said to me, "What were you going to do with it? Sell it to the gooks?" And I said, "No, sir, I'm going to eat it." He said, "I told you not to lie to me. Nobody eats that crap." I told him, "I do. I like it."

Then he asked me where I was from. I told him New York, and he asked me if I was any relation to the fight referee. I told him that the ref was my father. Now, I figured a McFadden from New Jersey who played football at Georgetown is not going to throw a Donovan from New York who played football at Notre Dame into the brig over a case of Spam. Sure enough, Major McFadden told me he was going to give me a week to eat the whole case, or, as he put it, "your ass belongs to me."

I ate the whole case in six days.

Thirty pounds of Spam. I was the company hero. The cooks used to come over to our tent and put the Spam in batter and cook it up for me. Twenty-fours hours a day I'd be eating Spam. And loving it. They let me off the hook, and I still have a soft spot in my heart for Spam.

But for a while, all of us wondered who was going to have a heart left to have a soft spot in after we invaded Japan. We all talked as if it was certain. What we didn't talk about, but what we knew, was that not a lot of us were going to be coming back from that hornet's nest.

Then they dropped the bomb.

I remember it was a rainy night in early August and we were all sitting around watching the comedian Charley Ruggles, who was entertaining as part of a USO tour. He was onstage when suddenly there was a big commotion. One general or another, I forget who the regimental commander was, got up onstage and announced that they had dropped the atomic bomb. We didn't know what the hell he was talking about. Then he said that he felt that the Japanese would soon sue for peace. Now we figured he was drunk, because everyone knew they were digging in on the beaches of Japan. In fact, I had a captain named Mike Heinz sitting next to me, and when the general made this announcement, I turned to him and asked him if this meant we were going home. And he laughed and said, "I'll tell you where the hell it means we're going. It means we're going to Tokyo."

But the general was right. And four months later I landed in California, in October 1945. I went in as a Pfc. and I came out as a Pfc. I suppose they just didn't recognize my leadership abilities. I was twenty years old and remember before I got on the train to Bainbridge, I tried to get a beer in a tavern in San Diego and the guy wouldn't serve me because I wasn't old enough. I'll never forget that. I'd nearly got my ass blown off in the South Pacific for twenty-four months but I was too young to drink in a California bar.

When I got to New York my cousins were waiting for me at the subway stop on the corner of the Grand Concourse and 202nd Street. And when I walked upstairs and into the apartment, my mother was cooking at the stove and trying not to let me know she was crying. I looked at her and said, "Here I am, Ma. I just won the war." My father was still on Guam. But my uncles and aunts and cousins all came over for a big party, and it was a very heart-warming reunion.

The first thing I did the next morning was head over to Fordham to speak to them about playing football. It was the only thing that was on my mind. I met up with Jack Coffey, who was the graduate manager of the football team, and I reminded him about my tryout when I was a junior at the Mount. I had written a few letters to people while I was overseas expressing my desire to transfer from Notre Dame to Fordham, and I had gotten nothing but positive feedback. Now, as I began to throw my spiel at Coffey, he pulled me up short. Fordham, he said, was planning to disband their intercollegiate football program. "If I were you," said Coffey, "I'd book passage on the first train to South Bend."

But in the meantime, a very wealthy man by the name of Biz Arnold had called me up and asked me to come into Manhattan and meet him for lunch. Arnold was a comic-book publisher, a multimillionaire, and had heard about me from mutual acquaintances in the Bronx. He had gone to Brown University, and his father had started the Arnold Foundation at Brown. So I went down to 200 Fourth Avenue (now Park Avenue South) and, holy Christ, his office was about as big as the inside of St. Philip Neri church. A real swanky deal. After the introductory amenities, he got down to business. "Arthur," he said, "would you like to go to Brown? My father's got an Arnold Foundation up there and I'm perpetuating it." Now, Brown didn't have any kind of good football team, but they had a helluva coach in Rip Engle, who later became a legend at Penn State.

Obviously, in his ardor to match Brown University and Arthur Donovan, Jr., old Biz hadn't checked my grades from high school or Notre Dame. But that wasn't my problem, it was Biz's. So I told him I'd consider it. Then he told me he was taking six boys up to Brown for the weekend and asked if I would like to come along to see the campus. I said sure, and when we met at the train station on a cold Friday morning in January, he handed me $1,000. "You're a veteran and the oldest," he said, "I want you to treat these young high-school fellows to a good time." Let me tell you, those young high-school fellows got treated to a good time, all right, but it wasn't by me. Biz Arnold stayed with us the entire time, from the train ride to Providence to the hotel suite, and picked up every bill along the way. A couple of times I tried to pull the money out of my pocket to pay for a tab, but Biz was either too quick or wouldn't hear of it. And there were quite a few tabs. Food was plentiful, and beer flowed like water.

When we got back to New York I said to him, "Here, Mr. Arnold, here's your money." But he wouldn't take it. "You keep it," he told me, and he just walked away. The next day I called him up and told him I felt very badly about my decision, but I'd always been in a Catholic school, and I'd prefer to go to a Catholic college.

"That's wonderful," he said. "Come on down and see me again." I figured he wanted his $1,000 back. I went back down to Fourth Avenue, and before I could say anything he told me that the coach at Brown prior to Rip Engle was a friend of his named

Denny Myers, who was now coaching at Boston College. Would I mind if he arranged an interview for me with Myers at BC? "Certainly not," I told him. "That sounds great." And then he gave me another $1,000.

Now I'm in trouble. I have $1,000 in my pocket that my mother had sent me down to give back. But instead of giving it back, I have another $1,000 in my hand. Biz Arnold then asked me what I thought about George Washington University in Washington, because he also knew the coach down there. And though I was sorely tempted to try for $3,000, I had to tell him I wasn't interested.

The following weekend I took Al Arater and one of his buddies up to Boston, met Denny Myers, and stayed for a week blowing the two grand Biz Arnold had staked me to. I loved the school and I loved the town. Denny Myers offered me a full scholarship, explaining that I could keep the money from my GI Bill to live off of and that the school would provide me with housing. And Boston itself was a great city. Considering we're talking about three returning veterans with $2,000 to blow, it's no wonder I fell in love with the place.

But there was one problem. When I got home there was a letter waiting for me from Notre Dame, asking when I expected to return. My mother opted for Notre Dame. Need I say more? I knew things hadn't changed much in South Bend when I got out there, and I was waiting in the administration office with four other football players. The registrar's secretary came out and asked us all to follow her, but when we got inside, she sent three of them into one room and me into another. I felt all those not-so-fond memories returning. I also got the distinct impression they were trying to tell me something. I wasn't wrong.

I had run into Moose Krause out in San Diego after the war ended. Krause was Notre Dame's athletic director for years, and recently retired. He was their line coach then. Each time I had seen him he was all fired up about me coming back to play for the Fighting Irish. But now that I was back, the trade winds had changed considerably. Krause told me that Notre Dame couldn't offer me a scholarship, but what they could do was set me up with a job in the kitchen and take care of my expenses. If I made the

team the following fall, we could talk scholarship then. I figured
since Krause hadn't come through before, he wasn't going to come
through now.

I told a friend of mine out there in South Bend, Tom Costello,
what had transpired. Costello had been two years ahead of me at
Mount St. Michael's and had gone on to play end for Georgetown
before the war. He and his brother were both held as prisoners of
war by the Germans in Italy. Anyway, Costello didn't like what he
had heard about my experience at Notre Dame, and both of us just
decided then and there to get the hell out of South Bend.

We put a collect call through to Georgetown's athletic director,
Jack Haggerty, but the sonofabitch wouldn't accept it. So on a
Friday night in January I called my mother in the Bronx and told
her I was coming home. I hitched a ride on a special train that was
taking the Hal McIntyre Orchestra back East, and two days later I
was back in the Bronx and preparing for Boston. Before spring
practice began I tried to pick up some spending money by digging
graves in Woodlawn Cemetery, but after a half a day of that crap I
decided I'd rather head North broke.

But before I could head off to Boston for four of the grandest
years of my life, tragedy struck our family. While out drinking late
one night with a bunch of wealthy men from the New York Athletic Club, my father got into an argument. Pushing led to punch-
ing, and before anyone knew what had happened, my father was
arrested for the accidental death of his best friend.

David Stanley Corcoran was the president of the Crockery
Board of Trade and one of the city's leading importers of Swedish
crystal. On Holy Thursday, April 8, 1946, Corcoran had just returned from a buying trip to Sweden and was out celebrating with
my father. I remember that afternoon, my father had called home
and I had asked him if he could make it home early that night, and
he said sure. But then he called again to tell us that Mr. Corcoran
was back in town and that he wouldn't be able to come home for
dinner. The two of them were the greatest of friends. And my
father was sure that when Corcoran returned from Sweden he was
going to ask my father to go into business with him.

At any rate, we all went to bed without hearing from my father that night, but that wasn't unusual. The next thing I knew, however, the phone was ringing at eight in the morning. That was unusual. It was my father. He told me he was at the 54th Precinct. He told me there'd been a fight and that it looked like Mr. Corcoran was going to die. At one o'clock that afternoon he did die. Corcoran was fifty-eight years old. My father was fifty-four.

What had happened was a bunch of them went out celebrating the evening before, and as far as any of the witnesses could remember, at sometime around five in the morning my father and Corcoran had gotten into a beef with a cabdriver at the corner of Fifty-seventh Street and Fifth Avenue. There were a few other people with them, including Corcoran's twenty-four-year-old son, D. Stanley, Jr. Somehow the argument with the cabdriver turned into a drunken argument between friends. My father hit Corcoran, the man fell and hit his head on the sidewalk, and he died of a cerebral hemorrhage eight hours later.

My father was devastated. He couldn't remember what had happened. His lawyer introduced evidence showing that my father's jaw was bruised and some of his teeth were loose, indicating that Corcoran had hit him first, but my father didn't care. It was all just a little horseplay between friends that had gotten out of hand. They were a rough, wild bunch, and they had done this sort of thing before. But no one had ever died before. I'll never forget the subway ride back up to the Bronx after we posted $2,500 bail. My father didn't say a word. I don't think he said a word for a week.

It was a horrible time for the family, the toughest thing we ever went through together. It nearly killed my mother. And no one seemed to know what really happened. They never really proved who pushed the man. On April 26, a charge of "technical homicide" was brought against my father. At the hearing my father and I sat there without saying a word. Toward the end, he began to weep. It was the first time I'd ever seen him cry.

On May 17, my father waived immunity and testified before a grand jury. He couldn't remember what happened. The grand jury refused to indict him. As he was leaving the courtroom he turned to a pack of reporters trailing us and said, "I don't know what happened. He was my best friend." And one of the hardest things I ever had to do was go down to the New York Athletic Club and see that man's son, D. Stanley Corcoran, Jr., to let him know how badly our entire family felt about his loss. He didn't hold a grudge. He was sad; he also knew how close my father was to his old man. That may have been the only time in my life I've been tongue-tied. What can you say to someone in that situation? After a few weeks of mourning, I needed a break. I found it in Boston.

I lived the life of Riley at Chestnut Hill. I partied and played and ate like a king, and going to school there was one of the best decisions I ever made in my life. Am I giving you the impression that I liked the place? Good.

I went up to Boston College in the spring of '46 with another New Yorker named Arthur Cesario, and we were the first New Yorkers to ever play football up there. They were used to guys from New England and, in the extreme, lower Connecticut and northern New Jersey. And unlike Notre Dame, they got a kick out of our accents and "New Yawk" ways.

They housed the veterans, three hundred of us in all, in jerry-rigged, double-decker Army barracks, which they built right on the campus. They didn't have any dormitories at the time, and you had to be a vet to live on the grounds. The place is unbelievably built up now, but in the late 1940s it consisted of just five buildings. I majored in education because they didn't teach phys ed, and education was going to be the easiest of all the courses. I wasn't trying to fool anyone with business courses or anything like that. I was there to play football.

At Boston College, I also met and played with the best athlete I may have ever seen in my life. His name was Edward (Butch) Songen, and he was a terror. He died just a few years ago, emaciated by cancer. But I'll always remember Butch as the Dave Winfield of my day, playing every sport and playing it well. After our junior season at BC, two different professional leagues tried to sign him up. First he was approached by the New York Yankees of the old All-American Football Conference. Dan Topping, of the baseball Yankees, was their owner, and he offered Butch a big bonus to jump. Butch declined, so the Boston Bruins of the National

Hockey League took that as a good sign, and they went after him. He blew them off, too. I think he was having too much fun at Chestnut Hill.

Not that I know why. If school was more or less a way station for a lot of us on our way to professional football, for Butch it was torture. He was about as comfortable in a classroom as a hooker in the Vatican. But he certainly made life fun for a lot of us, including a few teachers.

We had a geography teacher—Maps Lyard, we called him—and one day in class he popped a quiz on us. One of the questions was: "For two points, define and describe the Khyber Pass." I was sitting alongside Butch, and he whispered over to me, "Hey, Fatso, look what I put down for this one." I peered over at his answer and he had written:

> *Dear Professor Lyard:*
> *I've heard of the forward pass. I've heard of the lateral pass. And I've even heard of the shovel pass. But goddamnit, you really got me stuck on the Khyber Pass.*

I read it and I started laughing, I swear to Christ I was crying I was laughing so hard. And Maps Lyard gave Butch the two points for his answer. He said anyone that clever deserves full credit. I think he thought Butch was kidding. No matter. It may have been the only two points Butch scored on that test. Seriously. Butch eventually was drafted by the Colts, but they screwed him royally. They cut him to keep a quarterback named Dick Flowers, who didn't throw a spiral the whole year he was with us. Butch, meanwhile, ended up winning a couple of Grey Cup championships in the Canadian Football League.

I don't know what it is, but throughout my entire life I've seemed to attract the fruitcakes of the world. Wherever I went I made friends with the crazies, and Boston College was no exception. One of my best buddies at BC was a kid named Paul Duff, the son of a brain surgeon from Beverly, Massachusetts. Duff was out-and-out nuts. Remember Rosie Ruiz, the girl who was caught cheating in the Boston Marathon a few years back? Well, Paul

Duff had that act down when Rosie was just a twinkle in her old man's eyes.

Duff had been in the service, so he lived on the campus with us. And one Patriots' Day, the morning they run the marathon, we were standing on Chestnut Hill, watching the Marathon and listening on radio for the finish that ends in downtown Boston. Unbeknownst to everyone, Duff, wrapped in a blanket, jumped into the marathon two blocks before the finish line. He was wearing Army boots, with some kind of square-root number on his T-shirt, and he ran the rest of the race and they dropped the tape for him as the winner. Then a couple of his friends hustled him out of the crowd and for two hours the race committee was searching for the alleged winner of the Boston Marathon. Later we found out the alleged winner of the Boston Marathon was Paul Duff of Boston College. Fortunately for Duff, the alleged winner was never found.

Another time Gorgeous George, the famous wrestler with the flowing blond locks, was headlining a match at the Boston Arena, and a bunch of us went down to catch the show. Well, as Gorgeous is walking down the aisle toward the ring, suddenly I see Duff sneaking up behind him with a pail of water. Sure enough, he doused George, straightened his hair right out, and the match was called off. The two Boston papers made a big thing out of it, especially after Gorgeous George put up a $5,000 reward for the perpetrator. They never did find that perp.

This goofy Duff didn't care who he insulted. Once a friend of mine named Ug Murray and myself drove through a snowstorm over to Worcester to watch Holy Cross play BC in a basketball game. This was during the era when the Cross had some fine teams and Boston College just couldn't compete. Anyway, Ug and I were sitting in the stands when who showed up but Duff. He was sitting with us and we had our BC sweaters on, and right behind us were all the priests from Holy Cross. We were losing badly and the priests were cheering politely when suddenly Duff turned around to them and said, "For Christ's sake, why don't you bunch of assholes shut up." Murray and I wanted to die. You never saw two bigger guys slink away as low as Ug and I did after Duff opened his mouth.

Then there was Dominick Papaleo. This guy was a pip. I played with Ernie Stautner at BC. Stautner is a Hall of Fame defensive tackle who played with the Steelers and is one of Tom Landry's assistants in Dallas now. Stautner had been in the Marines with Papaleo, and Pappy, who was from Boston, convinced Ernie to come along to play at BC. Pappy was a hoodlum from the word go, but he was one tough sonofabitch. He was six-two and about 260 pounds, and once, in a game against Tennessee, he single-handedly won the game for us. He beat the crap out of the entire Tennessee defensive line.

But Pappy was more renowned for his exploits off the field. First of all, the guy couldn't drive. When he first came to school he had an old Ford Model A. He used to stop it by running into walls. He didn't know how to use the brake, I swear to God. Then he got a new car. Within a month it looked like a junker. That crazy bastard must have had eighteen accidents.

Another time, Pappy and I were taking a Spanish test, and we sat alongside Harry Ernst, who was the smartest boy in the class. The first question on the exam, written in Spanish, was, "What is your name and where are you from?" We were supposed to answer in English. Harry Ernst wrote, "My name is Harry Ernst and I am from Newton, Massachusetts." Papaleo peered over, then he wrote, "My name is Dominick Papaleo and I am from Cambridge, Massachusetts." I peered over and I put down, "My name is Dominick Papaleo and I also live in Cambridge, Massachusetts." When Papaleo looked over at my paper he went nuts. "You stupid sonofabitch," he said, "get my name off your paper." Then, when I realized what I had done, holy Christ, did I start laughing. I laughed so hard I got caught by Dr. Azwolla, our Spanish teacher, and the bastard flunked both of us for the year.

Because Papaleo flunked math also, he was required to take math or Spanish in summer school. These two courses were given at the same time, so Papaleo was advised to join the dramatics society to get enough credits to play in his junior year. He said, "The hell with this bullshit, I'm not going to join those queers." Father Maurice Dullea, a great priest, talked Pappy into joining the dramatic club, as he was needed on the team.

The first time I saw Papaleo after this I asked him how he was doing. He said, "Terrific—they're putting on a Shakespearean play, and all I do is open and close the curtains. The play was about Roman centurions. I'm meeting a lot of good-looking broads." Dress-rehearsal night went over great. On opening night, before a packed house, one of the actors, a centurion who had some lines to say, became ill and didn't show up. The director of the play approached Pappy to take his place. "Hell, no. It's bad enough I have to pull curtains back and forth, but I'm not going to say lines in the play." Father Dullea sat Papaleo down and gave him the same line of blarney he had given him before. It was only a couple of lines he had to say.

The first act was a great success. In the second act, first scene, Pappy was dressed as a Roman soldier. When he got the cue, he had to step forward and say the line "There he stands by the side of the ship" by William Shakespeare.

Now, before Pappy got the cue he was getting nervous, starting to shake and sweat, and he stepped forward and the words that came out of his mouth were, "There he shits by the side of the ship by William Shakes—it—I mean snake shit. Oh, bull shit, I didn't want to be in the play anyway."

It was a great success: Pappy passed the course, and BC had their offensive right guard.

But Papaleo was only one of the crazies I went to BC with. Fourteen people from my college team went on to play pro football, including Eddie King, the former governor of Massachusetts, and my best friend and roommate Walter Boverini, who's a big-shot state senator up there now. I still talk to Walter often, and King invited me to Boston to make a speech for him the last time he was running for governor of Massachusetts. King was a beaut. The guy was smart as hell, but I never saw him walking around the campus with anything deeper than the racing form. As I recall, old Dr. Azwolla flunked Eddie, too. For some reason King hated Azwolla. I never knew why. King lived right across the street from BC, and Azwolla had an apartment up at the top of Chestnut Hill. Every morning Eddie would park his car so Azwolla couldn't drive down the hill, and naturally it really burned the teacher up. He knew King was doing it on purpose. So he flunked him.

The three of us—Pappy, King, and I—ended up being tutored by a man named Mr. Antiqua. Antiqua was a big man, but he was lame, and he used to limp down to my dorm room and meet us for class. Finally he gave us a final exam, and he flunked us, too. I said to him, "Jesus Christ, what the hell are you doing? This doesn't make it look too good for your tutorial skills." And he agreed. "You got a point there," said Mr. Antiqua. "So I'll tutor you again. Besides, I need the money." Needless to say, the second time around we all passed.

Listen, let's be frank. I went to college to learn how to play football. I got an education, a good Jesuit education. You know, morality and philosophy and everything else. But everyone on both sides of the teacher's desk knew the score. One time one of our teachers, a history professor I only remember as Father O'Conner, gave it to me straight. "Arthur," said the priest, "I'm going to tell you the one thing you have to do in order to get by here. Don't cut my classes. You cut my class, I'll flunk you. As long as you come to my class, you're going to learn something, at least through osmosis." And I went to class for four years and graduated and, yes, I did learn things, quite often through osmosis. I wonder how many kids at today's football factories can say that.

I didn't play much my first year. The second year I played more than anybody because I played guard and tackle and because Boston College had some good returning starters and partly because there were guys who came in with me who were just as good as I was. Coach Denny Myers knew that the men he brought in after the war were much better than the kids who had played along the line for him the previous season. But they had taken him to the Orange Bowl in 1943, so he felt some loyalty to his former linemen. Plus, he was genuinely a nice guy who didn't want to hurt anyone's feelings. So he ended up rotating seven or eight really good football players along the defensive line, including me, Papaleo, and Ernie Stautner.

Stautner was one tough dude, and though Papaleo was the reason he came to BC, Pappy really didn't have to do all that much convincing. You wanted ten steaks at BC, you got ten steaks. Lobster? Prime ribs? Dozens of oysters? They were yours for the asking. They knew my sweet spot, and I was never at a loss for baloney and kosher franks. There was plenty to do in Boston, too, especially for a returning veteran.

I mean, they used to have a book on me. They knew I'd be at the movies on Monday and Wednesday and at the Lithuanian Club dance Friday and at a certain Irish bar every Saturday night. You wanted Arthur Donovan at any time during the week, consult the book and you knew where to find him. At first the school administration tried to give us proctors who imposed a 10:00 P.M. curfew and banned beer from the barracks. But we gently explained to these priests that some of us had been away fighting for three and four years and it just wasn't right to treat us like kids. Those we couldn't drive back to the rectory we bribed, and everything always went smoothly.

I played at nose tackle as often as Myers would let me in his rotating-linemen system, and it was at Boston College that I picked up my habit of puking before every game. I can't explain why, I'd never even gotten seasick on the *San Jacinto,* but my stomach would get so tight prior to a game that I'd be dry-heaving while the coach was giving his last-minute pep talk. I carried that unfortunate habit all the way through my playing days in the pros, too. And this happened even if I wasn't starting. And that occurred more often than I'd have liked at BC.

To be honest, I was Pop Warner League compared to guys like Papaleo. In that Tennessee game I mentioned, our coaches had seen that their blocking scheme could be disrupted if we could crash through their pulling line at an angle. All we needed was a man to do it. That day, Pappy beat the crap out of every Volunteer offensive lineman half a dozen times, and we won going away. But we were probably as scared of him as those kids from the University of Tennessee.

Pappy dropped out our senior season to pursue a more lucrative occupation. He led a life of crime and ended up hanging himself in a Danbury, Connecticut, prison. But before that he once came to visit me while I was living in Baltimore. He brought two of his underlings with him. They stopped at a local gas station for directions to my liquor store, and soon after they left, one of the liquor salesman who worked for me pulled in to fill up his tank. The guy at the gas station asked him, "Hey, is Donovan in some kind of trouble?" And when my man asked why, the gas station attendant replied, "Because there's three torpedoes that just pulled out of here and they're looking for him."

At Boston College I didn't even start until my junior year, although I played a lot under Myers' rotating system. I was a guard and tackle on offense and a middle guard on defense, and I remember in the last game of my freshman year, against Holy Cross, our traditional rival, who did I meet up with on the other side of the line but Tom Costello, the fellow who left Notre Dame with me. He's a lawyer in New York now, and his claim to fame, so to speak, is that his picture was once on the cover of *Life* magazine. No, not for his gridiron exploits. You see, Tom ended up marrying a girl from Worcester, and her brother turned out to be a Marine drill instructor, the sergeant who marched a bunch of recruits into the swamps around Parris Island in the early 1950s and ended up killing a couple of them. Tom was one of his defense attorneys.

Then as now, the NFL allowed teams to draft players as soon as their graduating class had matriculated. And since I had started at Notre Dame in 1942, I was drafted by the New York Giants in the 1946 lottery following my freshman season at BC. I never gave the Giants a second thought. I was having too much fun at BC. One summer I stayed in Boston to attend summer school, but the rest of my summer vacations were spent on construction work in New York.

I worked for two people from my neighborhood, Mr. Palmieri and Mr. Puzio, who were both mason contractors. They kept a job open for me every summer. I was their mortar mixer. Fitting, I guess, because a lot of people from the neighborhood always considered me something of a cementhead. They'd put me in charge of a crew that was right off the boat from Sicily, and we threw up garden apartments all over New York City. In fact, there's an apartment complex out in Flushing Meadow, Queens, on a site overlooking the old World's Fair grounds, that still has my initials carved into the cornerstone.

Meanwhile, most of the gang from the neighborhood had all married and had a few kids, and the only guys still hanging out were some of the younger fellows I knew. So every night, as long as they didn't mind baloney, we'd head up to Moocho's bar in the Bronx and sate ourselves with kosher cold cuts, beer, and pizza. Once in a while, just for a change of pace, I would go out to Long Beach, Long Island, or maybe over to Rockaway Beach. But most of the time I just stayed right in the neighborhood.

By my junior year I was the starting middle guard and was beginning to make something of a name for myself. We were playing in the old Braves Field (called Nickerson Field now) before crowds of forty thousand and fifty thousand. And though the teams I played on were never better than mediocre, the people of Boston loved us. After the '48 season, my junior year, ended, the Buffalo Bisons of the All-American Football Conference offered me a guaranteed contract to quit school and join the pros. It was a tempting offer.

Their coach, Clem Crow, came in with what was then an outstanding offer. The whole package came to about $25,000, including a $15,000 contract, a $5,000 signing bonus, and a brand-new car. Now, the most money I'd ever made playing football was $100 one of the Jesuits at Boston College had given me before a homecoming game to take my mother and sister out to dinner. Some people may have been receiving under-the-table payments to play at BC, but I sure wasn't. The only thing they'd really do for us is the same thing all these colleges are getting in trouble for today: ticket scalping. They'd give us maybe four tickets and let us sell them outside the stadium on game day. I remember a guy named Al Cannava would be out their scalping ten minutes before game time, then he'd run in and get dressed just in time for the national anthem. He said the money was always better the closer you got to game time.

There was a bidding war over college players raging between the NFL and the All-American Football Conference, which was why Clem Crow's offer was so delectable. But my mother wouldn't let me take it. She wanted me to finish my education. What a mistake. The AAFC folded after the 1949 season. Three of its teams, including the Baltimore Colts, were assimilated into the NFL. And by the time I was drafted by the Colts in the fourth round of the supplemental draft in 1950, Clem Crow was now their coach, the bidding war was a thing of the past, and the bastard offered me an unguaranteed $4,500 contract, take it or leave it.

I ended up taking it, but not before wondering what the hell I was doing playing with the big boys. I didn't even make All-New England my senior year. I was beaten out by a guy named Irv Heller from Boston University, of all places. And I felt terrible about graduating from Boston College. My experience had been truly a four-year picnic, and I made friendships I keep up to this day. But all good things must end. So one Sunday in July 1950 I returned from Mass and packed up my car and got ready to head for Baltimore.

I hadn't accepted their contract offer. I figurred I could negotiate when I got down there for training camp. Of course, I figured wrong. I remember the day I left the Bronx like it was yesterday. The car was packed in front of the house on the Grand Concourse when my father walked home and said to me, "Where do you think you're going?"

I told him I was leaving for Baltimore, and he asked me what the hell for. I informed him that I was trying out for the Colts, and he started yelling up to my mother at the second-floor window, "Mary, Mary, do you know what this kid is doing? He's going down to Baltimore to play football! Those big guys will kill him!" I had spent four years in the Marines, had played four years of major college ball at Boston College, and my father still thought I was just this big, overgrown sissy. I had to laugh.

I walked upstairs and kissed my mother good-bye and said, "See you soon, Ma. I'm going to give it a shot and I'll be back in a couple of weeks."

Thirty-seven years later I'm still here.

6

The Real War Years

I drove to Baltimore in the summer of 1950 in a brand-new car and with $45 in my pocket. The car was a Ford my mother had bought with the allotment money I'd sent home from the Pacific. She'd bought war bonds, saved them all, and spent the money on me as a going-away present. The forty-five bucks was all the money I had saved from my construction job. I had no more idea of making the Baltimore Colts than the man in the moon. Three days after I arrived I signed a one-year contract for $4,500, conditional upon making the team.

The Colts' training camp has always been out in Westminster, Maryland, on the campus of Western Maryland College, about twenty miles northwest of Baltimore. I arrived three days late, and who is the first person I see but Clem Crow, the very same Clem Crow who had tried to sweet-talk me into jumping school a year and a half earlier. Let me tell you something: The Clem Crow I met in Westminster was not the same man who had promised me the moon and the stars to play in Buffalo. This sonofabitch was crazy, and my first training camp immediately became one of the worst experiences of my life.

First of all, Crow must have had 150 players in camp, and all we did was scrimmage. No drills. No chalk talk. No run-throughs of plays. Just hot, humid, bone-breaking, full-pad scrimmages. The All-American Football Conference had folded after the previous season, and the NFL had swallowed the Cleveland Browns, the San Francisco 49ers, and the Colts en masse. There were a lot of unemployed football players out there looking for work, and about 90 percent of them seemed to be in the Colts' camp kicking the living shit out of each other.

For my first couple of days in camp I wasn't even issued pads. I guess they figured I was just this big, fat lump who wasn't going to make the team anyway, and pads were at a premium, as was everything in those days. Finally, enough guys left or got cut and I was given shoulder pads and a helmet. What luck!

I'll never forget the first scrimmage I took part in. Western Maryland's practice field was down in a hollow, and when I reached the edge of this hollow and peered over, I kind of got the feeling I knew what the Christians were thinking the first time they saw the Coliseum in Rome. I had walked out of the locker room with my new roommate, another defensive tackle named Sisto Averno, a guard from Muhlenberg College, and a Jersey boy. The two of us stood there at the edge of this hollow staring until Sisto finally turned to me and said, "Fatso, let's get the hell out of here." That was enough for me. But as we turned to leave, the line coach, Wayne Milner, caught us and asked where we thought we were going.

"How many people do you have practicing down there?" Sisto asked Milner.

"About a hundred and fifty," Milner replied.

"And how many people are going to make this team?" asked Sisto.

"We keep thirty-three men," said Milner.

"And out of those thirty-three, how many new defensive linemen might make this team?" asked Sisto. And when Milner said two, maybe three, Sisto called, "Good-bye." But in those days, I guess authority meant something. Because when Milner, an old Notre Damer, threatened to kick our asses unless we dragged them down into that death hole, we both sheepishly complied.

It was a Saturday morning in August, a hot and humid sonofabitch, and being down in this hollow made it feel like you were swimming through practice. We began scrimmaging at nine-thirty in the morning. And we didn't stop until quarter to twelve. So this was pro ball! Now, think a minute: There are roughly twelve minutes of football action during the average sixty-minute game. And we were out there, nonstop, for two hours and fifteen minutes. That's over eleven games of football in one morning, without even considering that in a real game the offense and defense aren't on the field at the same time.

Up and down, up and down the field they drove us; it got so bad that the defense finally said, "Screw this," and we started letting the offense score at will. I turned to another rookie defensive lineman, Don Colo, and told him I didn't think I was going to make it. He urged me on, and with the help of about a dozen cold towels we finally staggered through to the end. As we were trudging up the hill after this ordeal, Crow grabbed about six of us and told us to start running around the track.

I began jogging, but one of the guys Crow grabbed, a big Polish kid from Villanova who played offensive tackle, turned to the coach and said, "That's it. School's out." And he went home. I never saw him again. He would have made the team, too. But I think that was Crow's way of weeding out the men from the pussies, and I think it helped me make the team.

Just prior to one of our first exhibition games, against the Browns, a starting tackle by the name of Jon Jenkins, a Western Maryland kid by way of Dartmouth, hurt his ankle and I got in the game. I sacked Otto Graham, the Cleveland quarterback, three times and my foot was in the door. What I didn't realize was that there was a buzz saw on the other side of that door. I wasn't a very good player those first couple of years. I fit right in. The fact is, the Baltimore Colts stank.

Teams played seven exhibition games in those days, and the Baltimore Colts lost every one of them. I hear these guys complaining about the travel in the NFL today and it cracks me up. One Thursday night during that exhibition season we came down from Westminster to play the 49ers in Baltimore. We lost, and after the game Crow bused everyone back up to Westminster, and the next morning we got up at 7:00 A.M. for the flight out of Friendship International Airport. We flew to San Antonio, Texas, on Friday. On Saturday the Rams beat us 70–21 in San Antonio, really pouring it on with tackle-eligible plays and all this other cheap shit. And Sunday morning we awoke and flew to Shreveport, Louisiana, where we lost to the New York Yankees on Monday night. Three games in six days. Please, don't bitch to me about travel today.

And all through this horrid season we had to deal with Clem Crow, who had, shall we say, an impersonal style of coaching.

Today they call him the Turk. He's usually an equipment manager or one of the lower-echelon assistants who is assigned to knock on doors and tell people who aren't going to make the team that the head coach would like to see them. The universal training camp phrase that makes grown behemoths shudder is: "And don't forget to bring your playbook." I've seen those words literally send shivers down a football player's spine. These days, it's all very polite. Players are usually axed very early in the morning to save them the embarrassment of having to skulk out of camp in front of their former teammates. Well, let me tell you how Clem Crow pared the Baltimore roster that first season.

We had played our last exhibition game, against Green Bay, in the old County Fairgrounds in Milwaukee. After the game was over we stayed the night and flew back the next day to Baltimore. As guys were coming down the ramp of the plane, Crow was standing at the bottom of the tarmac, pointing: "You made it. You didn't. You're okay. You're gone." Guys were afraid to get off the goddamn plane.

That final exhibition game was also my first taste of Y. A. Tittle, who was one of the best quarterbacks ever to play and one of the cheapest bastards ever to live. Nobody liked Tittle, even though he was the only drawing card the 1950 Colts possessed. He was a jerk. He once asked a bunch of us if we would like to have a chicken dinner, and when we said sure, he told us to bring the chicken over to his house and his wife would cook up a nice dinner for us. Swell fella.

Another time, when we were playing the Rams on the Coast that first season, the three rookies—Colo, Averno, and I—were assigned to the same suite with Tittle. As I said, we didn't like him very much, probably because he was making the only good money on the team and he let everyone know it. Anyway, we checked into the Beverly Wilshire Hotel, and you talk about class, they had shaving and lather kits in the hotel gift shop that probably cost as much as I was making for the year. We saw all the movie stars out there—in fact, we saw Al Jolson the day before he died. But what really set us on our ear was the swimming pool. Man, we were ready for a dunk after a long, cold winter in Baltimore.

So we asked the manager if we could go swimming, and he said sure—until we told him we didn't have any swimming trunks. He wouldn't let us go bare-assed—and believe me, we would have— and he also turned down our request to dive in in our underpants. So to make do, we decided to frolic around in the bathroom in our hotel suite. Now, this thing was about ten feet square and six feet deep, and the reason it was in our suite was because we were sharing a room with Tittle. The bathtub had a swinging gate, and we filled it and the four of us are knocking around in there when someone hit the latch, the gate flew open, and we wrecked a good two floors of the Beverly Wilshire Hotel.

I mean, the ceiling of the room below us collapsed and the ceiling of the room below that collapsed, and the damage came to something like two grand. Guess whose money ended up paying for the damage? I could never figure why if four guys horsing around were responsible, why only three of them were docked. I could never figure it until I learned about the NFL quarterback star system, that is.

Anyway, we got back at him up in Wisconsin. We had flown up from Shreveport to a lodge in Sturgeon Bay, about forty miles northeast of Green Bay. And while Tittle was asleep in bed, we threw a burning log under his covers. Smoked old Y.A. but good. After the season, when the Colts folded, Y.A. was considered the plum of the dispersal draft. He went to San Francisco and from there to the Giants and had a tremendous career. And from what I understand, he stayed a cheap bastard.

But Crow is the sonofabitch I recall best from my first season in Baltimore. One of his character flaws was that he didn't trust anyone. Averno, Colo, and I would go to Mass every Sunday morning. And if we were on the road, every time the three of us would try to leave the hotel, Crow would be guarding the lobby. "Where you going?" he'd bellow as we tried to sneak out a side door. "We're going to Mass," we'd tell him. "Bullshit," he'd say. "You guys are going to drink beer." Then he'd send an assistant coach along to make sure we actually went to church. The guy was on us all the time.

But I suppose he had good reason. The Baltimore Colts of 1950 set an all-time record for points allowed in twelve games: We were outscored 462–213, including losses of 55–13 to the Chicago Cardinals, 70–27 to the Rams, 55–20 to the Giants and 51–14 to the New York Yankees. We finished the season with a 1–11 record. And the one game we did win, a 41–21 upset of Green Bay late in the season, Christ, the fans carried us off the field on their shoulders as if we had just won the world title. If I remember correctly, there were just about two fans for every player. We didn't go over real big in Baltimore that season.

Part of the reason, I suppose, was our losing ways. But a lot had to do with our owner, Abe Watner, who had made a lot of money in railroads up in the Northwest but who just didn't possess the business acumen to run a football team. This guy used to issue these absurd edicts like he was Il Duce himself. At one point, for instance, he decided that the chewing gum budget was too big, and he rationed gum to half a stick per man per day. Another one of his doozies was the tape drive. He felt we were wasting too much of it. So he had an assistant trainer scour the field after practice for the rolled-up, discarded tape. The trainer then tried to straighten it out and reuse it.

Like Mussolini, Abe Watner made his trains run on time. But the Baltimore Colts became his personal Albania. I guess we all realized that Abe was not long for the franchise—or for football, for that matter—when he closed down the Colt headquarters near Memorial Stadium and moved the team's offices into a cemetery he owned on the outskirts of town. Talk about omens. We should have known that Abe and Clem weren't the most astute observers of the game when they used a seventh-round draft choice to pick up a college kid named Arthur Bok as a linebacker. It turned out Bok had never played defense in his life and hadn't even played in the college game Crow had scouted. I recently met him in Dayton, Ohio. He is a practicing M.D. How lucky he was to get cut and become a doctor.

Nonetheless, for a twenty-five-year-old rookie out on his own for the first time, Baltimore was the Garden of Eden for me. It was love at first sight between the town and me, and I haven't lost the feeling since. In 1950, I lived in an apartment in a downtown hotel named the St. James with Sisto Averno. The hotel was old but nice. It was a great place for us to live.

The funny thing was, Sisto was never there. He ran off and got married without telling any of us. The way we found out was when a cop pulled us over after a bunch of us had been drinking in a bar up in Wilmington, Delaware. We were driving back to Baltimore, and after the guy pulled us over for speeding, we tried to get out of the ticket by explaining to the cop that we were Colts. "Goddamnit," said the trooper, "I just pulled another one of you football players over last week after he got married up in Elkton." He described the guy, and sure enough, it was Sisto. We busted his buns for some time after that.

Some nights I'd head down to a firehouse in South Baltimore, where an old Marine buddy of mine named Chuck Vallee worked. And we also discovered a joint right near the stadium named Kuzen's Bar, which was to become a home away from home for me for many years. Yet despite our love affair with Baltimore, the Colts only averaged sixteen thousand fans per game, and toward the end of the season the writing was on the wall. This team was on the road to El Foldo.

After the season that writing became etched in stone, as Watner sold the rights to all his players for $40,000, and Sisto and I were drafted by the Cleveland Browns. I signed for about $5,000, but the Browns were coming off a world title and just had too many defensive linemen already on the team. Midway through the exhibition season Paul Brown called Sisto and me into his office.

"Donovan, I know you're from New York," said the coach. "And Averno, you're from New Jersey. So I'm doing you both a favor. I'm trading you home, to the New York Yankees."

That night we drove from Bowling Green up to Ripon, Wisconsin, where the old Yankees trained. Ripon's other claim to fame: home of the Republican Party. This is also where I first came into contact with one of the funniest men in football, Jimmy Phelan. Jimmy was the coach of the Yankees, and although the game had really passed him by, he was a pisser. He had made his name coaching St. Mary's College in California. And though Jimmy didn't stand a chance of picking up the innovations in pro football, I'll never regret playing for the man. The Yankees were scheduled for an exhibition game in Chicago the day after we arrived, and Phelan told Sisto and me that we wouldn't be playing but to come along for the ride anyway.

Fine and dandy with us, we figured. I already had about fifty stitches down my face as a result of a cleat I had taken in the mouth the week before the Browns traded me. Of course, we got there, and five minutes before game time, Phelan walked up to me and told me I'd be starting. All I remember about the game was playing with Al Pollard, a maniac back from West Point who I believe had been thrown out of the academy. He was some kind of physical-fitness nut, and between plays he'd stand there doing jumping jacks or handstands or some such nonsense. He didn't last in the National Football League too long.

If the 1951 New York Yankees weren't exactly world-beaters (and they weren't—they went 1–9–2), I was certainly a happy man. I was home. I knew the local bars fairly well. And it was nice to see my family again, with whom I lived that winter. I was the baloney and beer king of the Bronx once again.

The Yankees were owned by Ted Collins, who was Kate Smith's manager. Old Kate used to come out to all the games. Bobby Layne once said that he used to worry more about Kate's throat than about opposing linemen, because once Kate couldn't sing "God Bless America" anymore we were all going to the poorhouse. Collins' son-in-law was the general manager of the team, but the real power on the club was Phelan, this feisty little Mick. He was an alcoholic at one time but is straight as an arrow now! And his best friend in the world was Casey Stengel. These guys were two peas in a pod: Neither one ever let much get in the way of a good time.

For example, we were a terrible team in those days. There was no way in heaven or hell we could even dream about staying close to the Rams, much less beating them. But one day we were out on the Coast prior to a Rams game practicing in Brookside Park, which is right alongside the Rose Bowl. And who walked out onto the practice field but Casey, the Old Perfesser himself. Jimmy stopped practice immediately and said, "Hold the phone, everybody up. We're looking so good we're just liable to beat the Rams. Better take it in." And when we got into the locker room he put his arm around Casey and announced, "Okay, boys, the bus is leaving for the racetrack in ten minutes. Don't miss it."

I'd often sit alongside Jimmy on the plane during road trips. And he'd turn to me and say, "Well, whattya think about this defense?" or "Whattya think about that play?" And when I'd tell him I didn't have the foggiest notion, he'd tell me I'd better get one quick. We went out after a Saturday night exhibition game in Houston and didn't get back to the hotel until 7:00 A.M. Sunday morning. Lo and behold, here is Coach Phelan waiting for us in the lobby to take us to church in a dump truck. Jimmy was a daily communicant and remained one for his entire life. A great man. And though we weren't as bad as the '50 Colts, we were still pretty bad.

But nothing seemed to faze Jimmy Phelan. I remember the first Pro Bowl game I went to, after the '53 season. We were in the Ambassador Hotel in Los Angeles, and Doak Walker and Bobby Layne had thrown a monster party in one of the suites. Well, as these parties will, this one had degenerated into an all-night drinking contest. Over in one corner of the suite there were about half a dozen guys just throwing up on the carpet. Jimmy Phelan and his wife walked in, took in the situation, and without missing a beat he turned to me and said, "Well, Donovan, you've certainly got a lot of fine athletes gathered here tonight, don't you. Mind if a broken-down old coach and his missus join 'em?"

That season I ran into Big Jim Farley, the chairman of the New York State Athletic Commission and the man who convinced my father to go into the refereeing business. Actually, I arranged a meeting with him in his offices down on Forty-second Street, in the old Coca-Cola Export Building. I had written to him and asked to see him. I wanted his advice on choosing a career. I'd been playing for two seasons with a couple of the worst dog-ass teams ever assembled. I was making $6,000. And I was having second thoughts about pro football as a career. Farley had no second thoughts whatsoever, only first thoughts. And he told me to get the hell out of the game. "There's no future in the game in general, and there's no future for you in the game in particular," was how he put it.

He was a great man—the postmaster general of the U.S.A. I saw him seven years later on the sidelines before our '58 championship game in Yankee Stadium. He was standing in front of the Giants' bench, and I went up to him and said, "Mr. Farley, I'm Arthur Donovan. I'm not sure if you remember a meeting we had several years back." And he just looked at me and said, "I sure gave you some bum advice, didn't I?" Yes, sir, you did.

I played fairly well that year, even though I still hadn't had a coach who could teach me any kind of technique. I was six-two and three hundred pounds, a big man in the game at that time, and I just overpowered offenses through sheer bulk. I still have a newspaper clipping from the old *Herald Tribune* describing my strengths. The clip reads,

Donovan does his best work against fakers, that is, backs who pretend they have the ball when they don't. Donovan figures that if he can make life miserable enough for faking backs when they plunge into the line, they will lose interest in their work. Soon they fake only halfheartedly and eventually they make sure Donovan knows they don't have the ball. Here again is an example of a man who roughs up players by calculation with a definite purpose, but he never intentionally injures.

The same couldn't be said for the clubs I was playing with. These teams were killing me. The Yankees fell from a third-place finish in 1950 to last place in '51. We played in Yankee Stadium, but we really couldn't compete with the Giants, across town in the Polo Grounds. Word was out on the street that Ted Collins wanted out. And one night soon after that miserable season was over, I was sitting in a bar and I heard on the radio that the franchise had been sold to a couple of Cowboys, Giles and Connell Miller, who were moving the team to Texas and changing our name to the Dallas Texans.

Don't forget, this was during a time when the NFL was still struggling financially. By this time I was what you'd consider the defensive star of the team, and I signed for $7,000 to play in 1952 and was happy for it. We were literally a dog-and-pony show, following geek shows and carnivals and playing exhibitions in out-of-the-way hamlets all over the country just to pick up a new fan or two. College football was still king. In national popularity polls, pro football ranked just above synchronized swimming and just below wife-beating. Team trainers are paid more today than the quarterbacks made in my time.

Anyway, after Collins lost his heart and his shirt in '51 and the franchise was sold to the Miller brothers, we became pro football's equivalent of rodeo clowns. We played in the Cotton Bowl but practiced at a place called the Shriner Institute, in a town named Kerrville, Texas, population eight thousand. They had all kinds of foreign stuff out there in the middle of God-knows-where. Rattlesnakes, armadillos, Gila monsters, things I never even heard of when I was a kid in the Bronx. Dead gophers scared the bejeezus out of me, and now I had to deal with this shit?

The Miller brothers owned a Mexican restaurant in Dallas, and to cut costs they hired one of their cooks as the Texans' equipment manager. The guy's name was Willie Garcia, and he had never even seen a football in his life. But he came cheap. Willie did have one saving grace, though. You see, he had a wooden leg, and he was good for one thing: Whenever we kicked the ball out into the high grass surrounding our practice site, we'd send Willie out there to get it because we figured he had only one of two chances of getting bit on the leg by a goddamn rattlesnake.

Once, midway through the season when we were taking off for the fourteen-day road trip to the Coast to play the Rams and the 49ers, Willie showed up at the airport and told Phelan he couldn't come along because his wife didn't think he was ever coming back. That rat bastard Phelan said to Willie, "No problem, *amigo*, you don't have to come. But just make sure that all the equipment is in order on the plane." Willie said sure, and as soon as he stepped onto the plane, Phelan ordered the captain to pull in the gang-plank—remember gangplanks?—and the sonofabitch took off. He actually kidnapped our equipment manager.

Phelan also brought in a trainer who was a full-blooded Indian he had used at St. Mary's. Chief Ray West was his name, and this guy made Phelan look like Carrie Nation. Old Chief would go off on benders and you wouldn't see him for days at a time. It got so you had to make an appointment weeks in advance to get a rubdown.

It was in Texas where I met George Young, who is now the general manager of the Giants. George was a big green kid out of Baltimore, and he's since become one of my best friends. He was an usher at my wedding, as a matter of fact. I remember he gave an interview to a newspaper once, and he started out really complimenting me. "Arthur's got that first step, that good quickness for the first ten yards," George said. "After that we're talking cal-ender speed. Arthur rarely makes a mistake on the field. In fact, he plays perfect games. He's strong and agile, and a pretty good athlete for a fat guy." A fat guy? Talk about the pot calling the kettle black. They haven't found the tailor yet who won't charge George double for a custom-made suit.

Anyway, we played but four home games in Texas before the Miller brothers began to realize that running a pro football team was like selling shamrocks in Shanghai. It just didn't pay. The few fans who did bother to come out and watch us treated us nice enough, but high-school and college football were still the draws in the Lone Star State. Every Monday morning when we were paid, Jimmy Phelan would stand there next to the paymaster's window and say, "Now, don't hesitate boys, get right on down to the bank and cash that sucker."

Maybe we just had too many characters on the team. One of my favorites was Chubby Griggs, a tackle who became my all-time hero one halftime by pulling a cape over his head and downing four hot dogs while Phelan was chewing us out. Not all these characters, however, were as good-natured as Chubby Griggs. Like I said, every team has its share of rats. Ours was a certain back whom the lawyers tell me I can't name. He was just about as rotten as they come. We were in Los Angeles to play the Rams that season when a girl came looking for this guy at our hotel. Her father came to the hotel, too. She was bearing his baby. Well, this sonofabitch wouldn't go down and see the girl.

"You chicken-shit, puffy-eyed weasel, get downstairs and talk to that young lady," I told him. No way, José. Years later he straightened himself out and became a fine man, but at the time he was a real bum. I believe he was on the lam from that poor girl for years to come. He once showed up at my apartment in Baltimore on the run. He said three different girls were looking to slap him with paternity suits, and he needed a place to stay. I didn't like the bum, but he was friends with my roommate, Don Colo, so he stayed.

Then there was our quarterback, a fellow by the name of George Ratterman out of Notre Dame. That sonofabitch was nuts. He shit in a guy's bed once. It was Joe Signaigo, of the sour-milk story at Notre Dame, and Signaigo blamed it on poor Buddy Young. Signaigo was going to kill Young, who kept pleading, "Check the footprints, Joe. Check the footprints." Buddy was about five-five, and Ratterman was about six-three with humongous feet. Well, Joe did check the footprints, and Buddy was spared. No one wanted to take on Ratterman. He was too crazy.

One time during the off-season he invited Sisto and me over to a party in his house in New Jersey, and when we showed up he got everybody a drink and we never saw him again for the rest of the night. I don't know where the hell he went. But I do know that his wife was just as wacky as he was. She came on a road trip with us once—we were playing in Cincinnati—and when George went back to the hotel to get some sleep she stayed out and partied with us until about five o'clock in the morning.

Those few months living in Dallas were some of the craziest times of my life. We all lived in these garden apartments, and there were parties every night. Girls would be coming and going. Guys would be playing strip poker. I remember a teammate named Bob Celeri, a real ladies' man, telling me he thought he had died and gone to heaven. We had one guy on the team, whom I'd rather not name because he was married at the time, but this guy would go up to New York, to Grand Central Station, and always have these "three cousins" meet him in the train station. We called them the Hook, the Crook, and the Snook, and this guy would go out with all three of them. He'd get off the train and head straight for a telephone booth in Grand Central, and either the Hook, the Crook, or the Snook would crawl in there with him and give him a hummer while he pretended to be making a call. The team would fall down laughing. I know, I know, real sophisticated humor. What can I say?

Finally, midway through the season, the Millers went broke, the team folded in Texas, and the Dallas Texans became wards of the league. We played the remainder of our schedule on the road and used Hershey, Pennsylvania, as our practice site and base of operations. My God, Hershey will never forget the Dallas Texans.

Practice was a joke. Phelan would work with the quarterbacks and backs while the rest of us just played volleyball over the goalposts. Twenty minutes was a grueling workout. I figured the Fates must have been making up for all of Clem Crow's sadism. We spent most of our time at Vince O'Connor's Place. Man, we broke that joint up more than a few times.

Just before our final game, Chubby Griggs got into a fight with Dick Hoerner, another one of our teammates, and our running back, little Buddy Young, ambled over to break it up. Chubby threw Young right through the jukebox. Another night Chubby got so plastered that he passed out in Vince O'Connor's. There was about three feet of snow on the ground, and eight of us carried Chubby home on a Flexible Flyer sled. It was like a funeral procession, four of us on each side carrying the sled with this 325-pound behemoth stone cold on top of it. We stayed in a motel called the Community Center, and when we reached the steps, at about three in the morning, we began serenading Phelan with Christmas carols. He finally opened his third-floor window, leaned out, and started conducting us, using a pencil as a baton.

The next morning Chubby was sitting on a couch in the lobby of the Community Center when suddenly he started turning very green. Sisty Averno spotted him first and yelled, "Watch out, Chubby's going to pop!" and sure enough, Chubby threw up all over the goddamn place. He ran to the elevator with his hands cupping his mouth, and just as the elevator opened up, there went the second gusher, all over the poor people standing inside.

If the Dallas Texans didn't win many games, they nonetheless took the title, hands down, for team Christmas carol chorusing and power puking.

And make no mistake, the Dallas Texans didn't win many games. We had no talent to begin with. And whatever enthusiasm we may have mustered was spent by the time the league took over our operation. The league management cut Celeri, for instance, because they thought he was making too much money. Then they offered to sign him back at a reduced rate. How do you fight a monopoly? Celeri signed and we all figured this team was through, and the league was just playing out the string with us to complete the regular-season schedule. We finished that season at 1–11–0 (which, by the way, made me 3–31–2 for my pro career).

The only game we won that year was an upset over the Bears in Chicago. Their owner, George Halas, the great Papa Bear himself, had promised the Bears a bonus the week before if they beat the Lions, which they did. Then, when he lost to us on Thanksgiving Day in front of a full house in Chicago, he threatened to take back those bonuses. And knowing Halas, I'm sure he did. I remember the last game of the season, we played the Lions in Detroit and they were beating us something like 40–0. And with about a minute and a half to go in the game we scored a touchdown. The unflappable Jimmy Phelan began hollering up and down the sidelines, "We got 'em now, boys! We got 'em now! Go for the jugular!"

After the '52 season closed down with that inauspicious thud, most of the team went back to Dallas to pick up our cars, and on the drive home I stopped in Baltimore to renew some old acquaintances. Even though I had only played one year there, there was something special about the town for me. And I had the feeling even then that that was where I'd end up spending the rest of my life. I went home to the Bronx for Christmas, but right after the holidays I packed up and moved back down to Baltimore, finding an apartment right near the stadium to share with Don Colo.

We lived right behind the center-field bleachers with another roommate, a basketball player from the Bullets by the name of Paul Hoffman, whom they called the Bear. And he was. Hoffman was big, wild, and trouble. He used to bring his basketball buddies back to the apartment after a game, and these guys would go on night-long benders. One night, tempers flared, and we told Hoffman and his friends that if they were going to have a fight, they had better take it across the street to the parking lot, because the landlady was about ready to throw us out of this apartment. So when they went across the street to rumble, we called the cops, who came and locked them all up. The Bear was more careful about who he brought to the apartment from then on.

I got a job selling auto parts to garages and gas stations, but my main business was sitting around Kuzen's bar wondering what was going to happen to the defunct Dallas Texans. I didn't have to wonder too long. One January night I ran into our quarterback coach, a guy named Cecil Isbell, and he told me there was a move to bring the Colts back to Baltimore. Two weeks later, on January 23, 1953, the Colts—the renamed Dallas Texans—returned to Baltimore to stay when NFL Commissioner Bert Bell persuaded a neighbor of his from the Jersey shore by the name of Carroll Rosenbloom to head a consortium buying the franchise and to become the managing general partner.

Rosenbloom was leery about the deal until a bunch of Baltimore civic leaders got together and sold fifteen thousand season tickets over a seven-week span. The great love affair between Baltimore and her Colts had begun. Keith Molesworth, who had coached the Bears, was named head coach. And a man named Don Kellett came in as the general manager. Moley was another coach the game had passed by. He was married to a very wealthy woman from Virginia, and we used to kid him all the time about being the best-tanned coach in football, because he'd never wear his shirt to practice. But in Kellett, the Colts had a winner. This guy knew how to build a team, and more important, he knew how to sell the team to Baltimore. He organized luncheons and banquets and charity speaking engagements, with players arriving gratis, and he really sold the "new" Baltimore Colts to this town. He was the master of public relations. He used to call these jaunts our "civic duty." Every place Baltimore had an affair, Kellett and a Colt were there.

At first we were a little skeptical about Kellett. Colo, Sisto, and I were the first three players to head into his offices and introduce ourselves to him. Colo was the first one in, and when he came out of Kellett's office he called us over and said, "Shit, this guy don't know nothing about football." But Kellett must have known something, for before the season began he engineered one of the biggest trades in sports history, sending five Colts to the Browns in exchange for ten players, including Don Shula, Carl Taseff, Art Spinney, and Bert Rechichar. Oh, yeah: Colo was one of the Colts who was traded to the Browns.

For my part, I liked Mr. Kellett just fine. That first time I met him, I went in and he said to me, "Well now, Arthur, the Texans certainly weren't very good, but you had a fairly decent year until you got hurt." Then I said the line I had been practicing in front of the mirror every hour for the past three weeks: "Mr. Kellett, I want to play for ten thousand dollars." I don't think my voice cracked, but it might have. And while I was lining up all the arguments I had for deserving a raise like tenpins in my mind, he turned to me, smiled, and said, "Okay."

Okay! That was that. I felt slighted. I had a million reasons why I was worth $10,000, and I didn't even get to use one of them. Kellett was always okay by me. The next season I went in to see him to talk money and he put a blank contract under my nose and told me to fill out the number, any number I wanted. I was too embarrassed, and I passed it back to him. Mother of Mercy, if I had known then what I know now.

At any rate, I began my career with the new Baltimore Colts on a high note. Molesworth may not have known much about the new innovations in pro football, but he knew enough to hold over only thirteen members of the 1952 Dallas Texans to play for the 1953 Baltimore Colts. Unbeknownst to me, after watching a couple of weeks of training camp Rosenbloom and Kellett had called together some of the older guys on the club and told them they were thinking about firing Molesworth. But first they wanted to get some player reaction. I think we all knew Moley wasn't going to take us anywhere, great tan notwithstanding, but at that meeting it was decided that firing your head coach before he'd even coached one regular-season game might not leave the greatest impression of organization on a city you were trying to impress. So Moley remained, and after our first game Rosenbloom and Kellett were wiping the sweat from their brows.

You see, the Baltimore Colts won. That's right, this is not a typo. Let me say it again. The Baltimore Colts won. Bert Rechichar returned an interception thirty-nine yards for a touchdown and he also kicked a fifty-six-yard field goal, a record at the time, and we beat the Chicago Bears, 13–9, in Baltimore in front of 23,715 disbelieving fans. Believe me, folks, there was joy in Mudville that night.

We lost to Detroit the following week, beat the Bears at Chicago in week three, lost in Green Bay in week four, but came back home to smash the Redskins in week five. After nearly half the season the Colts stood at 3–2. The town was on fire. But the ecstasy was short-lived. We lost our last seven games of the season to finish at 3–9. My highlight of the second half of the season was getting thrown out of the Rams' game for belting a guy named Skeets Quinlan. He had smacked me from behind, and when I retaliated, the referee caught me and whistled our team for a fifteen-yard penalty for a personal foul. I turned to the ref and told him, "My old man's a ref, a better ref than you'll ever be, and I know a bad call when I see one." That got me flagged from the game.

But even before the big second-half slide, everyone on the team knew Rosenbloom was going to get rid of Moley, ease him out of the coaching job and into scouting and personnel. And after we lost our last seven games, he was more than willing to go.

The only question remaining was just who was going to replace him. Despite the team's collapse, it was obvious that the Colts had a core of solid if not spectacular players, especially on defense. You could see we were starting to come along. And Rosenbloom wanted to find someone who could mold that core of psyches into one winning attitude and build on it through the draft and trades. Easier said than done.

But he did it. He hired Weeb Ewbank, a frugal Dutchman from Hoosier country in Indiana. Ewbank had been Paul Brown's tackle coach in Cleveland when the Browns traded me to the Yankees in '51, and though I really didn't personally remember much about the guy during the cup of coffee I had with the Browns, he had a reputation around the league as both a tremendous coaching talent and a rat bastard. I've never judged a man by other people's assessments, however, and I wasn't going to begin now. I was waiting until I had a chance to know the guy before I formed an impression.

During the off-season between '53 and '54, I was making a personal appearance at a synagogue outside Baltimore when someone came up to me and said, "Arthur, I'd like you to meet your new coach, Weeb Ewbank." Weeb shook my hand, said he remembered me from the Browns, and then looked me up and down and said, "I'd guess that you're at about three hundred pounds, and that's a conservative guess. If you expect to play next year you're going to have to lose a lot of that weight. You're coming into training camp at two-seventy or you can forget about coming into training camp at all."

My assessment of Ewbank's coaching ability would have to wait. But I had immediately come to one conclusion about the man: He was, indeed, a rat bastard.

7

Weeb: The Reins of Terror

When Arthur Charles Ewbank was hired by Carroll Rosenbloom in January 1954, Ewbank was forty-six years old. He had been a high-school coach for thirteen years, a backfield coach at Brown University, a head coach at the University of Washington at St. Louis, and an assistant—tackle coach—under Paul Brown in Cleveland for the past five seasons.

Upon taking the job, Ewbank promised Rosenbloom and the city of Baltimore that he would build a championship team within five years. None of us believed that crap, but as Weeb liked to say, he only missed by eight minutes and fifteen seconds. But more important to me than that championship season of 1958 was what Weeb Ewbank and his defensive coach, Joe Thomas, did for my career.

In short, they saved it.

Throughout my professional life I had been coached by a string of guys whose ideas were, shall we say, primordial in their execution of strategy. Frankly, none of the coaches I had played under were on top of the changing nature of the game. All had been good old guys, from Crow to Phelan to Molesworth, the kind of football people who had grown up with Bronco Nagurski and Jim Thorpe and, really, the game of professional football itself. The only thing I'd ever been told to do was pin my ears back and go after the passer, like *el toro* going after Manolete. I did that all right, I suppose, and did my share of goring, to boot. But that strategy never took advantage of my strengths, which were quickness for a man my size and an ability to instantly read the offensive play.

When Weeb and Joe Thomas came in and introduced the keying defense—one that *depended upon* quickness and a player's ability to read offenses—man, I was in hog heaven. Weeb Ewbank made Arthur J. Donovan, Jr., a Hall of Fame football player. I loved him for that; I always will love him for that. I can honestly say that Weeb Ewbank became and remains one of the most important, cherished people in my life.

With that out of the way, I can also honestly say that Weeb was a screwball who held insane grudges, concentrated too much on what I considered the unimportant aspects of the game, thought he was smarter than God, and deep down inside was one mean sonofabitch.

Take the weight thing. All right, I knew going into training camp in '54 I was going to have to drop about thirty pounds. And I did it. That spring I gave up beer and baloney for Lent, and I continued my diet right on through the summer. I reported at 270 on the button. Weeb wasn't happy. For the rest of my career, Weeb was never happy. I think he wanted a squad of 160-pound guys out there. The man was a royal pain in the ass about weight.

I hadn't really gotten to know him when I was in Cleveland's camp in '51. I was only there for a couple of weeks before being traded to the Yankees. And though he was teaching the keying defense to the Browns at the time, in those days a coach didn't give away tricks until he was sure a guy was going to make the team. Football was still evolving. There was nothing like the cookie-cutter offenses and defenses you see on the field today. Each team had its own personality, style, and strategy. Throughout my career the running joke was to steal someone's playbook and hide it, because losing your playbook would not only get you fined, as it does today, but more than likely would also get you cut somewhere down the road.

So in Cleveland, Paul Brown knew he never really had a roster spot for Sisto Averno and me, and he was afraid if he taught us the keying defense, even its rudiments, we'd take it to the next team we were playing with. Paul Brown was not the kind of man to surrender that edge. So the whole time we were in Cleveland's camp we served more or less as cannon fodder. They used to call Sisto and me the live tackling dummies.

But when Ewbank and Thomas came to their first Colt camp and began showing the defensive linemen how to read the footwork of the center and the offensive guards playing in front of us in order to figure out which way the play was moving, the defensive line of the Colts, which had always been strong, became great. It was like someone had given a mule team a cumulative brain. During the exhibition season Weeb had traded for a madman named Don Joyce to play defensive end. So our front line of Joyce, myself, Tom Finnin, and Gino Marchetti, if I do say so myself, was probably the best in the business.

And the funny thing was, because the keying defense had such a simple premise, we lined up the same way every place, day in, day out, for eight years. I'll never forget the big wop, Marchetti, constantly turning to me during the middle of a game and asking, "Hey, Fatso, what defense we in on this play?" "For Christ's sake, Gino," I'd say, "what goddamn defense we been in for the last five years? Nothing's changed." Sure enough, a couple of plays later there'd be Gino turning to Joyce or Finnin or Ordell Braase and asking what defense we were in for the next play. Jesus!

In retrospect, the keying defense appears rather academic: Where the blocking went was where the ball carrier was coming. Read the blocking and weep for the ball carrier. But at the time I thought Rosenbloom had tapped into the Albert Einstein of technique coaches. In fact, Rosenbloom took to calling Weeb "My crew-cut IBM machine." And that keying defense kept old Fatso in the league for eight more years. Need I say more?

Yet for all his strategic genius, Weeb wasn't exactly the smartest sideline coach I've ever run across. Basically, he eventually built a team that was like a finely tuned racing-car engine. We put together our game plan all week and, considering the talent the Colts amassed over the next few years, on Sunday we just went out and executed. If there was a need for Sunday afternoon tinkering with that engine, well, just like at Le Mans, you could pretty much rest assured that the race was already lost.

But even after the Colts became the greatest team in football, Weeb's sideline gaffes were the stuff of legend. Once we were leading the Bears by three points late in the game and we moved deep into their territory. It was fourth down with a couple of inches to go and Weeb turned on the sidelines and hollered, "Okay, field goal team out there!"

So Bill Pellington, who was standing next to him, turned and said, "Weeb, what the hell are you doing? We don't need a field goal. We need a touchdown." And Weeb said, "Pellington, you play and I coach. We need three points to tie the goddamn game." Pellington just about went out of his head. "Weeb, for God's sake," he screamed, "we're fucking *winning* by three points! A touchdown locks it up! A field goal does just about nothin'!" And Weeb sort of looked around and blinked and said, "Oh. Oh, yeah. Okay, men, go for the first down." We made it, scored, and locked it up.

Another time, during our great comeback against the 49ers during the '58 season, the score was tied in the third quarter, we got the ball, and John Unitas called time out and came over to the bench. He said, "Weeb, what've you got?" And Weeb just stared at him and said, "What've *you* got?" So John said, "Well, I'm not sure, so what've you got?" And Weeb, he just started walking away. He wouldn't answer his own goddamn quarterback.

So John, who was naturally nervous at this point, ran after him and yelled, "Weeb, for Christ's sake, what've you got? What do you think I should do?" And Weeb just turned to him calm as hell and asked, "Well, John, what do *you* think you should do?" John just looked at him, said, "Aw, this is bullshit, Weeb," went back in, drew a play in the dirt, and threw a long pass for a touchdown.

And, my right hand to God, a couple of days later Weeb got up at a banquet and somebody asked him about that play and he started saying, "Yeah, well, John was a little nervous at that point but I told him to get back in there and try that thirty-eight-deep pass because I had noticed a flaw in their defensive back-field . . .," and the bastard was going on and on taking credit for a play he didn't want to have anything to do with. It broke me up. But that was Weeb.

Unfortunately, no matter how well we played, Weeb was never satisfied. Of course, that first season under him we didn't play all that well. Not much was expected of the Colts in '54. We had gone 3–9 in '53 with a team of castoffs, rookies, has-beens, and never-was's. Weeb realized this right away. Of the thirty-nine players who had been on the roster at one time or another in '53, only nineteen played for the Colts in '54. And thirteen of the new faces were first-year men. Still, our team really wasn't very good yet.

We opened the regular season at home against the Rams, and they just murdered us, 48–0. On the first play of the game they pulled the old sucker pass play. That's when you put ten guys in the huddle and leave one just a few inches in bounds on the side-line to streak downfield when the ball is snapped. Nobody on our defense knew what was happening when a Ram end, Sheets Quinlan, kind of dallied over by their sideline. Weeb saw it and began yelling at Shula at the top of his lungs, but Shula caught the gist of what was happening to him too late and Quinlan breezed by him all the way for a score and the rout was on. The NFL out-lawed the sucker pass play after that season, but by then it was too little, too late for us. After the game I sat down and thought, "Jesus Christ, here we go again. I should have stayed in the Ma-rines."

I didn't know what to think. I was making pretty good money. I think I signed for $12,000 that year. But I didn't know if I could take another black hole of a season. I remember following the opener, we watched films of the massacre and Weeb kept trying to make excuses for me. "Lookit here," he'd say, "there they are holding Donovan again. They got away with holding him the en-tire game." They may have been holding me; they may not have been. But I finally had to tell Weeb that I didn't think the Rams' holding one defensive tackle was really the reason we lost 48–0.

Somehow, though, it got better as the season wore on. We won our second game of the year, against the Giants. And though we lost our next seven, everyone could tell we were an improving team. We weren't losing them by all that much. I mean, we had the makings of a killer defense. We were just waiting for the offense to catch up. In fact, we had but two serious problems that season: scoring touchdowns and stopping the other team from doing same. We surrendered 279 points while scoring just 131.

In our last home game we edged the 49ers, 17–13, and they had a helluva team that season. Then we went out to the Coast and got a measure of revenge for opening day by beating the Rams by a point, 22–21. Now people were beginning to get excited. In our final game of the year we traveled up to San Francisco and beat the shit out of the Niners even though we lost, 10–7. The refs killed us in that game. In those days, they had two West Coast officiating crews that flip-flopped between L.A. and San Francisco. Those were the only teams they reffed.

It was a little disheartening for an East Coast squad to travel West and find all the refs calling the hometown players by their first name and chatting about the wife and kids. I remember playing the Rams once and the official was so engrossed in a conversation with Norm Van Brocklin about a new movie they were both going to see that night that the official stepped on my foot as he passed me. He tripped and turned to me and shouted, "You clumsy sonofabitch!" In exasperation I said to him, "You're cursing me like that when you're nothing but a bunch of thieves who take care of the West Coast players?" He just walked away without saying anything. He knew it was true. Of course, we lost that game on a penalty. So even though we lost to the Niners in our season finale, we felt we had ended the year on a high note.

Perhaps more important than how we were doing on the field, however, was how we were doing in the city of Baltimore. The relationship between our team and the city was one of love at first sight. And like a good marriage, that love affair grew stronger with each passing year.

Don Kellett, the general manager, was constantly setting up public appearances for the Colts. There was a group of guys, local

Baltimore businessmen, who called themselves the Colts Associates, and they tried to help the players in any way they could—off-season jobs, housing, that kind of stuff. I always got my own job; I never looked for people to help me out. But some of these guys were okay, and I got to know a few of them well. Then there was the deal Kellett made to revive the Colt Band, a seventy-piece orchestra that had been formed during the team's old All-American Football Conference days and that played at all our home games. To this day the Colt Band still assembles in an empty Memorial Stadium in Baltimore and plays whenever the Indianapolis Colts are at home.

Then we had these leggy cheerleaders, the forerunners of the Dallas Cowgirls. I swear, they had skin-tight blue uniforms and five-gallon cowboy hats, and there was more than one Colt whose eyes wandered away from the football action on game day. It was really an amazing bonding between the team and the city. Thousands of fans would think nothing of traveling hundreds of miles to watch us play our road games. And down the road Weeb would always say that their presence on enemy turf often made the difference between victory and defeat. I don't know if I'd go that far. I still think most games are won by the better team. But he may have had a point. Sometimes the right sort of psychological boost can be decisive in a game between two evenly matched teams.

By the end of the season, after we held our own on the West Coast trip against two pretty good teams, people were panting for next season. We finished at 3–9 again, but it was a good 3–9, if you know what I mean. Plus I was still having a helluva lot of fun playing the game, despite Weeb's ban on fun.

I remember that year we drafted a guy named Jack Bighead, a full-blooded Indian out of Pepperdine College, to play offensive end. And Bighead was supposed to be the second coming of Crazy Horse. Bighead had a real tough-guy reputation. But during the third game of the season, Bighead went up for a pass near the end zone and a defensive back for the Bears dropped him right on his head and then stomped on it for good measure. With the swelling and all, Bighead really lived up to his surname. His face looked like something out of that Texas chainsaw massacre. He was carried off the field and that was the end of the big Indian. I think he caught six passes for the season and never played again.

But for every Bighead there was a Buzz Nutter, a scrawny little kid out of VPI who went on to become one of the best centers in the league. Buzz had the opposite problem I had with weight. He couldn't keep any on. He weighed about 230, and Weeb was always harping on him to get up to 250. I used to have to go all week without eating just to get down to 270, and wouldn't you know I'd be drooling come weigh-in day watching Buzz stick two ten-pound weights under his armpits and wearing a T-shirt on the scale to keep Weeb happy.

One night a whole bunch of us closed up a bar and headed back to training camp, where we tried to drive our cars up the front steps and into our dorm rooms. We had gotten sloshed at the Silver Run Inn, in Silver Run, Maryland, right near the Pennsylvania border. I knew the owner of the place and he had closed up the joint and left the keys with me. About one in the morning we finally locked up and began weaving back to camp. There were seven of us driving two cars, and we knew we had to be quiet sneaking back in, even though Weeb wasn't in camp that night, he was back in Baltimore. But Herman Ball, the assistant coach Weeb had left in charge, caught us trying to drive the goddamn cars into the dormitory, and first thing in the morning reported us to Weeb.

So Weeb sent word he wanted to see me, Marchetti, Tom Finnin, Don Joyce, Ordell Braase, and Art Spinney. All of us were defensive linemen except Spinney, who was an offensive guard. So we headed down to Weeb's room and knocked on the door and Weeb said, "Everybody come in except Spinney." Then he started in.

"You guys are making fools out of me and a mockery out of this football team, a football team that could become the greatest football team ever assembled." He went on and on and got all excited and finally he said, "But damnit, how can I fine people that I think more of than I do my own son?" Then he started crying and carrying on. Only we knew this whole act was bullshit and that he was really steaming at us but he didn't want to get the entire defensive line pissed off at him by laying a huge fine on us.

So finally Braase stood up and said, "Weeb, cut the crap. Fine us, for Christ's sake, but spare us the hearts and flowers routine." Weeb went nuts. "Get the hell out of here! Get the hell out of my sight!" he started yelling. And as we were walking out he yelled, "And goddamnit, send Spinney in here." And that poor bastard Spinney, he went in and Weeb fined him $500. That's what Spinney got for playing offense. But that's what I mean about Weeb being selective in his disciplinary stances.

For as long as Weeb coached the Colts, our routine during the week was to meet at Memorial Stadium, have a team meeting, watch film, and then go out and practice. But one day, for some reason, Weeb decided to hold practice first. I think it was going to snow or something. At any rate we went out, practiced, came back, and split into offensive and defensive groups on each side of the locker room to watch game films of our upcoming opponent.

So Weeb was setting up the projector for offensive films when Lenny Moore, a great halfback but a real flighty guy, said to me, "Shit, I ain't going to stay here. I know all I need to know about these guys." So he told Big Boy Sherman Plunkett to answer for him every time Weeb pointed to something on the screen and said, "Lenny, you see that?" When the lights went off, Lenny bolted.

Four or five times Weeb took his pointer and pointed to plays and asked, "Lenny, you see that?" And on each occasion Big Boy would answer, "Got it, Coach." Finally Weeb said, "Goddamnit, that's not Lenny," and flicked on the light to see Moore's empty chair. He asked, "Who the hell is answering for Lenny?" Sherman said, "I am, Coach." And wouldn't you know it, he fined Plunkett $500 for being deceitful and never bothered Lenny about a thing.

I read in a magazine once that during those early years if fans wrote to Weeb telling him off, or arguing about a play he called, he'd get their phone number and call up these critics to explain why he had done what he had done. That sounds like it came from a public-relations man's fantasy world, because the Weeb I knew trusted no one and explained himself to even fewer. After we used to break training camp but before we could get into Memorial Stadium, we would practice in the Pikesville Armory, just northwest of the city of Baltimore. Christ, Weeb would have his assistant coaches crawling up through the cubbyholes in the garage roofs where they kept the Army trucks in order to make sure no one was spying on us. I think that's where Al Davis picked up the practice of bugging the visiting team's locker room.

Weeb was also a perfectionist. He had started out in life as a schoolteacher, and that's what he remains to this day. You had to play by the rules as long as they were his rules. I still have a mimeographed menu announcement he used to hand out to the hotel staff of the places where we stayed on the road. What do you think a Freudian psychologist would make of this pronunciamento?

> *Please place at separate tables the various orders to facilitate service by waiters. It has been found in the past that things run smoother if the tables are labeled with cards listing the food to be served and the names of the men to be served at that table.*
>
> *Please serve beef bouillon to all persons eating the pregame meal. Also, French, Roquefort, and Russian dressing is to be available on each table, along with toast, butter, honey, and pitchers of coffee. No milk is to be served at the pregame meal.*
>
> *No one is to be served the lettuce salad or the baked potato, since a number of the boys do not want either. Therefore, please place on a separate table fifteen baked potatoes and thirty lettuce salads—and those persons who desire either may help themselves.*
>
> *Please place the steaks (and other orders) on the respective tables promptly at 9:00 A.M., making sure that the well-done meat is really* well done *and will not have to be returned to the kitchen for additional cooking.*
>
> *If it is necessary for you to hire more help to get this meal out on time, then please do so. Thank you. Weeb Ewbank.*

I mean, you'd think the guy was a hotel management trainee, not a football coach. And Weeb must have sensed that that was how a lot of people felt about him, because, for Christ's sake, that little Dutchman always thought he was tougher than he really was. Once, when John Henry Johnson of the Lions broke Carl Taseff's nose and the Gaucho nearly died (seriously—he was hemorrhaging during the entire plane ride back to Baltimore), Weeb was strutting around saying he couldn't believe a football player could miss any time because of a little thing like a broken nose.

And Weeb had one great saying that kills me to this day. He'd go through roll call in the morning, and if a guy wasn't there, he'd say to his roommate, "So where is (So-and-so)?" "He had to go home, Weeb," the guy's roommate would say. "His wife's having a baby." And then Weeb would say, "What a load of horseshit. Don't worry about being there when they have the launching. Just make sure you're around when they lay the keel."

When we were on the road he used to make us stay in these old ladies' hotels. The Green or the Huntington in Pasadena. The Windemere East in South Chicago, right on the lake. He figured we'd get in less trouble staying with a bunch of blue-hairs right out of *Arsenic and Old Lace*. Christ, old ladies even used to run the elevators in these joints. Nonetheless, we used to manage to get over. The old birds would help us sneak out through the basement if we'd bring food and perhaps a medicinal bottle back for them. Arthritis, you know.

After the '54 season ended in San Francisco, we were so sky high about our closing thrust that we decided to have a party in the locker room after the game. We were going to get beer, and Weeb was going to treat. But Garry Kerkorian, a quarterback out of Stanford, said he wanted to get some hard liquor, some whiskey, in there, too. Then somebody else said that maybe we ought to bring in some food. Now, this was too much for that cheap bastard Weeb. Things were getting out of hand and he saw this party was going to cost him some serious money. So he canceled the gig.

To the rescue rode Carroll Rosenbloom. Over the years before he died, Rosey got the reputation both with the Colts and, later, the Rams, as an owner who meddled in his team's football operation. It was a deserved reputation later on, but at the time we hardly ever saw or heard from Rosey. He didn't really start getting involved until we began winning big time. Then it became *his* team. In fact, early on he was a benign owner, whom I best remember for instituting a series of bonuses for interceptions, touchdowns scored, sacks, that kind of thing. He also began fining players for stupid mistakes on the field, and he fined himself right along with the player, matching the pot. After the '54 season was over he gave every player on the team a $500 bonus, the granddaddy of all bonuses. And he also threw us a party.

It was a big production in the St. Francis Hotel in San Francisco, and Rosey wasn't even there. I remember the whole team standing on line waiting to get on the phone to talk to Rosey and thank him for the bash. After the party we got on buses in front of the St. Francis, proceeded to the airport, and flew back to Baltimore.

In 1957 we lost to San Francisco in the last fourteen seconds of the game. After the game we went back to the Cow Palace Hotel on Market Street to meet our friends and California relatives. We met General George Usher and his wife. The general was my father's best friend who had fought with him on the Mexican border and in the trenches in France. He had returned to Santa Rosa and came down to see the game.

We had heard that three hun'dred people had developed ptomaine poisoning from eating hot dogs at Kezar Stadium. General Usher and his wife were with us when Mrs. Usher went to the bathroom and never came back. My cousin went to find her and discovered that she had passed out in the ladies' room, very sick from the hot dogs, too. Because of so many people becoming ill, the hotel was filled up and there were no rooms available. Mrs. Usher was out cold and the general was telling us he had to go home and feed the dogs. Can you imagine this shit? Here the poor man's wife may be dying, and he's going to leave her to open a can of goddamn Alpo for the Dobies back home. I couldn't believe it, I'll tell you that. But I told the general that his wife could sleep in my room. And after we got her up there, off he went to feed the pooches.

I was rooming with Art Spinney, whom I couldn't find at the time we carted Mrs. Usher up to our room. In fact, we were so worried about her that I called my aunt, who was a volunteer in St. Francis Hospital, and told her to send over a doctor to take a look. The doctor arrived, gave her a shot or something, and told us to let her sleep it off. Then I went out to find Spinney, normally one of the quietest and most gentle men on the team. I wanted to warn him not to come back to our room.

I also wanted to warn him that in case he did have to stop in, not to be concerned about the woman in bed staring at him with one eye. You see, Mrs. Usher had a glass eye, and we couldn't get her eyelid closed when we put her to bed. So, of course, I never found Spinney, and a few hours later I was standing at the bar drinking when here comes Art, white as a sheet and drunk as a skunk, screaming something about this shriveled up old lady dead in his bed. He knew she was dead because she was staring at him with this eerie grin. I was trying to get hold of Spinney to calm him down, but I was laughing too hard to really get an explanation across. And I'll never forget the look on his face as he ranted and raved up and down the bar that somebody had killed an old lady and thrown her in his bed.

After the '54 season I played in the Pro Bowl in Los Angeles. And the night after the game they threw a banquet back in Baltimore in my honor. I was voted the "most improved Colt." Evidently the joint went crazy. I understand I received a wild standing ovation *in abstentia*. And one of the people present and extremely impressed by all this foofaraw was a guy named Mike Strouse, who owned a wholesale liquor house in the city. Soon after he got in touch with the Colts and I went over to see him. He asked me if I wanted to go to work in his wholesale house as a goodwill ambassador.

I told him I was certainly interested, but I had my heart set on being a cop in New York. After the Pro Bowl I had gone home to the Bronx and taken (yes, and passed, for all you wise guys out there) the civil service exam. And the mayor of Baltimore had gone so far as to write the mayor of New York, Robert Wagner, and request that I be given a special dispensation to work six months of the year playing football in Baltimore and six months as a policeman in New York.

New York was really the only place I wanted to be a cop, because we had it all worked out with my uncles that I would put on a uniform and walk a beat as a probationary police officer for six months before they'd bring me in to work with them in the Detective Bureau in the Bronx. But just when I thought it was going to be gravy, Wagner turned down my request. And since I wasn't ready to give up playing football, my dreams of wearing a badge and becoming part of New York's Blue Wall were over. Sometimes I laugh to myself today wondering what I would have looked like chasing some burglar or mugger down the Grand Concourse. Maybe things worked out for the best.

Actually, there is no maybe about it. I took Mike Strouse up on his offer and over the next few months I attended tavern openings, liquor store dedications, warehouse parties, the whole nine yards. I soon realized, however, that standing around shaking hands and talking to bar owners about the Colts wasn't my cup of tea. Don't get me wrong, I've been doing that my whole life and I love it. It was just the idea of getting paid to do it. I felt like a whore or something. If I was going to get paid, I wanted to work for the money. So I asked out. I wanted to get into sales.

Churchill Ltd., owned and managed by Mike Strouse, was a multiple-line house that distributed the Melrose line that was a subsidiary of Schenley Industries. I went from being a goodwill man (that I didn't like) to a distillery representative selling Melrose. They asked me if I wanted to be a salesman and I told them "Only full time. I want to work during the football season, too." And that's exactly what I did.

For the next five years I'd get up at 7:00 A.M., meet a salesman on the street at 8:00 A.M., and the two of us would work our area until 11:30 A.M., time for practice at the stadium. After practice he'd pick me up again, and I'd sometimes work until ten or eleven at night. On Mondays, when we had the day off, I'd spend the whole day making calls.

I worked for Melrose until 1958. The day after the "Greatest Game Ever Played" I met with the Schenley people down in their offices in the Empire State Building, and they made me a district manager for their import operations. Now, instead of getting paid for chatting with bar owners and warehouse managers, I was earning my keep by selling to them. I liked that a lot better.

It was also between the '54 and '55 seasons that I met my wife, Dottie. In fact, it was on a blind date, and she wasn't even supposed to be my date. I had fooled around with a couple of girls, of course, but none had ever knocked my socks off like this broad did. My only other love in life had been a high-school sweetheart who years later ended up marrying Art Modell, the owner of the Cleveland Browns. And, of course, there had been a fair share of females at Boston College and down in Dallas.

But from the moment I met Dottie it was love at first sight. She had it all: big boobs, she didn't smoke, and she was Catholic.

She was a beautiful girl, and I don't know what she saw in a big, fat defensive tackle like me. But I'm glad she saw it. Our meeting was really pretty much fairy-tale stuff. Some sandlot football player I knew from Baltimore said he was going out on a blind date and asked me if I wanted to go with the other girl. She was supposed to be his date, as a matter of fact.

I had a public appearance scheduled the night I met her, and when I got out it was really late. The other guy, and I don't even recall his name, he wanted to just forget the whole idea. He said it was too late to meet the girls. But I told him we couldn't just leave two girls waiting for us, and we eventually went down to meet them at this nightclub, Andy's Lounge on York Road and Cold Spring Lane. Dottie was supposed to be his date, but what sandlot player was going to argue with a 270-pound defensive tackle for the Colts? When Dottie told me she was a licensed pharmacist, I didn't believe her. After all, this was 1955, and there weren't a lot of women in the work force, especially pharmacists. But sure enough, I went down to see her the next day and there she was behind the counter in her drugstore.

Dottie was also playing piano in an all-girl orchestra popular in Baltimore that called themselves the Queens of Rhythm. Who couldn't fall for a girl like that? Among football, my job with Schenley, her drugstore, and the band, we saw each other as much as we could. I'd usually meet her late at night and we'd head down to Kuzen's bar for a drink. Dottie and I dated throughout the '55 season, and on February 4, 1956, we were married in the basilica of a Catholic cathedral in downtown Baltimore. It was the Cathedral of the Assumption, and we had to get special permission to use it on account of I had so many family members and friends coming down from New York for the ceremony.

I was thirty-two years old, and it was the best decision I have ever made in my life. In January '57 we had our first child, Debbie. In December '57 we had our second, Chris. I found out how these things happen real quick. Weeb said he never heard of a boatwright launching two ships in the same year. Just goes to show, I was always a little bit different.

Meanwhile, while I was out selling Scotch and dancing to the tunes of the Queens of Rhythm, Weeb the IBM computer was holed up in the Colts' offices laying the foundation for a team that was soon to become the best in football. He dissected the team, realized what we needed, and in the 1955 draft went out and plucked an amazing twelve rookies who made the team, seven of whom became starters. That college draft was just about automatically responsible for turning the Colt franchise around.

What made it even more remarkable was that back then the college draft was really a hit-or-miss type of thing. Today they put so much money into scouting and body-fat counts and forty-yard-dash times that, combined with the fact that the schools the pro players come out of today are basically minor-league franchises, it's a wonder there's ever a blunder on draft day. Today you have a 95 percent chance that the kid you choose on the first round is going to make the team, because even if a scouting crew has mistaken badly and plucked a dud, the club is still too embarrassed to cut these turkeys because of all the money they're paying them. Christ, any kid chosen on the first round of the NFL draft today can leave his family rich as Croesus as long as he doesn't snort his signing bonus up his nose.

But back when I was playing, the colleges weren't so refined. Sure, there were football factories. But good pro players could still come out of the small schools like Muhlenberg and the College of the Pacific. If you were good, you played. If you were bad, you were cut, no matter what round you had been drafted in.

Some of the rookies we signed that year went on to become all-time Colts. There were names such as Raymond Berry, the all-everything end out of SMU. George Shaw, a quarterback from Oregon. Alan (the Horse) Ameche, the Heisman Trophy winner from Wisconsin who ran for a seventy-nine-yard touchdown on the first play of the first game of the '55 season. Ameche went on to be rookie of the year. Then there was halfback L. G. DuPre out of Baylor, and lineman Dick Szymanski from Notre Dame. Throw them together with the guys we picked up to play offense the following season—especially halfbacks Lenny Moore and Billy Vessels—and there was really only one missing ingredient from a championship stew.

We found that ingredient, of course, playing quarterback for a sandlot team outside of Pittsburgh called the Bloomfield Rams. Before John Unitas was through, he had nearly single-handedly carried the game of football into the modern era. To this day the man remains the standard by which quarterbacks judge themselves. And the funny thing is, when we first saw this guy, we all thought he was a bum who was never going to make it.

That must have been what the Steelers thought also, because after they signed John out of the University of Louisville they cut him in favor of a quarterback from Detroit named Ted Marchibroda. When Weeb first brought Unitas into training camp in 1956 he had a sore arm. The kid was always on the training table. I remember asking Gino Marchetti what the hell Weeb thought he was doing bringing in a quarterback who couldn't even lift his throwing arm above his shoulder. That's just another example of my keen player personnel evaluation skills. How wrong can you be? But still, Unitas didn't beat George Shaw out right away.

Shaw, as I said, had come in the year before. And the Colts began that year, the '55 season, like a house afire. We won our first three games, and the town was going nuts. But truth be told, I think the players, especially the defensive players, knew the Colts weren't quite there yet. The defense was great. But the offense had a lot of catching up to do. In the fourth game of the season, our worst fears came true. The Bears, who we had edged by six Opening Day in Baltimore, stomped us but good in Chicago, 38–10.

That was the beginning of the end. I don't know what the hell happened, but we only won two more games for the rest of the year and finished at 5–6–1, in fourth place in the Western Conference.

People began blaming Weeb for the big collapse. And there was a movement afoot to fire him and bring in a new coach. After that '55 season, Weeb was in deep trouble. Rosenbloom wanted to hire Buddy Parker, who had just been fired as head coach of the Lions. And late in the '56 season, as we were on our way to a disappointing 5–7 year, Kellett came around to ask a couple of the veterans what they thought of Weeb, whether the team should keep him or not. I remember we were practicing in Santa Barbara for a game against the Rams, and Kellett began pulling the veterans aside, one by one. I told him straight out, "Jesus, Don, the man's got another two years left on his contract. The least you can do is honor that." Values, especially contract values, were certainly different back then, if you know what I mean. Today coaches are like commuters, breaking contracts and rushing from job to job. And management's no better, as any sports fan over the age of six can tell you.

Anyway, the Steelers hired Parker, and Weeb kept his job. I'm not sure who else Kellett asked except for a defensive back named Bert Rechichar, who along with Ameche and myself had been the Colts' three All-Pros in 1955. And Bert told Kellett he thought Weeb should go. Weeb found out about it, and that was the end of Bert with the Colts. Weeb never did like Bert. And though Bert was too good to be just outright cut, his playing time diminished yearly until Weeb finally saw his chance and waived him in 1959. Weeb was one ornery little Dutchman who knew how to hold a grudge.

Let me give you another example. Tom Finnin was a guy Webb never liked. Finnin always gave him a tough time. He used to call Weeb up in the middle of the night and tell him he was going to quit the game. Weeb would massage Finnin, you know, "You can't quit, Tommy, the team really needs you, you're one of our leaders," that kind of thing. But it really burned Weeb to have to be doing this. But Weeb's credo was "I can put up with anybody until I can replace him."

So when Tom Finnin got married in 1956, he went on his honeymoon and never showed for training camp. Actually, he had called Weeb about a week before he got married and told him he'd be late because he was on his honeymoon, and while Weeb would sweet-talk Finnin over the wire, he'd be calling him nuts once he slammed the receiver down. The guy could talk out of two sides of his mouth better than anyone I've ever met.

So anyway, our first exhibition game was against the Eagles in Hershey, Pennsylvania, and Finnin told Weeb he'd meet the team at the game and come home with us. Weeb just said, "Fine, fine, anything you want, Tommy." He told Tom not to even worry about playing, just meet the team in Hershey and spend the following week easing himself into game shape. Then Weeb told our equipment manager to pack up Finnin's uniform and bring it on the road with us. I remember Weeb saying, "He won't play, but we'll dress him anyway." Sure enough, Finnin showed up with his new bride, and just to punish him, Weeb made him play the entire game.

Finnin hurt his shoulder that season, and Weeb, figuring he was washed up, saw his chance to get his final revenge. He traded Tom to the Chicago Cardinals. Weeb never let a grudge stand in the way of getting something out of a player. But once he thought you were through, he'd throw you away like a piece of garbage. Actually, though, his Finnin deal backfired. Tom was from Chicago, he didn't mind going back at all, and he eventually became a Chicago cop. Since then I've been advising Coach Ewbank to steer clear of the Windy City.

Weeb was a terrible bullshitter. He used to grade the players after every game, and he once told an interviewer that I was always the first guy to ask what his grade was. "Art's a pro's pro," he told this interviewer. "He's tried to get the one thing every great player must have: pride. Art is always the first to ask how he did, and he's never satisfied." Now, that was a very nice compliment to read in the papers, but none of it was true. Well, I guess some of it may have been. Weeb and his staff did grade us. But I never asked about my grades in my life. As early as my experiences in St. Philip Neri I had learned not to tempt Fate, especially Fate regarding grades of any kind.

But that was Weeb, a real manipulator. I suppose that's what made him such a great coach. He did everything he wanted to do his way, but he tried to make it seem that we were actually doing it our way. He wanted total control, from game plans to the menu for team meals.

Another time we were flying to the West Coast with a chance to win the conference crown, and Weeb was more worried about a stupid thing like the in-flight meal than he was about the Rams. I told you, I think he'd rather have a good weigh-in than a good game, which I suppose had a lot to do with his food fetish. Anyway, during this flight most of the team wanted a regular meal, but Weeb just wanted to have sandwiches. So, typically, he spent hours concocting this great plan. He went around to a couple of the vets and matter-of-factly said, "Hey, you know, we'll eat before we leave, then we'll have a meal when we get out there, so let's just order sandwiches for the flight. Whattya say?"

Nobody really gave a damn, especially me, who couldn't eat anyway, because I had a weigh-in coming up. So I remember telling him, "I don't care, Weeb, order any food you want. I'm concentrating on the game." Then he'd get up in front of the team and announce, "Well, I talked to some of the veterans like Donovan and they said they'd prefer sandwiches. They don't want a lot of meal. They want to stay in fighting trim. And I think that's the way it should be."

Well, this particular time, you should have seen the look on his face when the airline rep who booked our flights loaded up that plane with about ten thousand sandwiches. Jesus, the flight was one huge food fight, and Weeb steamed the entire trip out. He got the rep fired from United Airlines. I'm serious. The guy was unbelievable.

Then again, the game was pretty unbelievable back then. In fact, it was during the Hershey exhibition game where Weeb burned Finnin that a massive brawl broke out between the Colts and the Eagles. About half a dozen players from each team were thrown out of the game, including yours truly. But what I remember best was we had just traded for a big center from the Giants named John Rapacz, a good ol' boy out of Oklahoma. And in the second quarter, somebody fell on him and broke his leg. So they made him wait out the game, and brought him back to training camp in Westminster in a bus—without even setting the leg! Can you imagine this shit?

It was a good two-hour ride from Hershey to Westminster. And when we got back that night they put him up in the trainer's room above a gym we sometimes practiced in, where it must have been 120 degrees. The next morning an ambulance picked up Rapacz, toted him down to Union Memorial Hospital, and operated on his leg.

Two days later a bunch of us went down to visit him in the hospital, and when we walked into his room he was just screaming in pain. We were shocked. I said to him, "John, does your leg hurt you that much?" And he said, "No, it's my ass. While they were working on my leg they decided to take out my hemorrhoids, too. And now with this cast I can't move and my ass is killing me."

Rapacz never did play again for the Baltimore Colts, but there is a postscript to his story. A few weeks after his operation, he hobbled into practice one day on crutches. And while he was standing just off to the side watching a tackling drill, Don Joyce picked up Tom Finnin and dropped him right on Rapacz. Damned if he didn't break the other leg. Poor sonofabitch.

But the NFL was a rough trade in those days. Despite all the moaning and gnashing of teeth over violence in the NFL over the past few years, I can safely say that anyone who didn't watch us play hasn't seen true violence in sports. In a way, I kind of miss it.

8

Coal Miners' Sons

The first thing you have to realize about the modern game of football is that it's a television event. Naturally, the networks want to protect their interest, so to the announcers broadcasting these games, everybody's a nice guy. You can be a thief, a murderer, a gangster, you name it, and these guys up in the TV booth can't do anything but sing your praises. "What a wonderful fellow," they swoon. "I had breakfast with him this morning," or "I met him in the hotel lobby last night," or "I sat in on a chalk talk with him yesterday at practice," and everything's painted peaches and cream.

Let's try reality, fellas. The guy they're canonizing down on the field is the same guy who tried to run his wife over in the driveway last week. Wonderful fellow, right? The kind of guy you'd like your daughter to bring home, right? Give me a break! Who needs that crap on television? Just once I'd like to hear the announcer say that so-and-so's a helluva safety, or a goddamn good quarterback, but he also has the nasty habit of kicking the hell out of his wife. Something like that.

But that's what television has done to the league. It's all show biz. It's become such a television event, with all the players realizing their images are being beamed into millions of living rooms, that when a guy gets hurt, he knows he's on camera and he lies down on the ground like he's been shot in the head. That stuff slays me. For fifteen minutes the guy lies there and they have three trainers standing over him and the team doctor is usually kneeling over him like he's giving him the goddamn last rites. Invariably the guy jumps up and runs off the field, or if he's really playing for the cameras he'll stagger off as if he's just had triple bypass surgery. I'd be embarrassed to hell to do something like that. So would most of the guys I played with . . . and against.

Christ, when Weeb Ewbank was coaching the Colts, he had a special squad stationed along our sideline ready to run on to the field and pull injured guys off so we didn't have to waste a timeout. They weren't instructed to handle the wounded with prenatal care, either. There were three guys in particular Weeb liked to use—Don Shula, Carl Taseff, and Bert Rechichar—because they were defensive backs and they were fast. Unless you had a broken tibia sticking out through your uniform, they'd be scurrying in there and dragging you off by your feet, arms, head, anything, usually leaving a trail of blood and a stadium of echoing howls.

Weeb would deny this; he does to this day. But he's bullshitting. That's the way coaches and management felt. Right or wrong, the game was always more important than the players. It still is, they just disguise it better. We were replaceable; cogs in a machine. You played hurt, or you went back to the coal mines. Given the choice between arthritis or black-lung disease at the age of fifty, most of the people in my day chose arthritis and played hurt.

I remember once when I was with the Dallas Texans, we were playing the Rams in the Los Angeles Coliseum. Tom Dahms missed blocking me but Bill Lange, the right guard, picked me up. With that, Tom Dahms turned around and jumped on my leg and broke it.

And Jimmy Phelan, that old bastard, he made me walk out of Los Angeles Coliseum, up about a hundred flights of stairs, with a broken leg. No stretcher. No crutch. No help. No nothing. I want to tell you, it hurt like hell. On the way home they gave me a pain-killing shot, and I didn't feel too bad. But when that shot wore off, holy Christ, did I start to get sick. I threw up all over the plane. So finally Phelan told the team doctor not to put the leg in a cast. Something about it healing better in the open air. Right.

I sat out two games, but two weeks later we're scheduled to play the Rams again, this time in Dallas, and Phelan asked me to suit up and stay on the sidelines. "Don't worry," he said. "It's just for morale purposes. We won't be playing you at all." Jimmy Phelan's morale purposes, maybe. Certainly not Artie Donovan's.

We were supposed to get a good crowd, and the owners needed all the crowd they could get in those days. As luck would have it, it was the only day all season it rained, and the field was a quagmire. Players were going down right and left. Suddenly Phelan ran up to me and told me to get in there. He said he didn't have anybody left to play on the defensive line. So they taped up my leg and sent me in. Not even a cast! Just a little adhesive tape. I told him, "I can't move. I got a broken leg." Phelan just smiled and said, "That's okay, Fatso. If they run a play at you, just fall down and try to get in their way." Try to get in their way! That's just what I ended up doing. Didn't play half bad, either. And not only was playing through injuries a way of life in the old NFL, but also hiding your hurts was really big on the survival list.

The only Colt who didn't make it to the '58 championship game was Dick Szymanski, a linebacker and one of my best friends. He was a helluva football player, leading the team in tackles when he hurt his knee playing the Bears in Wrigley Field during the eighth game of the season. He was operated on and missed the rest of the year.

But what I remember best about Szymanski being hurt was his denial that he was hurt. We were coming out of the locker room at Wrigley to get on the team bus and I offered him a hand. I think I asked him if I could carry his shoulder bag or something innocuous like that. At any rate, he got all indignant, yelling at me, "Don't you worry about me, Fatso, I'm just fine! I'll be seeing you at practice Tuesday and I'll be kicking your ass!" Yet whenever that bus hit a bump on the way to the airport, I noticed old Syzzie was squirming in pain. In those days, you just didn't want to show it.

We drank beer all the way home on the plane, and that seemed to improve Syzzie's outlook. But sure enough, when I called his apartment the next morning to check up on him, his landlady told me he had checked into Union Memorial Hospital. I found out he was being operated on, so I stopped by that afternoon just in time to see him being wheeled back into his room on a gurney. He was in pain, yelling for more shots. But as soon as he saw me standing at his bedside, suddenly there was nothing wrong with him. I told him to take the shots while he could get them. But suddenly he didn't need shots anymore. I figured I better get the hell out of that hospital before Syzzie went into shock from refusing pain-killers in front of a teammate. And I was the guy's best friend. Imagine if a coach or an owner had walked in. He probably would have been doing jumping jacks.

I'm really not bragging or anything, that's just the way it was when I played. There were only twelve teams in the league, and only thirty-three players to a team. Those jobs were good . . . and scarce. Nobody wanted to lose one over a little thing like a torn tendon or a crushed cartilage or a bone protruding through the skin.

Early in my career—the Colts' first year back in Baltimore, as a matter of fact—I played with a defensive lineman named Barney Poole. He was a tough guy, but by 1953 he was pretty much over the hill. And he was doing anything he could to hang on. In one game he tore up his hand. He caught his fingers in someone's face mask and it nearly yanked a couple of the digits out. That hand was a mess.

This happened sometime early in the second quarter, and Barney was led off the field and into the locker room and soon thereafter an ambulance carried him off to Union Memorial. He got his fingers stitched up. I swear to God, he got out on Thirty-third Street and hitchhiked right back up to Memorial Stadium. Damned if he didn't return in time to play the fourth quarter. And he did play, too, with a big wrapping on those twisted and mangled fingers. He was one tough player, and the Colts rewarded him the following season by cutting his ass.

But by no means were most of the injuries inflicted in the early NFL accidental. During the 1950s, the NFL's rules regarding violence were loose, officials were looser, and we had homicidal maniacs running onto the field aided and abetted by devious coaches who'd spill anyone's blood to win a game. I have to laugh when I read about how violent football has become. If some of these boy-wonder commentators think the field is full of blood and guts today, I don't know how long they would have lasted watching the carnage before the NFL set out on a deliberate course toward "family entertainment." Christ, we didn't have locker rooms. We had charnel houses.

The mentality of the league kind of operated along the lines of those famous words from the great Chicago Bear middle linebacker Dick Butkus, who once admitted, "I never intentionally try to hurt another player unless it's during something real important like a league game."

The Colts' answer to Butkus was Bill Pellington, a middle linebacker whose credo was pain. After a game, Pellington's breath smelled like quarterback. If Pellington had played in New York, no one would have ever heard of Sam Huff. Now don't get me wrong, Huff was a tough, if dirty, sonofabitch. But that old West Virginia mountain boy was neither as big nor as tough as they've made him out to be. The New York media made Huff. When CBS put a microphone on Huff during a game and brought all the league's blood and guts into the living room via a documentary called "The Violent World of Sam Huff," his name was secure atop the list of tough guys. Sorry, Sam, but it just wasn't so. Same goes for Philadelphia's Chuck Bednarik, the only man when I came into the league who was still going both ways, playing sixty minutes of offense and defense.

Bednarik was a center on offense, and he couldn't block my grandmother. But as a linebacker he was a really good football player. But I think there was even a better linebacker on the Eagles playing with Bednarik, a guy by the name of Wayne Robinson. Man, he could hit. But because Robinson was from Minnesota and Bednarik was from the University of Pennsylvania, Bednarik got all the ink.

I guess what made Bednarik's reputation was the famous picture sequence of Chuck laying out Frank Gifford and standing over the Giff's prone body, arms shooting skyward, like some kind of barbarian whooping out a death song. There was also another time, when he creamed Y. A. Tittle, and they shot Tittle on his knees, blood streaming down his face. But guys hit other guys just as hard. Yet because it happened to two New York players and because Gifford and Bednarik still talk about it on television, it's developed into some kind of football folklore. What bullshit.

I tell you, if you listen to Bednarik, he's the greatest thing that ever happened to pro football. I like him, he's a nice guy, but what an awful bullshit artist he is. A real pisser. I admit he was a hell of a linebacker, but whenever I see him these days he starts in with that, "They tell me I'm Mr. Philadelphia, I'm Mr. Eagle." Come on, Chuck, give it a rest. Recently I was down in Jamaica with Dick Syzmanski, and we ran into Chuck. He started in with this Mr. Phildelphia crap and we both told him that if he was going to drink with us he'd have to do one thing: Shut up.

Personally, I don't think Sam was in the same league as a lot of linebackers I played with and against, such as Chuck Bednarik, Bill Pellington, Detroit's Joe Schmidt, the Bears' Bill George and Dick Butkus, the Packers' Ray Nitschke, and Dick Szymanski.

Schmidt was a real sweetheart. A savage coal miner out of Pittsburgh, he had a neck like a killer turtle and was about as subtle as a heart attack. One time when his quarterback, Milt Plum, threw an interception in the last two minutes of a game, Joe stewed about it for weeks. Every time the offense would pass the defense coming onto the field during the change of possession, Schmidt would say to Plum, "Pass, Milt, three times, and then punt. Let the defense win it for you." Schmidt was really one of the prototypes at the position. When he came into the league teams were just going to a formation of four down linemen and three linebackers.

Joe was always trying to outguess our offense. And he seemed to have a sixth sense about where we were going to run. Unitas would check off and call another play at the line, and sure enough, Schmidt would move right into the hole Unitas had called. Then Joe would start in with this singsong taunt to Alan (the Horse) Ameche: "Horsey, Horsey, Horsey, here you come and I'm waiting for you." I swear to Christ, John would be up there moving players to the left and right and Schmidt would move right along with them, as if he knew our goddamn plays. And Schmidt wasn't even that big a guy. But he could level you.

It's real hard to make the call, but the best linebacker I've ever seen play may have been the Bears' George. He was wild; he'd psyche himself up into a frenzy when he played. Then you'd meet him off the field and he was a completely different guy, another Clark Kent. And he'd line up anywhere on the field, kind of similar to the way Karl Mecklenburg of the Broncos does it now. Quarterbacks would be going out of their mind looking to find out where the hell Bill George was.

In today's game, since most of the defenses play with four linebackers, what's left of the true middle linebacker has too many assignments. Pass coverage, run coverage, it's hard to come up with a guy today as brutal as the guys I played with, whose primarily responsibility was to puncture kidneys and spleens and stuff the run, in that order. I guess the Raiders' Matt Millen comes about as close as you can get.

There used to be a lot of tough guys I'm sure you've never heard of who still make my bones ache when I think of them. And they weren't even tackling me! Do the names Roger Zatkoff and John Martinkovic ring a bell? Didn't think so. But they sure rung a few when they were playing for the Packers. How about San Francisco's Hardy Brown; ever heard of him? He was one tough bastard. I can't count how many people Hardy put in the hospital. His style was an intent to maim. He had this knack, this technique of slamming a shoulder into a running back's face; to this day I don't know how he did it. He was like a snake uncoiling. He'd get under your chin and, bang, you'd be seeing stars. Ball carriers looked for Hardy, rather than an opening, coming around that corner.

And in San Francisco, if Hardy didn't get you on defense,

Bruno Banducci would get you on offense. That guy, if he hadn't retired I would have. He was a graybeard by the time I got into the league in '50, but I still had to go up against him twice a season for four years. He was a tenacious offensive lineman. He'd grab and claw and basically knock the shit out of me, that's what he did. I could never believe he was doing this to me. I always thought he was holding. But then I'd see the game films and, nope, Bruno wasn't holding. He was just kicking my ass.

In 1950, when I was a rookie, we played the 49ers, and Banducci and a guy named Don Campora were playing across the line from me. Campora was a big-name rookie out of the College of the Pacific. He made all the All-Star teams, the whole works. As the game wore on, this kid kept holding me, and finally I said to him, "Hey, you sonofabitch All-American, don't hold me." But he kept doing it. So I punched him right in the mouth and knocked his front teeth out. Campora was jumping up and down and yelling, "You dirty bastard, you knocked my goddamn teeth out!" nice things like that. So Banducci ambled over and said to me, "What the hell did you do that for?" And I told Bruno that I had warned the guy to stop holding me and the guy hadn't stopped holding me. Finally Banducci turned to Campora and said, "It serves you goddamn right for holding Donovan. You don't have to hold Fatso here. Shit, he's easy enough to block as it is."

Players weren't above trying to get an extra competitive edge out on the field, either. Ernie Stautner, the Pittsburgh defensive tackle and my old teammate from Boston College, used to tape cardboard up and down his forearms to deliver a more lethal forearm shiver. When he retired, he taught his replacement, Ben McGee, this little trick. The Steelers were playing the Giants the year after Ernie quit, and suddenly McGee and poor Rosie Brown jumped up and start swinging at each other. They were both heaved from the game, and afterward, when they asked Brown what happened, he said, "Man, I been taking those blows from Stautner for ten years, and that was bad enough. But when this rookie started beating on me, I decided enough was enough."

But the true King of Pain had to be Pellington, 250 pounds of killing machine. We were playing Detroit in Baltimore on opening day of the '57 season, and on the third play of the game a Lion named Tom (The Bomb) Tracy swung out of the backfield and took a flair pass from Bobby Layne. Well, Pellington tried to clothesline Tracy, but he missed his throat and caught him square on the helmet. He knocked Tracy down and out. And I mean out. Tracy was lying on the turf unconscious for a good fifteen minutes. The Detroit trainers and team doctors were afraid to move him off the field until they made sure all his parts were still assembled.

Finally the game continued, and we huddled up. And in the defensive huddle, Pellington said, "Jesus Christ, I hurt my arm on that sonofabitch." He played five more plays before coming to the realization that his arm was broken in two. Snapped like a twig. He missed the rest of the season, which wasn't good news for opposing ball carriers, for that gave Pellington a whole year with nothing to kick but his dog and stew about what he was going to do to people when he came back.

When he returned in 1958, the team doctor outfitted him with a steel cast over his arm. During pregame warm-ups, he would wrap this cast with a big, thick foam rubber tubing. The officials would check his arm—cast, tubing, and all—and tell him it was okay to play with the wrapping.

But when we'd head back into the locker room for a final prayer and last-minute instructions right before kickoff, Pellington would take the thick wrapping off his arm and replace it with this little, quarter-inch foam rubber sleeve. He'd hit somebody with that cast and it would be like hitting them with a sledgehammer. Midweek game films turned into horror movies as we'd all sit around and count how many blocks Pellington would knock off each week. I'll never forget Billy Howton, a wide receiver for the Packers, walking up to an official and telling him, "Why don't you just give the sonofabitch a gun and let him do a clean job on us?"

It reached a point where everybody in the league was out to get Pellington, really hurt him. And that crazy bastard loved it. He knew guys were going to crack-back block on him—that is, go after his knees when he wasn't looking. So after he'd take two steps in one direction, he'd wheel around and kick before even looking. A lot of people in the stands must have wondered just who the crazy guy was kicking at air out there on the football field. But let me tell you something: More often than not some offensive lineman wound up with a mouthful of football shoe.

I don't know if he ate pills or what, but he was just absolutely out of his mind. Born crazy, I guess. Sure, some people in the league liked to hit other people and hurt them. But Pellington liked to do anything to other people to hurt them. Then he'd get this sick grin on his face.

The NFL champions used to open up the following year's preseason schedule with a game against the college All-Stars. And after we won in 1958, we opened the exhibition season against the college kids in August 1959. There was a fullback from Houston, the kid's name was Don Brown, and late in the first quarter as he swung out of the backfield on a pass pattern, Pellington hit him a forearm shiver that sent him to the turf like he was shot. The kid swallowed his tongue, and he was lying on the ground, jerking spasmodically, and finally he stopped breathing for a moment. It was a sick sight.

All these guys were screaming and hollering at each other. Otto Graham, who was coaching the All-Stars, came running out on the field yelling, "What the hell are you guys doing? They're only kids!" And we're yelling back at him, "Whattya want us to do, Otto? We're just playing the game!" Meanwhile, Big Daddy Lipscomb had walked over to the All-Stars and yelled to them, "Don't look at him! You won't want to play anymore!" And all the while this kid Brown is lying on the ground, dying. Christ, after seeing him, I didn't want to play anymore. And the only guy who wasn't concerned about anything was Pellington. He was just standing there and snorting and probably picking out the next kid he was going to send, if not to the morgue, at least to the hospital.

Needless to say, after that incident the All-Stars quit. We beat them 29–0, but we could have beaten them 150–0 if Weeb had wanted to run up the score.

Vendettas are big in football, and just about every team has at least one enforcer, the guy whose job it is to pay back for crimes, real or perceived, against your team. For his first couple of years with the Colts, Gino Marchetti was our enforcer. Gino was a tough kid from the ghetto. He went to school at Antioch College, right outside San Francisco, and they recruited him right off the racetrack. He was a war hero whose Italian immigrant family had been interned with the northern California Japanese-Americans during the war until the local papers started running stories about all the medals Gino was winning in the Ardennes Forest. They let his folks out then.

An Antioch recruiter had spotted the big hulk at the racetrack one day and brought him along to the head coach. He immediately became a star. He could also kick some ass, and that particular talent gained him quite a reputation as not only perhaps the greatest defensive end to ever play the game, but also as a dirty, cheap-shot artist. Then one day Gino was born again, so to speak. He had just brought down Detroit's marvelous halfback Doak Walker, and he couldn't resist digging the heel of his hand into Walker's schnozz as he was getting up off the ground. But instead of starting a fight or yelling or anything, Walker just looked at him. Didn't say a word, just stared at Gino. Gino felt like a piece of shit.

"I could see it in his eyes," he said later. "A big guy like me, with probably eighty pounds and six inches on Walker, having to resort to a mean, lowdown trick like that. That look of disgust reformed me. I'm no longer the hatchet man around here." Which, of course, did not mean that Gino stopped getting his licks in. Everyone gets their licks in playing football.

Unlike other sports, you're decked out in an armor-type uniform that shields a lot of inside action from the officials. There's always mass piles of bodies lying around, great cover for a swift kick in the groin. And you only saw your opponent maybe once a year, twice at best. There was no time to get friendly. When I was out to get someone, my modus operandi was to nail a guy right in the groin. In a football fight, you didn't want to hit the guy in the face. In my day you could still get a punch in there. They didn't have that birdcage face mask they all wear today. But the really big thing in football fighting was to hit the guy in the stomach or kick him in the balls. I've yet to meet the man who has calluses on his balls. You'd break your hand hitting some of those monsters in the face.

But a lot of guys were, and still are, headhunters. Lyle Alzado, who retired from the Raiders a few years ago, probably perfected the head shot. He would practice ripping off an opponent's helmet, snapping it back like a pop top on a beer can, and then he'd let the guy have it right in the chops with his own helmet. I once saw Don Joyce, this animal I played with on the Colts' defensive line, split a guy's head open with his helmet. It was Les Richter, who played for the Rams, and Joyce claimed Richter had kneed him in the groin. So Joyce ripped his helmet off and hit him right in the face with it. Gave him about eighty-five stitches right down the middle of Richter's kisser. We were playing in the Los Angeles Coliseum, and the crowd is screaming for Joyce's head and he's just standing there with the innocent look on his face and saying, "All I was doing was defending myself." Right, Don. I told him I'd pay to see him take that one to the judge.

Although I can't specifically recall if Richter ever paid Joyce back for the compliment, I'm sure he tried. Grudges were a way of life, and they died hard. You may recall my little tête-à-tête with Green Bay's John Symank earlier in this book.

Anyway, in '57 we were playing the Lions at Detroit in the fourth game of the year, and their big fullback, John Henry Johnson, took a cheap shot at Carl Taseff on an extra-point attempt. He hit him a shot in the nose and broke it, and Taseff didn't play for the rest of the '57 season. The next time we played the Lions, the following season, Johnson tried to do the same goddamn thing to Taseff. But this time he missed. I said to myself, yet again, "I'm going to get this sonofabitch sooner or later," because I really like Taseff. We called Taseff Gaucho because he was bowlegged. He was only five-ten, but if you hit him in the knees he'd be six-four. So anyhow, I told Ray Krouse, a teammate on the Colts who had played two seasons with the Lions, "John Henry Johnson is a marked man."

Krouse warned me that Johnson was a tough bastard. But it didn't matter. Honor was honor. Besides, I was no weeping willow, either. So a year after this, we're playing in Detroit, and

Johnson brings a kickoff back and is run out of bounds right in front of our bench. I was wearing one of those football capes that obscured my numbers, but I knew if I punched the guy I'd get caught. So when our special teams ran him out of bounds, he was still traveling fairly fast, and I hit that black bastard so hard with my shoulder, smashing it right into his face, that I figured, "Uh-oh, here's one I finally killed."

I was wrong. He laid there for a while. But he got up. And when he got up, whoops, watch out. I got out of his way real quick. Krouse was right. John Henry Johnson was a tough alley fighter.

For all his seeming reserve today, while he was playing, Don Shula was another mean sonofabitch, and a wild man to boot. He was a defensive back who would throw an elbow into a receiver's eye as soon as look at him. In '56 we were playing the Rams in Baltimore, and Shula had a little thing going with Los Angeles' great end Tom Fears. He must have been holding Fears every time he ran downfield, because all day as we were walking back to the defensive huddle after the play we'd hear Fears screaming, "Shoes, goddamnit, keep your mitts off me. Don't hold me anymore." Finally Fears had had enough, and toward the end of the game he coldcocked Shula with an elbow that put his lights out. Smashed Shula's jaw.

Pellington and I were sharing a house with Shula during that season—this was before I was married—and we went to the hospital with him that first night, just trying to be nice guys. And when they released him we took him home and asked him what he wanted to eat. Naturally, he said something soft, so we cooked him some eggs. But that choosy prick didn't like the way we cooked them. He told Pellington they were too hard. So Pellington said, "Screw you, cook your own eggs," and threw the whole plate at him. So much for being a nice guy. It was probably the only time in Pellington's life that he had actually tried.

And all this violence on the field encompassed everyone, even the quarterbacks. You might be able to argue that these quarterbacks playing today are as good as guys like John Unitas, Charlie Conerly, Bobby Layne, or Norm Van Brocklin as far as technique and arm strength and natural evolution. But you'll never convince me that today's quarterbacks are as tough as the guys who played with me.

You show me a quarterback today and I'll show you a surfer. They all look like beach boys, for Christ's sake. Dan Marino, John Elway, Joe Montana. These guys look like they'd pass out at the sight of blood. Especially their own. Montana's even a guy from the Pennsylvania coalfields, and he still looks like he just walked off the beach at Malibu and is on his way to serve Mass.

Believe me, this isn't just some old fart spouting off about the "good old days." I know for a fact that these guys aren't as tough, because years ago the officials used to let us get away with murder. You had five officials instead of eight. None of them were instructed to protect the quarterback. And nobody ever got caught throwing the odd elbow, fist, or knee into a quarterback's groin during a pileup. If you ever get the chance, check out some of the old films of things that happened to quarterbacks in those days. He'd drop back, pass the ball, and five seconds later we'd hit the shit out of him. Defensive players would step over the poor quarterback, who usually looked like he had a sucking chest wound, and say, "Hey, really sorry, I won't do it again." And the official would say, "Yeah, try not to, huh?" Today, as soon as the ball is released they have one referee in the backfield whose job it is to start yelling as soon as the quarterback passes the ball so everyone knows not to nail him.

In 1955, we had George Shaw at quarterback. George wasn't a big guy, but he was talented, a lot like Francis Tarkenton. We were playing the Bears out in Chicago, and Shaw took a mighty rap as he dropped back to pass. Ed Sprinkle, a grizzly old defensive end who had come into the league in 1944 out of Hardin-Simmons, broke through and hit Shaw low. Sprinkle kind of had him around the knees and was holding him up. No in-the-grasp rules in those days, although old George sure could have used a rule like that right about then. Because as Sprinkle was keeping him upright, linebacker George Connor got about a fifteen-yard head of steam up and bulled through and hit George high, right in the mouth. I mean put a shoulder right in his face and leveled him.

Connor broke Shaw's face mask, broke his nose, and knocked his teeth out. George was a mess. They dragged him off the field, and his nose was spurting blood, and he didn't know where he was when he got to the bench. I said to Gino Marchetti, who was standing next to me, "Well, there goes one pussy. We won't be seeing him anymore today." When George finally regained his senses, he said to Szymanski, "Hey Syzzie, how do my teeth look?" And Syzzie said, "I don't know, George, they aren't there." And you know what? George Shaw went back into that game. There was at least one fat defensive tackle on the Baltimore sidelines that gained a lot of respect for him that day. In fact, the Bears nailed Shaw the following year also, ripping up his knee. And it was that injury that paved the way for us to start the kid off the Pittsburgh sandlots by the name of Johnny Unitas.

No one ever saw John Unitas "sliding" into the grass after a scramble to avoid being tackled. Quarterbacks who did that were automatically labeled a sissy. Plus, when I first came into the league, you weren't ruled down until your forward progress was stopped. Today, it's when your knee touches the ground and an opposing player touches you. During the 1950s, you used to see guys clawing for that extra yard with tacklers sitting on top of them trying to smash in their skull. Running backs and quarterbacks naturally learned to give as good as they got.

Unitas dished out punishment when he ran. And he ran a lot. This business of not allowing your quarterback to run with the football is relatively new in the game. I realize it's because of all the money they pay these guys today. Owners want to protect their investment and all that. But I kind of agree with Steeler linebacker Jack Lambert, who said, "If they don't want 'em to get hit, why don't they just put a dress on 'em?"

In my day quarterbacks would look to punish the guy who was tackling them after a scramble, sort of a payback for all the hits they took while they were passing. Aside from Unitas, whom I never tackled, of course, the two Norms—Snead and Van

Brocklin—come to mind as quarterbacks who could really make a would-be tackler pay. Both of them were slow as molasses. I think I could have beaten them in a footrace. But they loved to lower the shoulder into your chin. If you hit them too high, or if they just didn't like the way you looked at them, they'd take a swing at you. Y. A. Tittle was another one of those guys. I didn't like him, but I have to admit he was tough. He played a whole game with a pulled muscle in his stomach one time. And people forget that before he got old he was one of the greatest running quarterbacks around. In his time he took a hell of a beating.

Bobby Layne was another great one for fighting. Bobby Layne was a great one for just about everything, as a matter of fact. Bobby would punch, butt, bite; he'd kill you if he thought that was what he had to do to win a game. He was about the last guy in the league not to wear a face mask. As I said, Layne was a certified nut.

Face masks were becoming popular around the NFL just as I was coming into the league in the early 1950s. I didn't wear one at first, but in '51, when I was picked up by the Browns, I got kicked in the face in training camp and took about eighty stitches across my eye and down my left cheek. A week later I was traded to the Yankees. And in the first 1951 regular-season game, against the Rams, a big fullback named Deacon Dan Towler caught me right in the same cheek with an elbow and I took another dozen stitches and broke a tooth. I said to myself, "Enough of this bullshit. Call me a sissy all you want, but I'm putting a bar on my helmet." It was just a single, Plexiglas bar, although later in my career I went to the double-bar style. And let me tell you, that bar kept out a lot of errant elbows, knees, fists, feet, and, on one occasion, a well-aimed football.

Norm Van Brocklin of the Rams was a tough quarterback, and in the huddle he'd hang in there taking all you had. Once, after I'd laid him low with one particularly vicious sack, he turned to me and said, "You hit me like that again and I'm gonna get your big fat ass." I soon got him again, and I gave him a little elbow while we were rolling around on the ground, just to show him a quarterback shouldn't make threats to a defensive tackle. Well, on the next play the offensive lineman in front of me just stepped out of the way. I didn't know what was going on. I had a clear path to the quarterback. But before I knew what hit me, Van Brocklin fired a line drive as hard as he could right into my face. But boy, it knocked me flat on my ass. I couldn't believe that he'd just waste a play like that. I guess he was mad. You have to have respect for a guy like that.

I think you may have come to the conclusion by now that fights were a way of life back when I played. And none of this yapping and yawing and pushing and then break-it-up-stuff either. Sure, we exchanged a lot of crazy talk at the line of scrimmage, just like they do today. But I'm talking about real fights. Christ, every time the Colts played the Eagles there'd be at least two free-for-alls during the game. It became such a tradition, I don't think either team knew why they were fighting after a while. It was almost like somebody wrote a rule that said that when Baltimore plays Philadelphia, there has to be at least one wild brawl. The officials never wanted to get near it. They didn't give a damn who got the hell kicked out of them.

The beginnings of the Colt-Eagle rivalry probably had something to do with a guy named Frank Kilroy. They called him Bad News Kilroy, and he was. The dirty bastard was a legend by the time I got into the league. It was the first thing you warned a rookie: Watch out for the Irish bum. He was really pretty unbelievable. He took kickoffs literally. He'd run downfield kicking people, just kicking them out of bounds. And he never got called for it. The officials would just let him do it. He was a gangster from Philadelphia. I heard he even carried a gun, the whole bit. Big hero in Philly, I think he went to school there, Temple or someplace like that. Once he came down on Giant quarterback Arnie Galiffa with a knee right into his back. This was after Galiffa had already been tackled. The Giants were after him for the rest of the game and, believe it or not, Bad News asked to be taken out. They started calling him No News. The Giants got him two years later, though, wracked up his knee so he missed a season.

Finally the league caught up with Bad News, just like they caught up with the rest of us maniacs. Violence was becoming such a problem that the commissioner, Bert Bell, finally had to step in and try to change some rules. I mean, star players were quitting rather than take the punishment. Alex Webster, the Giant fullback, had begun his career with the Montreal Alouettes of the Canadian Football League, and in 1955 he threatened to return after being knocked cold in a game against the Steelers. I've heard talk recently about an innovation in the NFL: the penalty box for miscreants. Let me tell you something; Gordy Soltau, a 49er receiver, was pushing that idea back in 1956.

That was the same year the coach of the Lions, Buddy Parker, threatened to resign after all the fights that occurred during the Bears' 38–21 victory in the Western Conference title game. During that game Chicago's Ed Meadows knocked Bobby Layne out of the game, giving him a concussion with a late hit. That same season, the Chicago Cardinals' owner, Walter Wolfner, tried to buy airtime to run films of a violent Bear victory. Bert Bell threatened to fine Wolfner, and he finally backed down, but the seed had been planted.

Earlier in that season, the Bears had nearly killed Charlie Trippi, a very tough halfback. The guy who did it to him was Ed Sprinkle, the same guy that got George Shaw. Sprinkle sucker-punched Trippi and shattered his jaw. He required a whole series of bone grafting. Then next season, Trippi broke Sprinkle's jaw. What goes round comes round.

So the league instituted new rules, the major one being that the ball was now dead when any part of the ballcarrier, except hands and feet, touched the ground after he made contact with the other team. There was also some subtle pressure on the refs to start blowing that whistle a little quicker. I have mixed emotions about that rule. On the one hand, yes, I suppose it did help clean up pro football's act. But on the other hand, I saw some amazingly exciting football played when the rule stated that the ball wasn't dead until you stopped a man's forward progress.

Halfbacks were used to hitting just as hard as the men who were tackling them, and the men who were tackling them knew that. Thus, before the rule changed, it was great to see guys getting knocked down and springing back up to keep running. I remember Shula intercepted a pass once against the Redskins and got knocked flat. But he was knocked forward, and he got up and ran for another thirty yards. It was a great run. And Buddy Young, our little running back from the early Colt years, was a great one for dragging guys along with him as they sat on his back. I once saw him go the last twenty yards for a touchdown on his knees.

I don't know if we'll ever see the likes of guys like Marion Motley and Jimmy Taylor and Jim Brown driving forearms, elbows, and knees into defenders and scattering tacklers again. They talk about Walter Payton making people pay for bringing him down, but Payton's nothing but a Fancy Dan compared to a halfback who used to play for the Bears named John Dottley, a tough big kid from Mississippi. And Howie Ferguson of the Packers was a fullback who only played a couple of years, but I'll bet you every guy who ever tried to bring him down remembers each and every tackle.

But the running back who was really something, the guy who could really fight, was a teammate of mine named L. G. DuPre. Louis George DuPre to his family; Long Gone DuPre to the rest of the world. Long Gone grew up in Texas City, Texas, the oil refinery town that blew up back in the 1940s. He was playing hooky from school that day and was out fishing at the end of a jetty, so he wasn't hurt. But L.G. had an amazing childhood, primarily because his father used to bring L.G. and his brother into barrooms and let them fight each other while he passed the hat. They used to whale the tar out of each other, from what I understand.

I met his father once. And I asked him if the story was true. Mr. DuPre said, "Sure is, son. We used to pass the hat. Turned quite a nice dollar, too." Now, that is one tough sonofabitch. And L.G. grew up just like his daddy. He wouldn't take a back step to anyone. All these other galoots in the league, they'd just swing and get swung at during a rumble. Their heads were all hard enough to withstand just about anything. But L.G., there was a scientific fighter. I can still picture him out in the middle of some brawl on the field feinting and jabbing and, boom, he'd unload that right hand and coldcock the poor sucker who was foolish enough to be mixing it up with him.

I guess John Riggins of the Redskins was the closest guy I've seen to those old-timers. Riggins is the kind of guy who, as we used to say in the Marines, got hit in the head one too many times with a hand grenade. But I've yet to see Riggins or anyone else in modern football mix it up like we used to do. Thank God.

The rule change helped, but it really took a while for it to come into effect. Mental attitudes don't turn overnight, and there were too many crazy people in the league for something written down on a piece of paper in the commissioner's office to immediately change traditions when people went out on the field to play professional football. There were insane people in the NFL, and Christ, it seemed to me we had most of them right on our own team. Either Pellington's spirit rubbed off on everyone, or the Baltimore management went out of their way to raid the lunatic bins to stock the Colts.

The defensive line itself belonged in a Fellini movie, what with me, Gino, and guys like Don Colo, Joyce, and Tom Finnin. Colo and I had been with the Colts from the beginning, and Colo was traded to the Browns in '53, so I didn't catch a lot of his mayhem unless we were playing the Browns. But I witnessed Joyce and Finnin firsthand, and the three of them were cut from the same cloth. They were crazy.

Finnin's main concern while rushing the passer was beating the shit out of the guy in front of him, and then at the last minute he'd jump up and tip the pass. It used to burn my ass that he'd get all the credit for putting pressure on the passer while I was busting my hump trying to get through the blocking. Finnin and Joyce both played like that. In a way, I guess it made it easier for Gino and me, because the other team was always looking for Joyce and Finnin. Even the guys playing opposite me and Marchetti always kept one eye peeled for a cleat kick or a wayward elbow from those guys. Finnin and Joyce were big buddies, too. Hung out together off the field. Great minds think alike, I guess.

But I'll never forget how tough those guys played. They'd do anything and everything to hurt people. Both of them, if they couldn't hit anybody on the other team, they'd hit us. Sometimes it was like you were playing against twelve guys out there with these two wackos running around looking to maim. Joyce would go after anyone, no matter what their uniform color. It made life tough in practice and training camp.

But the best training camp fight between teammates I've ever seen took place in front of sixty-two thousand people, and it didn't involve Finnin or Joyce. It was between Big Daddy Lipscomb and an offensive guard by the name of Ken Jackson, and it was one of the most brutal fights I've ever seen. Big Daddy got the shit kicked out of him.

To be frank, Big Daddy was pretty much of a bully as a football player. Baltimore brought him over from the Rams in 1956, and for all the legends that grew up around Big Daddy, he never really played for Los Angeles except on special teams, when they would send him in to try to block a kick. He was six-seven, about 290 pounds, and I don't think he liked to hit. At any rate, when Weeb brought him in here, Weeb got the public-relations machinery rolling to try to build Big Daddy into the second coming of Colossus. To an extent, it worked. But it didn't fool anyone who played with him.

The other protagonist in this drama, Ken Jackson, the Tall Texan, was a man with a long memory. Back when I was with the Yankees in '51, we were on a road trip out to the Coast to play the Rams, and on the Saturday before the game we all took in a game between the San Diego Naval Training Station team and Loyola University. Jackson, who was about six-two and 260 pounds and had played at the University of Texas before going into the service, was on the Navy team. And Loyola had an All-America defensive tackle by the name of Ernie Cheatham. Dirty Ernie Cheatham they called him, and today the guy is a three-star general in the Marine Corps.

Anyway, during this game Dirty Ernie hit Jackson a shot. Jackson had to leave the field. And even though he came back to play again in the second half with his mouth all stuffed with cotton wadding and bandages all over his face, we could tell that he was still pretty woozy out there. The Yankees drafted Jackson that season, and two years later, when we moved to Baltimore for good, we made a trade with the Steelers for Dirty Ernie Cheatham. He really wasn't that good a football player when he came to finish the season with us. Jackson remembered what Cheatham had done to him, and he wanted to get him. We knew he wanted to get him. More important, Cheatham knew Jackson wanted to get him. Cheatham eased around that locker room on cat's paws for the rest of the season before retiring and going back into the Marine Corps. He was lucky. Jackson never got his revenge. Nothing ever came of it.

Not so with Big Daddy. Two years later Jackson had this fight with Big Daddy up in training camp. Actually it wasn't really a fight. Big Daddy took a sucker shot at Jackson and decked him. By the time Jackson scrambled back up into the fray, there were people already breaking it up, so Jackson never really got any licks in. But he turned to Big Daddy and said, "I'm gonna get you, you dirty bastard. You're dead meat." No one doubted that he meant it.

Every year the Colts would play an intrasquad exhibition game for the benefit of various Baltimore charities—the Boys' Club and whatnot—and sixty-two thousand fans would fill Memorial Stadium. So the 1957 game was perhaps three weeks after the fight, and nothing had happened between Big Daddy and Jackson. Then, right in the middle of the game, Jackson did it. He butted Big Daddy—broke his face mask, shattered his nose, and knocked a couple of teeth out. They dragged Big Daddy off the field unconscious. And when he woke up on the bench he began mumbling, "I'm gonna kill that Texas bastard. I'm gonna go back in there and kill him."

Jackson heard about it, went over to Big Daddy on the sideline, and told him, "I hope you come back in for more. 'Cause I ain't through with you yet. I'm gonna murder you." And he had this gleam in his eyes that really shook Big Daddy. Hell, it shook me, too. We went up to Big Daddy and told him, "Gene, stay away from that guy. He will kill you." And from that day on Big Daddy avoided the Tall Texan like the plague.

Jackson was a crazy bastard. We were playing the Lions once on national television up in Detroit on a Saturday night in Briggs Stadium. It had rained all week, Boys' Town had played a high-school football game on the field that afternoon, and the turf was just a mess. The Lion defensive line was throwing mud at our offensive guard, another Texan named Jack Little. Little had great blocking techniques, but he wasn't really cut out to play football. He didn't like to rumble and, in fact, retired after the season. Jackson was playing tackle right next to Little, and he was berating him right on the field for taking that shit. He couldn't believe a guy from Texas would allow that to happen to him. Gil Mains was the Detroit defensive tackle who was throwing the mud, and on the sidelines Jackson told Little to watch him, he was going to show him how to take care of a team that throws mud at you.

On our next punt, Detroit took the ball, and a good five seconds after the play was whistled dead, Jackson came barreling down and absolutely laid out Mains. So help me Christ, I thought he killed him. Mains was still unconscious when they carried him to the team bus after the game. Jackson was thrown out of the game, and a couple of the Colt owners—we had five—wanted him heaved from the league. I think what kept him in the league was the fact that Mains was such a dirty player that a lot of people figured he got what was coming to him. People in Baltimore took up a collection to pay Jackson's fine.

As a matter of fact, in 1960 I was running onto the field late in a close game with the Lions and I drop-kicked Mains right in the face. He had hit one of my teammates, Alex Hawkins, late. And though Hawkins wasn't my favorite football player, you have to stand up for your teammates. So I drop-kicked Mains in the chops and got thrown out of the game and on the next play Earl Morrall threw a touchdown pass to Jim Gibbons and they beat us, 20–15. I still think it was worth it.

But Ken Jackson was not the craziest football player I have ever met, not by a long shot. That honor goes to a guy named Jim Winkler, whom I hope I never meet again in my life. During the exhibition season of '53, we made a trade with the Rams for Winkler, who was supposed to be an All-American from Texas

A&M. They said he was going to be a helluva defensive lineman, but he never really panned out.

When he joined us, we immediately dubbed him the Perch, because he had a face like a fish. Plus, he was always twitching his neck and his jaw and contorting his face. He always swore he had a broken jaw. And he was constantly socking himself in the mouth to try to straighten it out. I swear to God, he'd haul off every few hours and punch himself as hard as he could right in the face. He acted like a true psycho. And he was a big guy, about six-three and 270.

Finnin beat him out for the starting position that season and Winkler didn't play much. But when the Rams came into Baltimore for the ninth game of the season, our assistant trainer, Otis Douglas, went up to Winkler and said, "Let's go. Time to get your ankles taped." Winkler said to him, "I'm not playing," and Douglas, naturally, asked him what the hell he was talking about. So Winkler screwed up his face and said in this deep, goofy voice, "But Otis, I once played with the Rams. Would you go out and try to hurt your buddies?" And I swear to Christ, he wouldn't play. He dressed, but he just stalked around in back of the bench for the entire game.

During the 1954 preseason, Jim Winkler became Weeb Ewbank's pet project. Weeb figured if he could get this animal stoking on all cylinders, he'd have the next King Kong. Weeb began the bullshit routine. Every day Winkler would walk into practice and Weeb would tell him he was going to make him the greatest tackle who ever played the game. But during practice one day, Winkler got a scratch on his face, and he turned to Ken Jackson and asked, "How's my face look?" It was just a little scrape, but Jackson turned to him and said, "I dunno, Perch, I think you need stitches."

So Winkler walked up to the trainer, Eddie Block, and told him he needed stitches for the cut on his face. Block said to him, "Jim, it's only a scratch, and we can't stitch a scratch." Winkler then began bellowing, "I want stitches! I want stitches!" He was off the deep end now. They sent him up to the training-camp locker room, and Freddie Schubach, our equipment manager, was now faced with a giant perch shouting that he needed stitches. Well, flipped. He began tearing the locker room apart, all the time yelling for stitches, and Schubach had to lock himself into the equipment room. They took him down to the airport and sent him home to Texas that night—without stitches.

We never saw Jim Winkler again. But a few years later in the locker room his name came up, and a new guy who had just joined us from some team out West said he had heard a story about the guy. He told how one night Winkler's father came home and the Perch was sitting on the front porch, carving up the family dog. When his father asked him what the hell he was doing, the Perch allegedly twitched, punched himself in the mouth, looked at his old man, and said, "Daddy, you're next."

I don't know if that's true or not, but that was the story we heard. I watch the game pretty good today, and I don't kid myself, there's a lot of guys playing today who would have fit right into the teams I played on—in the locker room and on the field. I admire the toughness in the Raiders' Howie Long and the recently retired Lyle Alzado. They were a couple of mean sonsabitches. And Joe Klecko, that truck-driving nose tackle from the Jets, he could play in any man's league. Same goes for the new kid in Denver who plays all the different positions, Karl Mecklenburg. And I've met Klecko's teammate Marty Lyons on a few occasions, and he strikes me as a type of throwback. But I don't know if any of them could match up with the Perch.

But let mè tell you about another guy, Mark Gastineau. Jesus, what a horse's ass. A one-way player all the way. He makes his living rushing the passer, granted, but against the run he reminds me of a guy I used to play with on the Colts named Johnny Sample. Sample was a real cutie. He's a line judge in tennis now, and I hope whoever's in charge of the line has an armed guard on it, if you know what I mean. Once the Colts found they were losing equipment at an enormous rate and hired the Pinkerton Detective Agency to find out who was lifting it. I don't know how much shoulder pads were going for on the black market in those days.

Anyway, even though he was a defensive back, Sample, like Gastineau, was good at one thing: defending against the pass. And like Gastineau, he was a hell of an athlete who wasn't looking for

Anyway, even though he was a defensive back, Sample, like Gastineau, was good at one thing: defending against the pass. And like Gastineau, he was a hell of an athlete who wasn't looking for any contact. You could run all day on both those guys, and if they ever did happen to get in the way of a ballcarrier—say, by accident—you could always tell in the defensive huddle from the cleatmarks on their foreheads. Sample would pile on after a guy was down, of course. I think that's maybe how Big Daddy became so proficient at coming in with the late hit. Sample taught him. But more often than not, even though he was the last line of defense, he'd wait for guys to get by him and then use his speed to catch up and tackle them from behind.

And Lord forbid if Gastineau ever went into that damn war dance with some of the guys I played with. We'd have yanked him off the field and asked him in no uncertain terms, if you know what I mean, just what the hell was going on. When we used to score a touchdown, we'd shake a guy's hand and say, "Good play." No jumping up and down like a goddamn lunatic with St. Vitus's dance. But Gastineau's a showman. I laugh like hell when I see that act, and if they let him get away with it, even with the new rules prohibiting excessive histrionics, more power to him. He's making a lot of money for jumping up and down like that, although I doubt if you'd catch his teammate Klecko doing that jig for all the tea in China.

In fact, most of the violent men I played with and against would catch a load of the bullshit that goes on today and have but one short sentence for all those dancing fools playing the game out there today.

"Daddy," they'd say, "you're next."

9

Those Championship Seasons

A funny thing happens to me when I try to remember all the good times on the great teams we had in Baltimore as we closed out the decade in the 1950s:

I can't.

It just seems that the really good times—and I don't mean football's good times, I mean life's good times—occurred when things were going badly for my team on the field. Life is so *yin-yang*.

Once the Baltimore Colts assumed the mantle of greatness and became the best team in football, things got a little staid. Maybe it's because bad teams breed individuality and good teams require anonymous regimentation. Maybe it's because by the time Weeb Ewbank turned the Colts around he had weeded out most of the characters who had inhabited our roster for so long. The guys who were responsible for the Colts being both crazy and bad. Or maybe it's just because the game of professional football was changing.

I already told you that the championship game of 1958, "The Greatest Game Ever Played," heralded a turning point for the National Football League. We became more of a business and less of a jock fraternity. In any case, the better we became, the less crazy

181

we also seemed to become, and believe me, it wasn't for lack of trying. We still had some lunatic *hombres* crashing the party.

There were guys like Billy Vessels, a running back from Oklahoma who had gone up to Canada to play after college. The Colts lured Vessels back to the States in 1956 with a big contract. Billy had earned a real big reputation in college and Canada, and right off Weeb didn't like him. Of course, Billy seemed like a slick con man, the type of guy always strutting around with an ostrich plume sticking out of his fedora and a thousand schemes for getting out of practice. Weeb tried to give the impression that it was Billy's Nathan Detroit act he didn't appreciate. But we all knew the truth. That weasel bastard Weeb didn't like Billy for the same reason he never liked Alan Ameche: They were both making more money than Weeb was.

And though the Horse was just too good a player for Weeb to do anything about (though not for lack of trying), Vessels only lasted a season with us. Weeb made life so miserable for Vessels that Billy quit football after the season. That was too bad, because the kid was one hot little player, ostrich plume or not.

Ameche, on the other hand, was one of the best runners the Colts ever had, so Weeb really couldn't afford to upset him too much. But that sonofabitch would do the little things to let the Horse know who was in the saddle, like bench him against certain teams. But though he might have been mean, Weeb wasn't stupid. Ameche would only sit against the patsies like Dallas or Green Bay. If we had a tough game to play, the Horse was suddenly a starter again, not to mention Weeb's best friend.

The Horse was the first great offensive player the Colts picked up. I remember asking Charlie Winner, Weeb's offensive coordinator, about this Heisman Trophy winner out of Wisconsin after we drafted him in 1955. And Winner just deadpanned, "Aw, he's just a short, fat-assed little guinea." I believe Charlie Winner changed his tune when the first time that short, fat-assed little guinea touched the ball for us he went over seventy yards for a touchdown.

But considering Weeb really wanted a team of choirboys, it's a wonder we became as good as we did. I mean, there's lots of sonsabitches out there who can play football, and you better have a few of them on your team. There's bums and gangsters playing on the best teams today, although you'd never know it from the stooges who announce the game on television. When you have an NFL franchise, you're not running a popularity contest. You're running a football team. And it's just a face of life that some bad men can play some good football.

Of course, coaches were an altogether different story. Before Weeb took over we had some beauties. There was an assistant named Tom Hughes, whom Weeb would send out on scouting assignments. This guy was a total flake. Say we were playing the Eagles on Sunday. Well, on the previous Monday Hughes would check in and Weeb would say something like, "Okay, Tom, what about this center Kelly Philadelphia's been starting? What are the kid's tendencies?" And with a straight face Hughes would say something like, "Oh, yeah, Kelly, helluva good-looking guy. Looks just like Dick Szymanski." That would be the guy's scouting report. In total.

But whereas Weeb would out-and-out fire coaches, he was a lot more subtle when he wanted to get rid of a player, especially someone who could help the team.

We had an offensive lineman named Dick Chorovich, who came along in 1955, and I swear, this guy could have been the greatest lineman to ever play the game. Chorovich had it all—size, speed, and a mean streak a mile wide. We used to joke that the Colts were hiding the fact that they had drafted him out of Joliet State Prison. With our defensive line, any rookie offensive lineman who came along was guaranteed to take a beating. But this kid Chorovich was pushing guys like me and Gino around like we were goddamn high-school kids. Anyway, Chorovich was from Miami of Ohio, and that's where Weeb had begun his coaching career. And Weeb hated this kid because he was a real wise guy. Plus, I think Weeb just wanted to be the biggest name to come out of Miami of Ohio. He ran Dick Chorovich ragged, and after two seasons he ran him right out of the league. He took the worst beating of any rookie lineman ever to come to a Colt camp.

If Weeb didn't like you from the beginning, he never liked you, and neither did his coaching staff. Weeb was a little man, and sometimes he acted like a little man (but he got things done right).

But despite Weeb's petty bullshit, by 1957 we knew we were legitimate championship contenders. The previous couple of years the Colt players had always *hoped* we were going to be pretty good. That '57 season we *knew* we were going to be very good. Thanks mainly to Johnny U., our offense had finally caught up with our defense. And man, the gears of the Colt steamroller were starting to mesh. The Baltimore organization had its first winning season ever that year, going 7–5.

We won our first three that season, lost our next three, and then put together a four-game winning streak that had us challenging for the title. Talk about a heady experience. But we really blew the whole thing during our fourth game of the season, in Detroit. Lenny Moore fumbled a pitchout late in the game, and as the ball was heading out of bounds, everybody who was chasing it kind of just eased up. Suddenly, right near the sidelines, the football took this crazy hop back back in bounds. The Lions recovered, scored a touchdown, and beat us, 31–27. The Lions went on to win the conference title and the league championship.

Sure, we were still in the race down the stretch, but it was really that Detroit game that took the wind out of our sails. Our final two games that season were played on the Coast. We lost both of them. The first, a defeat in San Francisco, was a rob job. I told you about those West Coast officiating teams, right? Well, here was another example of their hometown bias. Late in the game, on fourth and ten, Hugh McElhenny just shoved our rookie corner-back, Milt Davis, out of the way and caught a touchdown pass from John Brodie to beat us, 17–13. It was a blatant penalty, but you don't think those guys were going to call it, do you?

That loss pretty much knocked us out of the playoff picture, and in our final game of the season we were killed, 37–21, by the Rams. Los Angeles totally kicked the crap out of us, and as we were walking off the field after the game Norm Van Brocklin caught up to me and said, "Sorry, Fatso. I had to do it." I looked at him in wonderment. "If you didn't play your best I wouldn't think much of you, Norm," I said. Then, as he trotted away, I added under my breath, "you dirty bastard."

In 1956 during the season we stayed at the Biltmore Hotel in Santa Barbara. We turned the town on its ear. I remember they had a female piano player in the hotel lounge who quit after the first night we were in.

One night we went out and were getting sloshed, and this guy Heap Peterson, a tackle who didn't play much, came with us. Heap didn't drink, but on this night we talked him into trying a beer. And when he wasn't looking, Gino threw two or three shots of vodka into that beer, and Heap downed the drink and collapsed. So we lugged about 320 pounds of Heap Peterson out into the night and tried to catch a cab.

Finally six of us flagged a taxi down, and as we rode back to the hotel, the back bumper of the cab got stuck on a train track. There are train tracks all over Santa Barbara, and every California train comes right through there. A couple of us disgorged from the car and pulled the hack off the train track, and when the driver, a Mexican American, got out to inspect the damage, we took off with his cab. I learned a whole new set of Spanish curse words that night. They come in handy when I pop down to Mexico City. And I can still see the guy running down the street after us in the rear-view mirror. I think Weeb smoothed over the stolen-vehicle charges with the police, who wanted to arrest us. After all, it was just a couple of guys who didn't win a football title letting off a little steam. Right? Right.

But despite our third-place finish, the Colts were ascending. We may have lost the title, but we had found a quarterback in Johnny Unitas. Unitas had played about half the 1956 season after George Shaw got hurt. In fact, John had about the most inauspicious beginning any player in the league could have had.

The first regular-season pass John Unitas ever threw went for a touchdown. For the other team. It was in 1956 in Chicago, during our fourth game of the season. The Bear defense had just knocked Shaw to the sidelines with a busted knee. Unitas came in and hit a Chicago defensive back by the name of J. C. Caroline square in the numbers, and J.C. ran it in for a score. When we got the ball back following the kickoff, Unitas bumped into Ameche while attempting a hand-off, fumbled, and the Bears recovered and went in for another score. Following the next Bear kickoff, Unitas fumbled trying to hand off to L. G. DuPre, and the Bears went on yet another touchdown drive.

That was a bad day all around. We lost that game to Chicago, 58–27, and it rained so hard that afternoon that on the team bus back to the airport we got stuck in a minilake under an overpass on the highway and we all had to strip to our underwear and get off the bus and push it out of the water. That must have been some sight for the motorists passing by. Afterward, none of us had any idea we had found ourselves anything more than a quarterback who had a great knack for leading the opposition on tremendous touchdown drives. But that was the beginning of the reign of Johnny U., and old George Shaw never did get his starting job back.

In training camp in '57, after Shaw had recovered from knee surgery, Weeb was going around telling people that the quarterback job was up for grabs. Right—like the tsar's job was up for grabs before the Red October. That was the bullshitting Weeb at his best, lying for no good reason at all. Everybody and their mother knew John Unitas was going to be the starting quarterback for the Baltimore Colts. But Weeb even went so far as to tell the reporters that there was a three-way fight for the position among John, Shaw, and Cotton Davidson, a 1954 draft choice from Baylor who had just been discharged from the service.

That's just the way of coaches. Nothing's changed. The coaching credo: Don't tell the truth until you're forced to, and then tell the writers you were telling the truth all along. I saw the same thing happen last season when Jim McMahon went down with an injury and Mike Ditka of the Bears began playing head games with the writers about who he was going to replace him with. Of course, the disinformation strategy is ostensibly used to confuse the opposition. But I really believe Ditka screwed up the heads of his backup quarterbacks—Steve Fuller, Mike Tomczak, and the ultimate starter down the stretch, Doug Flutie—to such an extent that they were as confused as everyone else. Naturally, the Bears watched the Super Bowl on television.

The same with Weeb. Davidson was a nice enough man, but to think he could even begin to compete with Unitas was absurd. The guy had a hole in his chest, for Christ's sake. I swear to God, it looked like Davidson had been hit with a cannon ball when he was a kid or something. At any rate, to the surprise of no one, John won the starting job with ease, and it was only occasional injuries that kept him out of the Colt lineup during the next seventeen seasons.

Unitas was always a quiet guy. Tough, but quiet. For instance, when he threw an interception he was a wild man going after the defensive man who had picked him off. And when he ran with the ball he'd inflict some major punishment, even if he did look like a wounded stork thrashing around in those black high-tops. But off the field he was as soft-spoken as a priest. My friends who played offense—guys like Raymond Berry and Jim Parker and Jim Mutscheller—they all told me that this kid quarterback we picked up off the sandlots was a leader, despite his soft-spoken demeanor. In a Unitas huddle no one was allowed to talk except the quarterback, although I've heard tales that Berry never shut up in those huddles, jabbering after every play about how open he was and asking why the hell he wasn't being thrown to on every play.

Sandusky tells me a story that during the 49er game in 1958 here in Baltimore, Unitas kept calling Lenny Moore's number in the huddle, and Moore kept slashing through the San Francisco defense. So after about half a dozen straight runs by Moore, Lenny came back to the huddle and told John, "Hey, man, cool it. I'm getting tired." Whooaa. Nobody tells John Unitas to "cool it." Parker says Unitas's face turned into a flinty stare, and his eyeballs nearly burned a hole through Lenny's head. "Listen, asshole, nobody tells me to cool it," Unitas said. "I'll run your ass till you die." He put the fear of God in him, and by this time Lenny's stammering, "Forget it, John. Forget I said anything. Give me the ball, please. Give me the ball on every play."

I know what made John Unitas the greatest quarterback of all time: his brain, his arm, his cunning, with a dash of Weeb

Ewbank's coaching thrown in. Weeb had smarts, and once he taught John his check-off system, how to call an audible at the line, there was no stopping Unitas.

Although Weeb tried often enough to send in selected pearls of wisdom from the sidelines, John called all his own plays in the huddle. If the play Weeb sent in happened to jibe with what John wanted to run, so much the better. If it didn't, John just ran what he thought would work and Weeb took credit for it later. I believe that's why Raymond Berry allows his quarterbacks in New England to call their plays today. Steve Grogan, the backup to Tony Eason, signals in the selections from the sideline right now. If Grogan's playing, he calls his own in the huddle. But Eason's young, and I'll wager for as long as Berry remains coaching the Patriots, the men playing the game on the field will be deciding what offense is going to work. After all, Berry saw that strategy work to perfection intimately for twelve seasons with John.

John knew how to take charge. Still does. A few years back I was a driver in a car pool, taking my daughter Kelly and some of her friends to school. Different parents were assigned to drive on different days. Unitas' twelve-year-old son was one of the kids who rode with us. Well, one day, in the middle of a blizzard, I stopped in front of the Unitas house and honked the horn, waited about five minutes, honked the horn again, and this little jerk was nowhere to be seen.

We waited long enough for all the kids to be late for school, and finally I got out of the car to find out where he was. As soon as I got out of the car two snowballs went zooming right past my ear and crashed onto my windshield. That little weasel had been waiting behind a snowbank for me to get out. Well, let me tell you, I wailed into little Unitas then and there. Called him every curse word in the book, and then some.

The bottom line: Sandy Unitas got mad about my language to their son and had me kicked out of the car pool. So it goes. And when I recall that story I still think of one thing: That kid's old man would never have missed a massive target like me with two snowballs. I guess accuracy isn't hereditary.

By the '58 season, of course, the Colts were on top of the foot-

ball world. Our offense was unstoppable. Our defense was un-
movable. Weeb had complemented Unitas with a bevy of talented
athletes, guys like Berry, Parker, and Moore, three guys who
joined Unitas (and me) in the Pro Football Hall of Fame. Berry
was a perfectionist who took pride in knowing every inch of the
field, Parker a decapitating blocker who lusted for defensive blood,
and Moore was one of the fastest little runners to ever play in the
league. The pass-protecting ability of Sandusky, Spinney,
Mutscheller, Preas, Nutter, and Szymanski made Unitas a star.

The first time I ever saw Lenny, donning his uniform during the
exhibition season of 1956, I nearly busted a gut laughing. He was
taping his ankles outside of his shoes, a common enough practice
today but unheard of in '56. We immediately dubbed him
"Spats," a nickname that stayed with him throughout his eleven
seasons with the Colts. But you could have nicknamed Lenny
Moore "Rasputin, the Death Bat from Hell" and it wouldn't have
changed the fact that he was one of the best goddamn runners to
ever carry the ball, a willowy little guy who could run, catch, and
block with equal ferocity.

And Lenny was a true gangster of love. He's cleaned up his act
since. I was recently on a plane with Lenny and when the flight
attendant came around for drink orders, Lenny asked for a Coke
and told me he didn't drink anymore. I almost fell out of my seat.
Lenny Moore not drinking is like the pope not praying. Then he
pulled out a Bible and began reading! He says he's a born-again
Christian. Well, maybe he doesn't drink anymore, but he still lies
like hell, because he was trying to convince me that the reputation
he acquired with the Colts was all a figment of the media's imag-
ination. Hey, Lenny, I was there, remember?

When Lenny Moore first came into the league as a number 1
draft choice out of Penn State in 1956, he was one wild man. I
mean, for all this guy's talent, sometimes just getting him to run
the correct pass pattern in practice would drive Weeb to banging
his head against a wall. To this day I still don't know if Lenny was
just wild or obstinate, but he loved to go against humanity's flow.
And he was always complaining about what we figured were non-
existent injuries. Basically the guy was a loony bird. His first wife

filed for a divorce after she claimed he tried to run over her with a car. I tell you, playing on the same team as a Lenny Moore surely reminded me of the old days. But Weeb allowed guys like Lenny to make the team once in a blue moon.

One of those guys, however, who did play a part during those championship seasons was Eugene Lipscomb, Big Daddy to his fans. Big Daddy was the Lawrence Taylor of his time when it came to physical attributes: six-seven and 290 pounds of solid muscle that could shoot through the air like a ballistic missile. But he was the Lou Costello of his time when it came to running his life. He was a drinker and a gambler and a skirt prowler who pictured himself the black Tyrone Power, and he ended up dead of a heroin overdose in a West End Baltimore apartment house. But what I remember best about Big Daddy was that he laughed easily and cried easily.

Big Daddy's mother was murdered on a Detroit street corner when he was eleven. She was going off to work in a laundry when she was stabbed forty-seven times by a man she knew while she waited for a bus. Lipscomb never knew his father. Big Daddy moved in with his grandfather after his mother died, and he once told me that his grandfather used to tie him to a bed and whip him with a strap for stealing the old man's whiskey. I never did ask him if that's where he developed his taste for VO.

When he was eighteen he went into the Marines and began to play football, real good football. He came out and went straight into the NFL. Weeb picked him up from the Rams in '56 for the $100 waiver price, and for some reason Weeb had a blind spot about Big Daddy. It was as if the coach's mind was split in half: His brain could never make his ego understand that this man with all the strength, power, and speed couldn't be molded into the ultimate football player. Coaches are like that. They see a perfect physical specimen and figure they can instill the desire and mind-set.

Of course, coaches who believe that are usually wrong. It takes more than a man with a whistle to change a person's character. Big Daddy was never more than a marginal player for us, although both he and Weeb did their level best to promote him as the black Colossus.

Weeb tried the same thing going into the '59 season. But it soon became pretty obvious that Big Daddy was the weak link of our defensive line. I mean, people were running right over him. So Donovan got the call again. Early in the season, after I had just returned from my mother's funeral, I came back to hear how Big Daddy had been spouting off his mouth all week about what he was going to do to Jim Brown when Cleveland came in the following Sunday.

Well, during that Cleveland game, the Browns turned Big Daddy every which way but loose. I never saw a defensive lineman get blocked from as many directions as Big Daddy was blocked that afternoon. He was screaming and hollering in the defensive huddle, and naturally we're all asking him what the hell they were doing to him. "They're triple-teaming me! They're quadruple-teaming me!" he cried, a statement that kind of took Ray Krouse and me by surprise. Because if they were triple-teaming Big Daddy, we were wondering where the hell the guys were coming from who were running over us.

In truth, Big Daddy never had more than two Browns blocking him in that game. And while looking at the game films afterward, Weeb saw that he was making a big mistake keeping Krouse and me on the bench. Big Daddy started a lot of fights with his mouth and with his fists, and he may have won quite a few of them. But on the defensive line he was nothing more than an overgrown kid, and men have a way of handling overgrown kids. A majority of the people playing the offensive line in the league were most definitely men. So for the remainder of the season the three of us shared the two tackle spots, and everything worked out fine.

Big Daddy Lipscomb was a flashy dresser who owned flashy cars and whose life eventually exploded around him. They found him dead in early May 1963, at the age of thirty-one. There was a homemade syringe next to his body and enough needle tracks in his arms to crisscross Santa Barbara. My friend John Steadman, the sports editor of the *Baltimore Sun,* once dubbed Big Daddy, "The Playful but Lonesome Giant." And that's exactly what he was.

I'm not going to bore you with a lot of mindless football palaver recounting a season nearly thirty years old. Let it just suffice to say that in 1959 the Baltimore Colts kicked ass and took names. Unitas was on the cover of every national magazine that season. Everybody knew John Unitas. One time John and I were out in Los Angeles for the Pro Bowl, and an ex-teammate of mine named Paul Salata, who lived in L.A., took us out for a Serbian Christmas party. The Serbs celebrate Christmas in January, and Salata took us from house to house in the Serbian community. Nobody knew me, but every one of those Serbs knew John Unitas. Everywhere we went it was like the Second Coming of the Lord.

But if Johnny U. was the most famous Baltimore Colt, I think the real heart and soul of the team was Gino Marchetti. Maybe I shouldn't be speaking for the offense, but I believe the Colts drew their strength from Gino.

But believe it or not, for all of Gino's bulk, his forte was his finesse. The sonofabitch was as strong as an ox, but he would finesse people right into the ground. He was probably the quickest defensive lineman off the mark that I've ever seen, and that includes Mark Gastineau and Karl Mecklenburg.

I look at the defensive linemen who make All-Pro today, and in my mind's eye I try to conjure up a comparison with Marchetti. For the life of me, I just can't. Nobody comes close to playing the game the way Gino played it. Christ, they handle Randy White in Dallas like he's not even there. White's always been like that. The only time he ever got to the passer was when he had Harvey Martin playing alongside him. Every time I watch the Cowboys play, all I see is Randy White going backward, being blown off the line of scrimmage.

The same with Rulon Jones, Mecklenburg's buddy out in Denver. Jones is a big, tall, skinny guy, and he gets buried when they run right at him. Then I have to listen to Merlin Olsen and all these announcers saying what great defensive linemen there are today. What bullshit! I think the best defensive lineman in football today is Chicago's Dan Hampton. I think Hampton's better than the Raiders' Howie Long, and Hampton's the guy—a two-way player who can stuff the run *and* rush the passer—who most reminds me of Gino in his prime.

One time in training camp one of our high draft choices, an offensive lineman, drew Gino one-on-one in a blocking drill. Well, on the first snap, Gino faked a move right, went left, and left this big college All-Star grasping at air. On the second snap Gino faked left, went right, and the rookie, who still hadn't laid a finger on him, was now frustrated as hell. Finally the rookie was ready to flat-out kill this sonofabitch Marchetti, and on the third snap he came roaring out of his set position, howling the Gurkha war cry. So Gino just put his hands on the rookie's back and leapfrogged over him, leaving him chewing on a mouthful of dirt. The rookie lifted himself off the ground, turned, looked at the offensive line coach, and asked plaintively, "So what do I do now?" I was standing over on the sidelines watching this and I yelled to the rookie, "Applaud! Just applaud!"

The only guy I ever saw give Gino as much as he got was Forrest Gregg of the Packers, who now coaches that team. Gregg was just as quick as Gino, and he'd give him fits. Gino would try a move right, and Forrest would be standing there. He'd deke outside and cut inside, and there would be Gregg just waiting for him. It got to a point where the two of them looked like dance partners on the game films, and there was no end to the taunts directed at Gino during film sessions. Of course, you could only bust Gino's chops when the lights were out and he couldn't move from his chair. Otherwise, he'd rip your spleen out and use it for a wine sack.

But off the field Gino was just one of the guys. Back then we pretty much all hung around together, drinking beer and whatnot, and there was really a great camaraderie to the teams. I guess winning had something to do with that. We went 9–3 in '59, winning our last five in a row and just destroying the Giants, 31–16, in the championship rematch in Baltimore two days after Christmas.

I remember people coming up to me on Christmas Eve and telling me how sorry they felt for me because I had to work on such a grand holiday. I thought they were crazy. I was playing football, making good money, around $17,500, and was on my way to a championship. Carroll Rosenbloom sent us all a basket of fruit that Christmas. I gave mine away. I would have preferred a couple of dozen hot dogs, or maybe a hunk of kosher salami.

Once the Colts began winning, Rosenbloom began getting more and more involved with the team. Carroll was a chain smoker who inhaled three packs a game: "one for the defense, one for the offense, and one for halftime," he used to say. He dressed in what I can only term the Jack Nicholson mode of fashion—dapper, dark clothes with just a hint of Hollywood. And sportswriters took to calling him a part-time owner, part-time hoodlum. That he may have been, but Carroll was always good to his players. He set about half the team up in business. Guys like Ameche and Marchetti became millionaires from the businesses he staked them to. It seemed Carroll always had an eye out for the little things that would make a football player more loyal.

The party in the St. Francis Hotel in San Francisco was a perfect example of that. In fact, before Rosenbloom got involved in the team's day-to-day operations, Weeb used to make sure the closest we got to San Francisco before game day was a hotel fifty miles outside of town. When Carroll heard about that policy, he stepped in and made sure that whenever the Colts traveled West they'd stay in the best hotels right in the middle of the city. He was also a real superstitious guy. Before every game he'd circle the field, pat Unitas on the head, and accept a piece of adhesive tape from Lenny Lyles, a defensive back, before heading up to his box. Don't ask me what it all meant.

Rosenbloom's business interests included everything from shirts to socks to stocks to toys, and the World Champion Baltimore Colts became his biggest plaything. He'd personally address the team about twice a year, usually when we broke training camp and before our most critical game. And though he never added anything close to football insight to our collective psyche, it was always nice to know the owner was with you in spirit. Once, while we were in the midst of a particularly horrid streak, Rosenbloom came into the locker room and told us he wasn't going to speak to us again until we played like the champions he knew we were. By the time he finished up his little speech, Big Daddy was all upset. "Ain't you ever comin' back, Carroll?" he kept wailing. "Ain't you ever comin' back?"

But the Big Daddy man always was a bit of a pessimist. We were good—the best, in fact—and I think it took about a week and a half before Rosenbloom was back glad-handing us after our latest victory.

During that 1959 season I remember running into the old Green Bay center, Jim Ringo, in an airport. We were at the top of the heap and the Packers were still a pile of dog shit. This was before Vince Lombardi turned things around up there, and I said to Ringo, "Jesus Christ, Jim, you and I have played with the worst goddamn football teams to ever come down the pike, and now I'm playing with one of the best. I hope to God someday you have the opportunity to know what it feels like to go from worst to first." Little did I suspect how the tables would turn.

But for now, the Baltimore Colts were at the top of the world. In the '59 championship game the Giants were actually leading us, 9–7, before we decided to get serious and play. Charlie Conerly was quarterbacking them, and we started to lay a terrible beating on him on defense, while on offense Unitas just caught fire. The defensive line was getting to Conerly so quick that when we weren't sacking him we were pressuring him to just heave that pig, and we must have had four or five interceptions in the second half alone. Not that we minded, but none of us could really figure out why their offensive line had suddenly collapsed.

I nailed Charlie good late in the game when we were up by fifteen points and victory was a foregone conclusion, and as I was helping him off the ground I whispered to him, "Charlie, I think you ought to get yourself out of this game before you get yourself hurt, or worse, killed." On the next play three or four of us hit him simultaneously after he released the ball, and we just about impaled him on the goalpost. That's when the goalposts were still on the goal line. So Jim Lee Howell, the Giants' coach, finally lifted a dazed and battered Conerly after that play, and with a few minutes remaining sent in Don Heinrich to quarterback.

Well, this should give you an example of how fierce our rush was back then. The Giants had the ball at about their own eight-yard line, and Heinrich leaned under the center to take the snap. He was giving a quick count when suddenly we faked a blitz for-mation—that is, faked as if everyone were coming. Heinrich turned white. I heard him say, "Oh, shit, here they come." The Giants' center, Ray Wietecha, centered the ball just then and the snap flew between Heinrich's legs and we recovered the fumble on their one-yard line. It was hilarious.

So was the Colts' locker room after the championship game. I have a picture of me and Richard Nixon in the postgame locker room, and in the corner of the snapshot you can see half my fa-ther's head. I wanted to get my father into the picture with the vice president, but he was too busy talking to the mayor of New York, Robert Wagner. Wagner asked him what the hell an old fight ref was doing in a football team's locker room, and my dad had to explain that the guy he wouldn't allow to become a part-time New York cop was now a world champion. I remember Nixon only being interested in how much money we made for winning, which was about $5,000.

That off-season, between '59 and '60, the Colts became the toast of Baltimore. They didn't exactly have the rubber-chicken circuit in those days. But every other night a different bar would have a different party for one of the Colts, and of course the rest of us would just pile in on that blast. I remember the day after we took the '59 title, I met Don Joyce at about ten o'clock in the morning, took him to my offices, and told my bosses that we were going to hit some taverns together.

Let me tell you, I wasn't going to these joints to sell liquor. I was in the mood to buy. That day was cheeseburger heaven for Mr. Arthur J. Donovan, Jr., and Mr. Donald Joyce. I was up to my protruding belly in burgers, hot dogs, French fries and gravy, and Schlitz—man, I bet you we gained twenty pounds apiece that day. At about midnight Joyce was still going strong, but I had to beg out. I felt like I was going to blow up.

Then, of course, there was always the club. The Valley Country Club in Towson, Maryland, was the scene of many a debauch. The proprietors were none other than (who else?) Arthur and Dottie

Donovan. When I married Dottie in 1956, her parents were already one-sixth owners of a tennis and swim club covering twenty acres in Towson, a Baltimore suburb. Six businessmen had gotten together and bought the place, a twenty-two-room colonial mansion that needed refurbishing. Dottie's father was a Baltimore policeman, and he also owned a diner—a truck stop, really—on the Pulaski Highway outside of town. The diner lay directly on the Baltimore-to-New York truck route, and Dottie's parents did okay.

After we were married, the family gave us a membership to the club, and I really took a shine to the place. A few months after our marriage, Dottie's father, Bud Schaech, approached me and asked me how much money I had. I asked him what he had in mind, and he told me he had an idea to buy out the other five partners. The place was going bankrupt and they really didn't have anyone to manage it properly. So I went to see Don Kellet, the general manager of the Colts, to ask him for his advice. Kellet told me to let the place go bankrupt and then buy it, but my father-in-law didn't want to do it that way.

Bud and I put our monies together and took over ownership of 100 percent of the Valley Country Club. He put his name on the liquor license because I was still working for Schenley, and it was against the law for me to sell liquor and have my name on a liquor license. Dottie sold her drugstore and began taking courses every summer in club management up at Cornell University. She went there for a month during the summers of '56, '57, and '58, and she still goes up there now to run workshops on club management.

We bought the Valley Country Club on a shoestring. It was twenty acres of prime land ten miles from downtown Baltimore. And over the past thirty years we've poured blood, sweat, and tears into the place, not to mention tennis courts, two swimming pools, a bathhouse, a snack bar, locker rooms, offices, a ballroom, a dining room, kitchens—all the things a kid from the Bronx feels real comfortable with.

From 1957 on, after every Colts' game, walking into this place was like stepping back in time. That's what really put us over the hump, the business the Baltimore Colts brought in. The parties we used to throw out at that club. We practiced the Five d's: drink, dinner, drink, dance, and drink. And after every away game, when the players got off the bus or the plane, there would be a caravan of cars to the Valley Country Club. And the thing is, I never gave the players anything free. Pro athletes are notorious moochers, but these guys just kept coming back week after week for more. They were having a good time. We'd throw a party once a year, on the arm, our way of thanking everybody for coming out.

There were a lot of nights when I was not only a bartender but a lifeguard and a medic to boot. One time Jackie Simpson, a defensive back on our taxi squad, came to pick up Fuzzy Thurston, and Simpson was so drunk he almost drove into the swimming pool. I saw him tearing down the driveway and I ran out, hollering, "Stop! Stop!" And damned if he didn't stop six inches from my goddamn diving board.

Everybody came, even the Unitases, and every Sunday night the lights would be blazing there until two in the morning, when I had to close up. Aside from the players, we'd pack in five hundred fans a night, and it was the best time of my life. I remember we had a party one night, and somebody came up to me and said, "You better go check on Don Joyce, I think he has a problem." So I went looking for him, and I couldn't find him anywhere. Finally I peered into the third-floor bathroom, and though there was no Joyce, the evidence surely pointed to his having been in the vicinity. You see, the sink basin was filled with puke. The bastard had thrown up in the sink instead of the john. Suddenly I heard a low groan from outside one of the third-floor windows. I looked out, and sure enough, there was Joyce, passed out on the roof, precariously near the edge. I almost wanted to push him off the roof I was so mad at him. Instead I crawled out there and dragged him back in through the window.

"C'mon, champ, c'mon, champ, wake up." I must have thrown cold water on his face for an hour before he finally came around. Then, when I finally got him downstairs and walked him down the driveway to his car, Ameche saw us and started pretending that he was falling-down drunk. Right away Joyce perked up, ripped himself out of my grasp, and began yelling, "Arthur, Arthur, I'm okay! You've seen me like this a few times. But neither of us has ever seen the Horse so loaded. I better drive him home." Of course, I was going to let Joyce drive a car only over my dead body. But he wouldn't let his wife into the driver's seat until we finally convinced him that the Horse was only acting.

Joyce was always one of the wackier Colts. His family belonged to the club, and one day one summer he threw his kid in the pool so many times that the lifeguard thought the kid was about to drown. My lifeguard went up to him and said, "Excuse me, Mr. Joyce, but you can't do that anymore." So Joyce threw the lifeguard in. After that I had to tell him, "Any more of this shit, Donny Boy, and you're out of here."

Life was literally a cabaret for the fat and happy crew from Baltimore, as it always is with winners. The Pro Bowls I used to go to were in L.A. every year, and every year we'd all get together out there for a Pro Bowl party in a restaurant called the House of Serfas, which was owned by a big football fan named Ernie Serfas. It was in Englewood, right on the corner of Stockton and LaBrea. And Ernie owned an adjacent motel, which despite the fact that it wasn't the official Pro Bowl hotel, nonetheless received *mucho* business from football players the week preceding the game.

One night the whole bunch of us were sitting in Ernie's bar when who walked in but Gorgeous George, my old buddy from Boston. And Gorgeous, with his entourage trailing him, started passing out buttons with his picture on them. So Charley Ane, a tough old tackle with the Lions who was sitting in the corner telling stories about Bobby Layne splicing porno films to the Detroit game films, called Gorgeous over and said, "No need for the buttons, fella. We all know who you are, and I'm gonna give you one minute to get out of here or your ass is going right through that window. Do you hear me?" Gorgeous George heard him, and, whoop, that wrestler swiveled on a dime and was out of that room in a flash.

Winners tell jokes. Losers say "Deal."

Meanwhile, while us fat old vets were rolling in clover after two straight championships, the team didn't really pick up any rookies of importance in the draft. Nor did Weeb pull off any blockbuster trades. And in retrospect, that kind of sealed our fate. We were a good, solid team. But we were getting old. And I think if we could have had some youngbloods in place waiting to step right in when the old guys started to fade, our fall from grace wouldn't have been quite so precipitous. While we were running around half bombed for two years, the franchise was crumbling beneath us.

The Baltimore Colts, favored in most publications to take their third straight NFL championship, began the 1960 season like a house afire. We opened the season with a 20–0 whitewash of the Redskins and then creamed the Bears, 42–7, and I just figured, "Well, here we go again." After eight games we were 6–2 and playing like the greatest team in the league. Then, poof, it all went up in smoke. We dropped our last four games to finish at 6–6, in fourth place in the Western Conference. Losing suddenly wasn't so ha-ha funny as it had been earlier in my career. I kept looking and looking, but I never could find that damn silver lining. I suppose once you taste the top, it's impossible to get used to the foibles of the bottom again.

There was nothing I could see about the team that had really changed. It was just like someone had pulled the rug out from under us. By 1960, Weeb's power had increased within the organization to a point where Kellett was general manager in name only. Whereas early in his Baltimore coaching career Weeb would start decision-making sentences with, "I'll ask Don to talk to Carroll about that," now those sentences always began, "I'll have to speak to Carroll about that." But for all his faults, Weeb was never accused of not knowing football. And I think he was as dumbfounded as the rest of us when the victories began to slip away from us.

The game that really broke our backs that season was the Detroit game in Baltimore. We were 6–3 when the Lions came for the third-to-last game of the season, and we were leading them, 15–13, when their quarterback, Earl Morrall, threw a touchdown pass to Jim Gibbons with fourteen seconds left. Three of our defensive backs all jumped to intercept it at the same time, and they all crashed into each other. They knocked each other off and Gibbons was left standing alone. He strolled into the end zone.

But in the locker room after the game it was me whom Weeb

laced into and blamed for the loss. You see, that was the game in which Gil Mains had hit Alex Hawkins after the whistle, and I just happened to be walking by and I drop-kicked Mains right in the face. There were fourteen seconds left and the Lions were out of time-outs. But my penalty stopped the clock long enough for Detroit to draw up a play in the huddle, and of course that play went for the touchdown that beat us.

Weeb threw a shit fit in the locker room. "Goddamnit, Donovan, goddamnit, you had to get thrown out and stop the clock and give them the game!" he railed. "Are you happy, Donovan? Are you proud of yourself?" Of course I wasn't. But I'll tell you one thing: If I had to do it all over again I'd still kick that sonofabitch in the chops.

Also, the Colts had been leading a charmed life in terms of injuries for the past couple of seasons. And Fate seemed to catch up on us in '60. There was a lot of smoke in the papers about how we were just fat and happy, more worried about our bank accounts and our outside business deals than we were about winning games. But it was just that: smoke.

I came into that season lighter than I'd been in ten years. I must have played at around 262 pounds, and I had a helluva season for a thirty-five-year-old bum. Hell, I had a helluva season for a twenty-five-year-old bum. But other people were falling left and right. It was like roll call at Gallipoli. Raymond Berry sprained an ankle during the Rams' game. Lenny Moore got knocked out in Detroit. Mutscheller limped through the season on a bad knee. And Ameche ruptured an Achilles tendon, an injury that finally forced him to retire after the season, while he was at the peak of his career.

Then nothing seemed to work. With the Horse hobbled and used mainly for blocking purposes, our offense was forced to rely almost completely on Unitas and the passing game. Even the greatest quarterback in the history of the game found that burden too much to bear. Defenses were just laying for Johnny U.'s heaves. And even when things appeared to go right, something turned them around. The slant-in pass to Lenny Moore had been Unitas's bread-and-butter play since he and Moore began exploding against defenses three years earlier. But in 1960, knowing that they didn't have to worry about Ameche rumbling out of the backfield, defenses just clogged up the middle and completely took that play away from them. Then, just to show the way our luck was going, the one time they did connect, the pass hit Lenny right in the hands and dislocated his thumb. *Oy vey.*

Also that season, what I had taken as just a snatch of conversation with Jim Ringo turned into an omen. If the Colts were on the skids, the Packers, with Vince Lombardi in his second season as head coach, were on the rise. In 1960 the Pack finished at 8–4 and won the Western Conference title for the first time in sixteen years. Lombardi was already starting to mold those squads that were to become the great Green Bay teams of the 1960s.

Bart Starr was in Green Bay, as was Paul Hornung and a killer offensive line that included Ringo, Gregg, Jerry Kramer, and Fuzzy Thurston, whom Weeb had let go the previous year. But the man I remember best was Jim Taylor, their chugging fullback and the first person I had ever played against to spark the thought in my mind that maybe I was getting too old for this little boy's game.

Taylor was, quite simply, a fullback with the mind-set of a linebacker. No, no, let me rephrase that. Taylor was a fullback with the mind-set of a polar bear on Dexedrine. They talk today about seeing stars after being hit by the Refrigerator coming out of the backfield. Let me tell you something: When Taylor hit you, you saw the entire galaxy. Man, he would block for Hornung, and his blocks put Hornung into the Hall of Fame.

When I first played against Taylor I didn't realize he was that tough a guy. After all, he wasn't playing the defensive line, so how tough could he be? I found out real quick. Hornung was running Lombardi's patented sweeps all afternoon, and all afternoon just as I was about to make the tackle this Clydesdale impersonating a fullback would literally burrow me into the ground. I kept turning around looking for the license plate, and every time it read "TAYLOR" across the back of the tractor-trailer that had run me over. I kept going back to the huddle and telling Gino that this kid from LSU was one tough sonofabitch, and the wop would just shake his head and say, "I know, I know."

I was beating Jerry Kramer pretty good off the line, and usually when you beat the offensive lineman you're picked up by a back, and I could usually just throw a blocking back's ass all over the field. But not Taylor. Every time I hit him he'd come back for more. So finally I hit him a shot with my goddamn forearm right in the chops. I figured that would teach him to stay away from me. Well, a couple of plays later he came right back and he hit me a shot in the chops, and then he did it again on the very next play. I was screaming in the defensive huddle, "I'll kill that jerk sonofabitch!"

Then I started screaming at him, and he just paid me no never-mind whatsoever. So we went on hitting each other the entire game, fighting our own private little war, and just prior to the final gun I got the last shot in. After the gun sounded, I started walking off the field with a fan from Baltimore. His name was Mr. Walker, he was a regular at Kuzen's bar, and he had brought his son up to Milwaukee to see us play. Anyway, I was walking off the field talking to Mr. Walker's son when this guy tapped me on the shoulder. I turned around and, whomp, I took another shot right in the chops. It was Jim Taylor.

"I told you I'd get you," he said. "We're evened up now." I couldn't believe the nerve of this rookie. I tried to chase after him, but he was too fast for me, as usual. Everybody was always too fast for me. Anyway, for as long as I played, which was only another year, Jim Taylor and I never said another word to each other despite the fact that we kept our private war going.

And about ten years ago I ran into him in an airport. He was going up an escalator and I was going down. I just looked at him and said, "You sonofabitch, you." And he smiled, the first time I'd ever seen him smile, and answered, "Aw, come on, Fatso, can't you take a joke?" That broke the ice, I had to start laughing myself, even though I think I still have bruises from where Jim Taylor used to lay me out.

After the 1960 season I sat down with Dottie and assessed my career. I always made my own decisions, but I wanted her advice. After all, I was still playing a pretty rough game, and I was watching a whole new generation of football players come into the league.

When we drafted Tom Matte out of Ohio State in 1961, the first day he showed up in the locker room Gino introduced him to me. "Very pleased to meet you, Mr. Donovan," Matte says. "I'm looking forward to playing with your son." I really needed punks like that.

Even though it was the hardest decision I ever had to make, I suppose in a way I knew deep down it was time to get out. I mean, by 1961 half the established coaches in the league were guys I had played with and against—Don Shula, Tom Landry, Otto Graham. I remember we played the Dallas Cowboys during the 1960 exhibition season, their first year in the league. They were a horrendous team, and after we smashed them I was walking down the runway toward the locker room when I passed Landry. I went to stick out my hand to shake and he walked right past me without even acknowledging me. He absolutely snubbed me. Jesus Christ, I couldn't believe it. What happens when you become a coach, your shit don't stink?

That was also the first game I saw Don Meredith. The Colts went down to the Cotton Bowl, my old haunt, and during warm-ups someone tapped me on the shoulder and said, "Hey, look at that rookie quarterback's legs." I've seen roosters with thicker legs. They were like number 2 pencils. And while we were warming up I went over to him and said, "Hey, Don, you got some balls playing with that pair of legs." He had on three or four pairs of socks just to make his calves look thicker. But he turned out to be a damn good quarterback, and a nice guy to boot. And I was right: He did have some pair of balls.

Once, during a Dallas-Washington game, Sam Huff, who had since been traded to the Redskins, hit Meredith a shot and knocked him flat. Don was slow getting up. And as he lay there on the turf, this big, red stain began to spread across the front of his jersey. Huff, the rough, tough, cheap-shot artist, looked down and began freaking out. He was almost crying. He thought he had killed the guy. But Meredith was wearing one of those chemical heating pads under his jersey, and he realized the thing had sprung a leak after Huff's hit.

So Meredith began playing the scene for all it was worth, gesturing histrionically for the staggered Huff to lean closer to him. "Sam," said Meredith, "I want you to tell my mother that I love her." Huff was tearfully promising to heed this dying man's last wishes when a Cowboy trainer trotted up, took in the scene, and started laughing hysterically. Meredith couldn't hold his smile back any longer and started giggling. I think Huff chased that sonofabitch all the way to Houston when he realized what was happening.

Also, in 1961 I was starting to get hurt. Aside from the broken leg I suffered while playing for the Texans in '52, and a few aches and pains here and there, I had had an injury-free career. But by '61 I was thirty-six years old, and time was starting to catch up with me. I hurt my knee in an exhibition game against the Steelers, and I couldn't practice for a week. I was really worried, and I thought, "Jesus Christ, what a way to end it all, going out with a bum knee."

Our trainer worked on it all week, but I still missed the next exhibition game, against the expansion Minnesota Vikings. As you well know, expansion teams are the pits, so when we went North and the Vikings tore us a new asshole, I mean really stomped us, Gino Marchetti called me up and said, "Well, Fatso, I guess you made the team by default this year, because we sure don't have anyone else who can play."

The wop was right. We finished the '61 season at 8–6. And even though we made a run at the title by winning four of our last five games, everybody kind of knew that glory days in Baltimore were over. I had always planned to play until I was forty. This was before George Blanda came along and kicked until he was forty-seven, and nobody had ever played in the NFL until they were forty years old before. But that dream was beginning to slip away. Nonetheless, I was a football player, and a football player, like a sled dog, runs until he drops dead in the reins. That's why I showed up in Westminster, Maryland, for training camp in the summer of 1962.

Weeb called me aside in the beginning of camp and told me I was still his number 1 defensive tackle, but he was going to rest me during the exhibition season and see what a couple of youngsters named Jim Colvin and John Diehl could do. "You don't get to the second guy through the hole as quickly as you used to," Weeb said. I knew something was in the wind, and the hurricane hit me in the face when Kellet, the general manager, came up to me and told me that if things didn't work out there would still be a job for me somewhere in the organization.

So it came to pass that I didn't play the first three exhibition games, and these two rookies, Colvin and Diehl, were being eaten up alive. I started our fourth exhibition game, against the Cowboys in Roanoke, Virginia, but I was lifted after the first quarter. And after the game Kellett called me into his office and said, "Arthur, tomorrow we're going to announce that you're going to retire and come to work for the team. You'll do some scouting for us."

On the morning of August 30, 1962, at the tender age of thirty-seven, I ended my career with the Baltimore Colts. A couple of the guys, just to let me know I wouldn't be forgotten, stole an old pair of purple trousers I owned and wore all the time and ran them up the flagpole on Western Maryland's campus. Somebody put fire-crackers under my car, but it was all false bravado. My buddies on the team cried. I cried. I got in my car and drove home alone to Baltimore. I was in a daze.

Twelve years of memories ricocheted through my brain on that long and lonely drive home. I thought about Clem Crow and Sisto Averno, Bobby Layne and Jimmy Phelan. I thought about the Dallas Texans and the New York Yankees. I thought my life had ended. The feeling didn't last, of course, but for that drive home I was the saddest man in the universe. The Colts had been my life and love, and now it was over. And I never did hear another word from those bastards about a scouting job or anything else.

10

Fooling Them Again

On September 16, the opening day of the 1962 NFL season, I made my final appearance on the field in Baltimore's Memorial Stadium. The Colts held an Art Donovan Day prior to their meeting with the Rams, and let me tell you, there wasn't a dry eye in the house. Including both of mine.

I was supposed to wear my No. 70 jersey out onto the field one last time before they retired the number, and before the game I headed toward the home team's locker room to change clothes. But when I got to the door I just couldn't do it. I saw Gino standing at the doorway, the tears started welling, and I decided that since I was no longer a member of the team I shouldn't be changing in the team's locker room. I threw the jersey on over my decidedly slumped shoulders in the officials' locker room instead, the closest I've ever come to needing those sonsabitches for anything.

Up in the stands 54,796 people cheered. Down on the field the team presented me with a Cadillac, telegrams from around the league, gifts, the whole shmeer. Finally they shoved a microphone in front of my face, and the words came slowly, painfully.

"Up in heaven, there is a lady who is happy that the city of

Baltimore was so good to her son—a kid from the Bronx. Thank you."

I turned and walked the final fifty yards over the Memorial Stadium turf, through the end zone, and into the tunnel under the stands. Then I put my head in my hands, leaned against a wall, and cried like a baby. Dr. Edmond J. McDonnell, one of my closest and best friends, the Colts' team physician, was waiting for me. He was like a brother to me . . . and still is.

My football days were through; no one wanted old Fatso anymore. Or so I thought. As they say, not so fast there, linebacker-breath. After a couple of games the Colts realized that Colvin and Diehl, my replacements at defensive tackle, were proving about as adept at stopping opposing rushers as I was at ballet. Kellett called. They wanted me back. But after getting my hopes sky high and asking me to return, goddamn if they didn't check and find out that league rules stated that once a player retires during the exhibition season, he must sit out an entire year before he can play again. "Jesus Christ," I thought, "I would have hoped they at least knew the rules before getting me all jittery like this."

So with that fantasy quickly squashed, I decided to get down to business. Real business.

While I was a rep for Schenley, I used to call on a man named Fred Zang, who owned two liquor stores in the Baltimore area. Fred was a crazy Colt fan, and he really took a shine to me. He was an old milkman—an old horse trader, really—and he had some street smarts. He had parlayed his two liquor stores into megabuck businesses, and he became a regular visitor to training camp and, of course, the postgame bashes we used to throw at the club.

One night over dinner during training camp of '62 Fred asked me what I thought I was going to do when my playing days were over. I told him I planned on staying in the whiskey business. I had a fairly good job, and when I could devote full time to it I was looking forward to getting into the national picture, traveling the country as a national brands manager for Schenley. But I also told him that that scenario scared me a little, because I was afraid I wouldn't be able to devote enough time to the country club. So Fred said to me, "Well, why don't you buy my stores?"

"Jesus Christ, Fred, I can't afford to buy you out," I said. But he told me not to worry about the money. He said his son was an electrical engineer who wanted nothing to do with the liquor business, and since he felt like I was also a son to him, he'd have his lawyer work out a deal I could afford. He loaned me capital to pay my bills and get my feet on the ground. Christ, the guy even left me money in the cash registers to make change for my first customers. So I bought those two stores in 1962. And over the next twenty-one years, before I sold out in 1983, I averaged about a million dollars' of business a year in them, selling mostly six-and twelve-packs of beer. No one ever said Baltimoreans couldn't hold their liquor. Those two liquor stores put my five children— Debbie, Chrissie, Arty III, Mary, and Kelly—through school and allowed Dottie and me to pour all the money we made on the club right back into the club.

We scrimped and saved trying to squirrel away a buck here and a buck there while we turned the club into a modern, moneymaking tennis and swim club. Once in the early 1970s, I was climbing down a ladder checking the main drains in the diving well when the ladder slipped and I fell into the deep end, *sans* water. My goddamn kneecap was broken and I must have been lying in there for an hour before anyone found me and called an ambulance. Then, to add insult to injury, the emergency medical team couldn't lift me out. They had to call the fire department, and it took twelve firemen to hoist me out on a stretcher and into the ambulance. I never hurt so much in my life.

However, despite the fact that I was concentrating on the business of providing for my family after football, that didn't mean I didn't have time for a little monkey business, too. After all, I was still Fatso Donovan.

The season I retired, the Colts finished in fourth place again, with a 7–7 record, and Rosenbloom fired Weeb and hired Don Shula as head coach. The following season the New York Jets of the American Football League hired Ewbank, and for the next couple of seasons Weeb would bring me up to the Jets' summer training camp at Peekskill Military Academy in Peekskill, New York, and have me pass on some tips of the trade to his defensive linemen.

I did that for a couple of years, and one of the craziest bastards to come through that camp was none other than Broadway Joe himself. Namath was the kind of character who could go out and get plastered the night before a game and throw six touchdown passes the next afternoon. In other words, my kind of guy.

I remember the Jets were playing an exhibition game against Houston in Birmingham, Alabama, and Namath stumbled into a quarterback meeting the night before the game drunk off his ass. Walt Michaels, then an assistant coach, wanted to kill him. As Michaels began to rise from his chair, he said to me, "Look at that sonofabitch. I'll nail his ass." But I pulled him back into his seat and told him, "You better not unless you want to get fired." Throughout the entire meeting Weeb wouldn't even look at his starting quarterback, he was so pissed. But what the hell, the kid was the franchise. And he never let his carousing affect his play on the field.

Joe's room in training camp was the only room with a re-frigerator in it. And it was always chock full of beer and cham-pagne. Joe also brought his dog to camp one year, a little scroungy mutt. And one time the Jets' backup quarterback, Mike Taliaferro, convinced a rookie quarterback named Pete Liske that Weeb al-ways looked after Namath's mutt. So right before practice here comes Liske holding Namath's dog and he walks up to Ewbank and says, "Weeb, Joe wants you to hold his dog for a couple of minutes while he gets dressed." Weeb was so steamed he didn't know what to say. I think it was the first time since he picked a fight with Sam Huff that I'd seen him rendered speechless.

Truth be told, the whole experience was like summer camp for me. I was no more a coach than Weeb was a player, but I sure taught those boys how to drink beer. I also taught the defensive linemen how to read an offensive key, so I guess I earned my money. But I think my most lasting impact on the game of football as a defensive line coach was holding off the onslaught of the foreign field-goal kicker for at least a couple of years.

I share with Alex Karras the feeling that these little sidewinders who come in and "keek ze futbol for touchdown" are nemeses to our way of life. And though it was inevitable that sooner or later the league would become inundated with foreign field-goal kickers—they are, after all, the best kickers; that's all coaches are looking for—I did my part in stemming the tide, for while I was a Jets' assistant, I was also in charge of coaching the field-goal holder. And every time a new foreign kicker would try out, the holder who squeezed the ball too tight, or lined it up on the tee just a shade off-center, or pointed the laces in a direction that would make a ball shank—well, that holder drank for free on Arthur J. Donovan, Jr. Let me tell you, I've never spent money better.

But before I became a part-time coach with the Jets, I nearly became a part-time player again with the Colts. Shula approached me prior to the '63 season and asked me if I was interested in coming back, maybe playing a down or two on each defensive series. Baltimore was still operating with a sieve in the middle of their defensive line, and Shula must have figured that the least a guy as big as I could do was fall in the way of a ballcarrier and slow him down a little. After all, I'd done it with a broken leg over a decade before. But after asking a few people whose opinions I respected about the comeback idea, I turned him down.

My father only gave me two pieces of advice in my life. One, when I went into the Marines, was that if I had to get a tattoo, get it on the bottom of my foot, where no people could see it. The second was never to let anyone pick my friends for me. And I haven't. So the people I talked to about making a comeback were really people I trusted. The general consensus seemed to be that I had gone out on top, and no one wanted to see some fat old man back in there getting the shit kicked out of him by kids half his age. That wasn't exactly how it was put to me, but that was the basic idea, and I agreed. I thanked Shula for asking, told him he had made me feel ten feet tall, and finally squashed the football-playing bug. I never played another game for the rest of my life.

Well, that's not exactly true.

In 1978, twenty years after we played the game for real, the Giants and Colts put on jerseys and game faces and replayed "The Greatest Game Ever Played" for laughs in New York's Central Park. It was touch football, six to a side, and CBS paid us all to come back and give it a whirl so they could televise the game as a halftime feature. Nothing changed but the score. The Colts still won and the Giants still lost, 28–14.

The Colts were represented by myself, Ameche, Marchetti, Unitas, Moore, Berry, Parker, and Myhra. CBS brought back such Giant old-timers as Gifford, Rote, Pat Summerall, Rosie Brown, Ray Wietecha, Alex Webster, Dick Modzelewski, and my old pal Conerly. Marchetti and Ameche had made a million bucks in the fast-food business, and as we spread out on the Great Lawn of Central Park, with the New York skyline jutting up over the tops of trees in the distance, I remember thinking that Gino and the Horse could buy a whole block of Manhattan and not even miss the money.

We all got together at a nightclub a few nights before the game for drinks (what else?), and everybody was lying about what great shape everybody else had stayed in. To tell you the truth, I felt it was more like forty years since we had played the game for real. I was 310 pounds, and it showed. We're not talking game shape here.

That night they showed a tape of the '58 game at the bar, and I'll never forget Unitas studying that film like he was taking down notes in his playbook. Everyone else was hooting and hollering, and there was John playing the professional, which I suppose tells you something about his character and why he was the greatest quarterback of all time. What a cunning bastard.

Just before the Horse scored the winning touchdown in overtime, Rote got up and went to the bar for a beer. "I've seen the ending before," he said. And as the Ameche on the screen went into the end zone to clinch it, the Ameche sitting next to me on a barstool covered his eyes and began to cry.

The game itself in Central Park was a joke. I announced to everyone beforehand that I was going to hold, grab, gouge, and cheat, just like the old days. I couldn't walk, let alone run. I mean, there was Gifford, this svelte, trim television star, and here was old Fatso, the man born fat, going to try to catch him twenty years after the fact? No way. Myhra brought a six-pack of beer over to our sidelines just before kickoff, and Ameche gathered everybody around for the pregame meal. We toasted Weeb, of course.

Sonny Jurgensen, the old Redskin warhorse and the honorary referee, set the betting line at six points, Colts favored, and on the sixth play of the game Unitas covered the spread by hitting Moore for a score. "Seven-nothing!" yelled Jurgensen, and when the Giants bitched that it should be 6–0, Jurgensen quietly reminded them that the man who was the ref and who also had set the line was betting on the Colts.

Conerly's first pass was intercepted ("Same old Charlie," cracked Webster), and Unitas found Berry open for two bombs to give us a 21–0 lead at the half. We coasted to a 28–14 victory, then hit the beer on the sidelines. Jurgensen was there first, though I gave it my best shot. I told you I could never catch anybody.

I enjoyed being around football players, whether they were old geezers playing touch in Central Park or young kids trying to make the Jets in Peekskill. There is a bond that has formed around old warhorses like me and my ex-teammates that seems to get tighter every day.

A few years back, around Christmastime, I received a phone call that made me weak in the knees. Alan Ameche's son had been killed in an automobile accident. He was home from school on Christmas vacation. A lot of Alan's former teammates from Baltimore went up to his house in Pennsylvania for the wake, and I have never witnessed anything as sad in my life. Alan owns a tremendous house in Malvern, Pennsylvania, and I'll never erase the memory of the Horse and his wife and the rest of the kids standing around that little boy in the coffin. I hope to God it never happens to me. I don't think I could take it. The Horse is such a strong man. And his wife is a strong woman.

After the wake ceremony, Gino and I were standing out in the kitchen with a few of the other guys, and I mean we got bombed. Then after the funeral, we went back to the Horse's house and a couple of us began talking out on the veranda, and then a few more joined us on the veranda, and the next thing anyone knew, war stories about the Baltimore Colts were gushing. Over on the corner of the veranda I spotted Alan, a sad smile creasing his lips as he listened.

As we were leaving, one of Alan's sons came up to me and said, "Mr. Donovan, that's the best thing that could have happened to my father, the fact that all you guys came up here to pay your last respects and comfort him. You let him know he has people in the world who love him."

That's the kind of bond football players develop.

Nonetheless, when Weeb offered me a full-time coaching position, I had to turn him down. I had too much going for me in Baltimore with the club and the liquor stores. But that didn't mean I didn't get my share of kicks in.

For about twenty years Ordell Braase and I did a Monday night radio talk show, the kind where people call in and ask questions. And my pregame regimen never varied: to the deli for two pastrami sandwiches and a case of Schlitz, then off to the station. The show was sponsored by Miller, so every time I popped a Schlitz on the air I had to make like I was drinking a Miller. We used to bring the Colt players on as our guests, and by the end of the night the studio was a mess. The producer used to complain that when I'd plop my case of Schlitz down on the table there was no room for the microphones. And I remember Bert Jones spitting tobacco juice all over the goddamn place one night. So they threw us out of there and we moved the show to Braase's Flaming Pit in Baltimore County. We'd get about four hundred fans drinking and hooting and hollering and I'm surprised that people listening at home knew what the hell we were talking about half the time.

And I guess Ordell and I disillusioned more people about the old Colts than anything else. One lady phoned and called me a buffoon. She said I didn't know how to speak correctly. I told her, "Listen lady, if you were from the Bronx, you wouldn't speak too good, either." When I got home that night my little daughter Kelly came up to me and said, "Daddy, at least you're a big buffoon."

Another time what sounded like this sweet old lady called in and asked why today's football players couldn't be more like the old Colts when it came to being solid citizens. She was all upset about drugs and whatnot. So I told her that Sample was on trial for income-tax fraud or passing bad paper or some such thing and Big Daddy was found dead with a needle in his arm and who else did she want to talk about? She hung up.

Then there were my halcyon days as a color man on the Colts' preseason television broadcasts. I did that for four years, and I tell you, I was never cut out to do TV. I tell the truth too much. That's what I've always liked about Howard Cosell. He really did try to tell it like it is. However, sometimes Howard's version and history's version differ. Whenever I see Howard these days he'll say something like, "Arthur, back when you and I were playing football they didn't have—" I have to cut him off to remind him that he played street ball and I played pro ball.

Howard's the kind of guy who if you ask him a question and he doesn't know the answer, he's going to give you an answer anyway. But that's all right. I like him. He's smart. I've followed his career since he interviewed me in the Chicago locker room after a Bears' game in 1957. He was a radio big shot then. And I think he was the only guy out there telling the truth about ballplayers. He might go overboard with all the big words and all, but I never knock a guy's racket as long as he tells it the way he thinks it is.

Perhaps that was my problem as a "television personality." Once we were flying home on the team charter, and I got half a load on and began flat-out telling guys that they stank. What the hell, I couldn't lie. The Colts did stink. The people listening to me on television knew they were terrible. What was I supposed to do? That's the trouble with announcers today. They think we're stupid and they think they can get away with lying to us.

I think the producers at WJZ-TV realized that about me a little too late. Prior to one exhibition game against the Redskins in the early 1970s, while they were playing the national anthem I noticed that one of the Washington players wasn't standing at attention. It turned out to be Duane Thomas, one of the true head cases of all time. And this bastard wasn't even standing up. He was sitting on his helmet and looking around like he was on a butterfly hunt. That really burned me, and after the anthem was finished I really let Thomas have it over the air.

In front of ten zillion fans, half of them Redskin fanatics, I told the audience that it was "Too goddamn bad somebody doesn't knock that dirty sonofabitch's head off." My partner, Dick Stockton, the play-by-play man, just about dropped a load when that went out over the air. He turned white, looked at me, turned his mike off, and asked me if he had heard me correctly. I repeated my opinion, and he turned his mike back on and began making excuses for me to the audience. I told him, "No, Dick, I mean it. If this guy don't like the country, let him get the hell out. If my son were in Vietnam right now I'd go down on the field and shoot the rotten bastard right between the eyes."

Well, that was it for my television career. They fired me after the game. Too bad, because doing that color commentary was kind of fun.

By the time I was doing all this media stuff Rosenbloom had traded his ownership of the Colts for Robert Irsay's ownership of the Rams. Now, a lot of nasty things have been said and written about Irsay, especially since he moved the Colts to Indianapolis. I'm sure a lot of that stuff is true. I remember him barging into the locker room after a game once and in front of the whole squad asking his quarterback, Marty Domres, who had thrown five interceptions, why he threw the ball so well to the other team and not his own. But I have to say that the man never mistreated me.

When Irsay first took over the franchise he made Dick Szymanski his general manager, and both Syzzie and Irsay liked having me around. I guess they would have called me a good-luck charm if the Colts actually had any good luck going for them. But they didn't. That, however, didn't bother me. I'd be doing the color commentary and we'd be on the road and Syzzie would call me up in the hotel and say, "Come on up to my room." I'd get up there and we'd order cheeseburgers and beers up the wazoo, and

Syzzie would just sign the tab, smile, and say, "This is on Robert." Great guy, that Bob Irsay.

Actually, Irsay struck me as being just plain nuts. He would fire Syzzie five and six times a month, and Syzzie would never pack up his office, because he knew the owner would forget about it in the morning. In fact, when he finally did fire Syzzie for good, he had to tell him two or three times to get the hell out because Syzzie didn't believe him.

The day after they sneaked in at midnight with the moving vans and moved the Colts out to Indianapolis, everybody was moping through Baltimore like some kind of tragedy had struck. I couldn't believe it. Flags were at half mast. People were wearing black. The whole nine yards. I thought it was ridiculous. Sure, I miss the team, but that's just it, all we're talking about here is a football team. I say save your half-masted flags and black armbands for days when over two hundred young Marines get blown to smithereens in Beirut. That's a real tragedy, not some goddamn football team moving out of town. You can bring back a football team. You can't bring back your dead children.

I spend my time these days running the club, doing speaking engagements, making an occasional commercial. Every once in a while they haul me out of mothballs and ask me to appear on television. David Letterman is a good friend of mine, and I've been on his show a number of times. The first time I was on, however, the guy surely didn't know who I was. Some director must have booked me, and when I walked out onto that stage I could read the look on Letterman's face: What the hell is this? But he liked my stories about the old days, and at the end of my eight-minute stint, during a commercial, the director came over and asked me if I could do another eight minutes. "Another eight minutes," I told him. "Hell, get me a couple of baloney sandwiches and a few beers and I'll do another eight months."

I've never lost my taste for the kosher deli. And every night, after Dottie and Kelly, my youngest, eat a regular dinner, I take a couple of cold-cut sandwiches into our den and just sit there and watch television and wash those babies down with a six-pack of

Schlitz. Sometimes Kelly will come in and ask me to help her with her homework. The rest of the kids have moved out of our big, old empty house, and Dottie and I don't know what we'd do without Kelly, who just turned eleven. When she asks for homework help, I can do the geography and the history. But when she comes in with that mathematics, I just tell her to go see her mother. It's the Irish in me. We know four school subjects: geography, history, philosophy, and fighting.

Or sometimes I'll sit in that den and I'll see myself on a commercial and I have to laugh at the shit they pay me to do. I did one recently for the Maryland State Lottery, and I spent the day in a dinghy floating in Chesapeake Bay. When the director finally yelled "Cut!" after about the four-hundredth take, I couldn't get out of the goddamn boat. My ass had fallen asleep. Two grips had to haul me ashore. I tried to tell the guy shooting the spot that we had it right after the first shot, but who the hell listens to what I say? All I do is make jokes about people. Well, just to set the record straight, I want you to know that times haven't changed all that much. Arthur J. Donovan, Jr., is still the butt of some pretty good ripostes. I do a lot of traveling around the country, speaking to different groups, and a good number of my former teammates often drop by to get their shots in at old Fatso. It takes a big man to allow these guys to make fun of me in my own book, but I'm nothing if not a big man.

So herewith a condensed version of an Arthur Donovan roast (I've cut out the boring political bullshit and the references to women's anatomy, which, believe it or not, embarrass me). Give it your best, guys, because you know I'll get the last laugh.

Marty Domres, former Colts' quarterback: "I saw Artie walk in today and I was shocked. I mean, yesterday when I ran into him down at the K-Mart he promised he was going to wear those Orson Welles designer jeans I saw him trying on. But instead, here he shows up in his four-piece suit. The first thing Artie says to me when he gets in here is, 'Check my shoes. I just had them shined and I had to take the guy's word for it.'"

Gordon Beard, Associated Press sportswriter and the master of ceremonies: "Since Artie's here today, I'd just like everyone to remember: No cuss words, okay? I'm sure the school board ban on nonstandard English will be thoroughly tested here today. Imagine if Arthur lived in California? With that new proposition they just passed making English the mandatory language, Artie would have to move back to the Bronx.

"Anyway, most people think of Artie as one of a kind. But I like to refer to him as a full house. Of course, you've all seen Arthur doing those Chesapeake Treasure commercials for the State Lottery. From the side it looks like those lottery tickets were sunken treasures. But Arty was a natural for the lottery commercials. He always plays his weight ever since it went to four digits.

"As Artie well knows, in the old days a football player was fined for being overweight. Today they make you a star. Look at William Perry. But let me tell you something, Artie was the original Refrigerator. He opens his mouth and a light goes on. And it never goes off. With his appetite and his legs, Artie reminds me of a charity: Meals Without Wheels.

"When Irsay left town with the Colts, perhaps the best departure line was uttered by Arthur. He said, 'It gives me an empty feeling in the pit of my stomach.' And you better believe it, folks, nothing could be more painful than that for Artie. This is also a real bad time of the year for Arthur. He's supposed to be a light eater, and there's only about nine hours of light per day in November.

"Looking at Artie, it's hard to believe he once played at two hundred and eighty pounds. It's also hard to believe he used to be a ninety-five-pound weakling. Then again, most kids are pretty weak at birth. Artie's mother used to tell him that if he didn't finish his meal, he couldn't go out and play. Artie played six, seven times a day. And then there was his father, Arthur Donovan, Sr., the man who taught little Arthur his arithmetic. Unfortunately, what with his father being a fight referee, Artie never got past ten.

"But he was smart enough to gain a scholarship to Notre Dame, and now Artie can count up to twenty-three. That's how he sells four six-packs. He's got to make a profit somewhere, doesn't he? But it doesn't matter what Artie can count to, because besides being a damn good football player, Artie was a national hero. He went and fought in the South Pacific during World War II and he was wounded twice. Once when he got caught with a stolen case of Spam and once when the ship bringing the beer into Guam sunk. That one got him right where he lives.

"And from the South Pacific he went to Boston College, where he was a red-shirt senior. And if you know Artie, then you know he's still wearing that same red shirt. Arthur has aged well, like salami. Which is only fitting, because the guy is about half salami by now anyway. And now he's a star again, almost a regular on Letterman and a hit in the movie *Two for the Money*, where he played both parts."

Chris Thomas, Baltimore sportscaster: "I walked in here tonight and the first thing Artie told me was that he had lost twenty pounds. I thought that was wonderful. Everyone should have a goal in life, and I'm happy to see Artie reach his. I, too, had a goal in life, and coincidentally I reached it the same time Artie reached his. Yes, sir, folks, just as Artie lost his twentieth pound Marilyn Monroe walked into my apartment and asked if anyone was interested in oral sex. It happened to Artie, it happened to me, it can happen to you. The day Artie loses twenty pounds is the day Marilyn Monroe shows up at your door.

"Here we all are, the day after Thanksgiving, and the only person who didn't eat more than he should have yesterday is Arthur Donovan, Jr. Before Thanksgiving some of us go to a turkey farm to order a bird. Artie orders the farm. 'What have you got?' he asks. 'A thousand? I'll take them.'

"I'm honored to be here today celebrating this man. And when I was asked to sit on the dais and speak, I figured I had better do some thorough research on this man's life. So here's what I came up with.

"Art was born on June fifth . . . and later on June sixth, 1925. At birth he weighed thirty-six pounds, had a crew cut, and slapped the doctor back. By the time he was one week old, he was up to ten bottles a day. Schlitz, of course. On his first birthday, his grandmother baked him a cake in the shape of a cow. On his second birthday, his grandmother baked him a cow. When Art turned three, his parents donated him to the Bronx Zoo. In the ensuing twelve months, the animals learned as much about young Arthur as he did about them. One day the elephant came up to

Arthur, who was as naked as the animals in the zoo, and asked him, 'So how do you breathe through that thing?'

"Now you have to understand, when you grow up in the Bronx and you're Irish, there are only three things you can do: You can become a cop, you can become a priest, or you can become a boxer. The New York City Police Department told Arthur they didn't want anyone on the force who looked so much like the people they were trying to lock up. As for the priesthood, the cardinal of New York said Artie would never be able to get through the communion ceremony because the sonofabitch would drink all the wine. And finally, as for the squared circle, well, Arthur's father figured his kid already looked like he had lost about forty bouts, so he refused to put him in the ring.

"I read in an old Baltimore Colt press guide that while at Boston College Artie was a 'brave competitor who majored in education.' Of course. If Art hadn't been a football player he would have been a teacher. Can't you see it now? Your child coming home and telling you that the teacher said that 'dey ain't no such ting as good vegables.' It also said in this press guide that Art's first roommate with the Colts, Sisto Averno, majored in philosophy at Muhlenberg College.

"Can't you just imagine the conversations these two had in their hotel room on the road? One night Sisto might say, 'Arthur, it's like Descartes said, "I think, therefore, I am."' And Arthur would reply, 'Fuckin'-A right. I think I'm hungry, therefore I'll eat.'"

Sisto Averno: "I was getting dressed this morning and my son asked me where I was going. I told him I was going to a roast for Uncle Artie. And he said, 'Well, they better roast two of whatever they're cooking. One for Uncle Art and one for the rest of the people.'

"But you've all been concentrating so much on Art Donovan's girth here tonight I believe you've overlooked a very important facet of his personality. Not that I disagree with you about Art's rotund being. I remember Arthur telling me he wanted to be a mounted patrolman in the New York Police Department. But I knew that would never happen. Because I'm from right across the river in Jersey, see, and I knew the NYPD had no Clydesdales in their stable.

"But what I best remember Arthur for is his cheapness. I mean, this guy still has the recess slips from St. Philip Neri in his back pocket. When Artie and I were traded from the Browns to the New York Yankees in 1951, we arrived at the train station and here comes Arthur carrying his father's old World War I suitcase. This thing was falling apart. And, in fact, it finally fell apart at the train station. But instead of buying a new one, he borrowed my knife, went up to a mailbag, cut the rope off the mailbag, and tied that old suitcase up. Then, when we flew to Houston with the team, they wouldn't let Arthur in the Shamrock Hotel with that suitcase. They made him go around back to the bums' entrance."

Ordell Braase: "As I look at the great man, Arthur Donovan, sitting up here on the dais with me, one thought springs to the forefront of my mind: In the thirty years I've known the man, I've never before seen Arthur wear a suit whose jacket matched the pants.

"You've all been sitting up here speaking about Arthur Donovan the football player. I'd like to tell you a little about Arthur Donovan the philosopher. Not too long ago, Art and I were driving up to Western Maryland to go turkey shooting. The fact that the fuel efficiency in my car soared after he made a pit stop has nothing to do with this story.

"No, after Arthur's pit stop we began discussing the state of the world. And Arthur said to me, 'This country's all screwed up, and you know who's to blame?' With bated breath I awaited the answer. 'It's them no-good, pot-smoking, drug-taking sonsabitches that sailed in from Liverpool, that's who's to blame.' I was taken aback. I asked him who the hell he was talking about and he told me: 'The Beatles.'

"'The Beatles got all these kids smoking pot since they came over here,' Arthur said to me. 'And they're what's wrong with this goddamn country.' I kept my mouth shut, not being able to connect the ills of the country to the four lads from Liverpool yet not wanting to incur Arthur's wrath. Then, about a year later, I received a call from Arthur. He was frothing on the other end of the line.

"'What'd I tell you!' he yells over the phone. 'Those guys from Liverpool are no damn good!' This time I had to ask him what the hell he was talking about. 'Whattya mean, what am I talking about?' he screams. 'Didn't ya see that riot over in that soccer stadium? Those guys are all from Liverpool. Those Liverpoolians are no goddamn good.' And someone here tonight had the nerve to say Arthur Donovan is not a philosopher?

"Also, if you look into Art's war records, you'll find that he is a decorated hero. Yes, sir, Artie received the Purple Heart. He was shot in the ass running away with that case of Spam. Artie's football career never really stabilized until he was chosen by Cleveland in the 1951 dispersal draft. Weeb Ewbank was the offensive line coach for the Browns, and Weeb quickly realized the talent that Arthur possessed and cut him.

"And of course I'm glad to see Arthur's notoriety continuing after his playing days are over. He's become a real celebrity on television. When I first saw his lottery ad on the tube I thought he was floating in a urinal. 'Good God,' I thought, 'Arthur's become the new Tidy Bowl man.' Then there's those national talk shows. You can't turn on television these days without seeing Art's lovely mug clogging up the screen.

"But if I may get serious for a moment, I'd just like to say that through the medium of TV the rest of the country is finally finding out what we in Baltimore have known all along. That Arthur J. Donovan, Jr., ain't nothing but a world-class bullshitter."

Chuck Thompson, "the Voice of the Colts": "I first became aware of the fact that there was something a little bit different about Artie Donovan on our first trip to California together with the team. At the time, there were no direct flights from Baltimore to California, so the squad would take Capitol Airlines to Chicago and then TWA over the Rockies to California. Now, it so happened that almost every time we flew to California, it was a Friday.

"So once we were on the ground at Midway Airport in Chicago waiting to change planes, and I spot Mr. Donovan in the airport, looking for a priest. He was seeking out a special dispensation to eat baloney at seventeen thousand feet.

"Or let me ask you ex-players out there: How many times in the wee, small hours of the morning, after you had been across the state line in Pennsylvania imbibing life's blood, how many times did you return to Colt training camp in Westminster and walk into Donovan's room only to find Arthur himself sound asleep and his television roaring a test pattern at you? And then you would walk over to do Artie a favor by turning off his television, only to have him jump up and scream at you, 'You no-good S.O.B., let that sonofabuck alone. That's the only way I can keep my pizza warm.''

Jim Parker: "I was a first-round draft choice out of Ohio State in 1957, and any rookie is nervous coming into his first pro camp. I'll always remember Arthur Donovan, the old vet of the team, walking up to me on that first day of camp, putting his arm around me, and saying, 'Boy, remember one thing if you want to make this team. Out on that field is the only place you can whup the hell out of a white guy and not have to worry about going to jail.' The man just inspired the hell out of me.

"Another time Arthur brought me under his wing and told me he'd like me to come out to his country club for dinner one night. Well, about a week later I took him up on it. But instead of coming alone, I brought four or five of my buddies out with me. My black buddies. So we got to the door and I knocked on the door and Artie answered. He took a long look at our party and asked me if I had a reservation. Then he told me he didn't have a table for us, but he'd be more than happy to sell us something to go."

Well, folks, that's about it. I got nothing more to say. I'll get back at those bums for their kind remarks when I see them personally. And have no doubt, I will see them personally.

On August 3, 1968, I was inducted into the Pro Football Hall of Fame. I went in with one of my old idols from Fordham, Alex Wojciechowicz. It was about the happiest day of my life. What I said then applies here as well. I'm just an average guy who happened to get very lucky in life. I had good family, good friends, and good teammates. I also have no regrets about anything.

Nothing's changed much for me since I made that vow back at Mount St. Michael's never to laugh at another man's endeavors. I'm proud to say I've kept that vow. I've never laughed at anyone but myself. I've always felt that in life, anything you take out of the pot you have to put back in. I hope in some small way I've put something back in the pot.

So I guess I'll see ya later.

Index